C000176005

A BETTER LIFE

Isobel Scharen

AN M-Y BOOKS PAPERBACK

© Copyright 2020
Isobel Scharen

A CIP catalogue record for this title is
available from the British Library

ISBN (Print): 978-1-912875-38-2
ISBN (epub): 978-1-912875-41-2

To the memory of my mother

CONTENTS

PART ONE—SINGAPORE

PART TWO—NEW ZEALAND

PART ONE

Singapore

Chapter 1

February, 1941

The taxi inched through a downpour, the wipers beating and beating, dragging the heavy sheet of water back and forth. Then as abruptly as the rain hammered down, it ceased.

When the car stopped, Ada remained seated and watched the steam begin to rise from the ground and unravel above the trees. She was reluctant to move. The driver's lack of interest in her meant there was no need to talk. She could brood without guilt, without being reminded how lucky she was.

"Can go no more, mem," the driver said. He could not take her right to the gate of the boarding house. Streams coursed down deep furrows made by bulldozers when pipes had been laid for the new housing estate in Geylang.

Grateful for the respite he had unknowingly granted her, she tipped the driver generously and stepped out onto the ridged earth in her thin sandals. Workmen, idling by the roadside, stared brazenly at her and called softly. She ignored them and made her way up the path to the boarding house, entered the gate and climbed the battered wooden steps. Ada noticed, as she always did, the flaking paint on the verandah posts and the crumbling plaster, and felt the usual flicker of despair even though she knew that there was no longer any need to worry. The old bungalow, with its mottled tiled roof and pillared base, had recently been sold to a Chinese businessman, buying it for his newly married son.

The house was quiet. Vera, her sister, had left for work, and their mother, Elizabeth, was taking her nap. Ada glimpsed the shy Eurasian boarder disappearing into his room along the corridor. He seldom spoke, although he'd stammered congratulations when she became engaged, and nowadays managed a timid smile.

The kitchen smelled of raw onion and coconut grated for sambal. Chicken curry simmered on the stove top, but the vegetables lay unsliced. The maid, Amah, had abandoned cooking for a task more to her liking. Through the open window Ada heard her voice, small and sharp as a razor, scraping across the thick midday heat. Ada rolled up the blind and leaned out, the scent of bougainvillea and jasmine coming up to greet her. Amah, her thin shoulders bent forward in belligerence, was scolding Abdul, the houseboy and gardener. He was knocking rambutans from the tree, wielding his long pole in extravagant arcs that threatened to end up on Amah's balding head. Ada could not hear what she was saying, but guessed it was to do with some unfinished job. Amah had this notion that Abdul was deceitful and lazy, and she was forever prowling about the house and garden in her soft black slippers and pouncing on him. Admittedly, he liked nothing better than to lean against the wall and smoke his pipe, his sturdy parang beside him, but he willingly did all the heavy jobs.

Ada was about to call Amah in, stop her from hounding the poor boy, when she reminded herself that this quarrelling would soon be a thing of the past - in two weeks' time, to be exact. After the wedding Abdul would go with her to the Woods' in Serangoon, and Amah would be with Elizabeth and Vera.

Ada let the blind down and hurried to the bathroom for a throw-over. She kicked her sandals off her swollen feet, stripped, grabbed the pitcher from the bucket, and began dousing herself vigorously. It was simply pre-wedding nerves, she reasoned. There was no need to feel apprehensive. She loved Michael, and he loved her.

She dabbed all-cure Tiger Balm on her temples and made a cup of coffee, sweetened with an extra comforting teaspoon of condensed milk, before seeking the shade of the front verandah. This overlooked waste land, and on the far side a Malay kampong, the thatched roofs of the huts partly screened from view by a fringe of king coconut trees. Ada could see a group of children from the kampong splashing one another in the rusty puddles. A few were chasing a ball, some racing beyond it simply for the pleasure of running. She heard their shouts and laughter and thought how she would miss them. Their fathers, too, when they came across to sell vegetables and fish, especially Ali, who had invited Ada and her mother to his son's wedding. "More the merrier", he'd grinned. She remembered the laughter and jests of guests trying to waylay the groom as he walked to the far end of the village where his radiant bride waited for him on a raised dais. Paper lanterns hung in the trees. She remembered how at ease people had been, and reflected wistfully that her own wedding day would certainly not be so relaxed.

She did not hear her mother come out from her bedroom that opened onto the verandah.

"Ah, you are back, Ada." Elizabeth sat on her cot. "I've been worried about you. You shouldn't have gone on your own."

Ada longed for more solitude, but tried to keep her tone free from irritation.

"I didn't have the choice. Amah was unwell. Complained of a headache. But I think she wanted to keep an eye on Abdul." Reluctantly, she added, disliking the need to be accountable, "I kept to the quayside." She was aware of the dangers lurking in a side-alley – the brothels, the gambling dens, the opium houses. "And I took a taxi to come home." She would not say that she'd paid the costly full fair, having instructed the driver not to stop for another passenger. After her episode with the godown keeper, she deserved the luxury.

"You look very tired, child."

"There's a new godown keeper. I had to use all my patience and hold my ground. Old Mr Lee," she said, referring to the previous keeper, "used to go out of his way to be helpful, especially when I first started going in after Daddy died. He knew Daddy of course. Respected him."

She would not tell her mother of the new keeper's leer, the way he had tried to touch her when she'd entered the musty warehouse. She was young, white and unescorted, and he might have thought she was a refugee from the war in Europe. It was said that many of the women were struggling to survive in the East. "He was shocked when I spoke to him in Malay. And he gave me a reduction on the oil. Though I paid what he wanted for the milk powder. I remembered Daddy saying that you should never let a Chinese lose face or you'll lose more."

Ada pictured her father now – the lightly crossed arms, the faint smile - emblems of his calm steadiness in the face of formidable guile. Noel Pendel had never been like other tuans and their wives – he had no need of theatrical gestures and huffy dismissals.

"Your father would've been proud of you, child. He always thought you would go far. If only he could've been alive to give you away." This was not the first time Elizabeth had said this, so Ada made no comment. "You'll never have to go to Boat Quay again."

"But I want to." Ada thought back to the morning - coming out of the dim warehouse into the glaring light of the riverside. The rotting egg stench of the river carried on the heavy air. And all around was bedlam - the barks of the lightermen jostling their wide-bellied craft, the excited cries of old men playing cards, the shouts of coolies heaving bales of sugar-brown rubber from sampan to the dockside. She would miss the productive chaos. She could not imagine Evaline Wood, Michael's mother, allowing her to go there.

Elizabeth did not hear her, or chose not to do so. "You'll get your life back. You'll never have money worries."

Ada did not brighten at this, which she instantly regretted because Elizabeth continued. "I know how hard it's been for you." Her mother's deep sigh encoded a frequently expressed guilty regret for taking a good-for-nothing as a second husband. "Never marry again if you marry well the first time."

"I know," Ada replied. "You're always telling me. And I've no intention of doing so. Michael's only twenty-four anyway." Only four years older than her. It was hard to believe sometimes. "He's not going to die for a long time."

"Young men sometimes do die. They're dying in the war now."

"We haven't got a war here."

"Good people are taken because they're too good for this world."

"Oh, Mummy. For goodness sake. What a thing to say! Telling me Michael is going to die young." Elizabeth had the knack of handling worry about the unpredictable future by imagining the worst. Ada understood her mother had grounds for pessimism due to her own experience, and perhaps it was wise to be constantly prepared for disaster, but it was still irritating.

"I wasn't saying *Michael* was going to die. He'll always be there for you. He'll give you an easy life." Elizabeth clasped her hands together. "You don't know how lucky you are. Every day I thank God my daughter is marrying such a thoughtful and generous man."

"Are you talking about the butterscotch?" Ada said. Michael always arrived at the house with small gifts, such as a tin of Parkinson's butterscotch, much appreciated and not seen in the Pendel household for some time.

Elizabeth, aware that Ada was teasing her, continued. "I'm thinking about him taking me out when he was so busy with his teaching and scouts, because he knows how confined I feel." He had driven her in his father's Vauxhall, once to Mt. Faber, another time to Katong Park. Ada had nearly cried with gratitude seeing Elizabeth so happy.

"He's very patient too. Hearing me going on." Elizabeth loved to talk about her life in service in Kent – where she'd met her first husband Noel – getting up at dawn to light fires and press clothes. She knew what hard work was. If Michael was bored he did not show it, Ada thought, and recalled the time when Elizabeth had said that she could never believe her luck now, having servants and all. Elizabeth was so thankful to Singapore and people such as Michael for sharing it with her. Michael's face had softened, and he replied quietly that his family had also come for a better life.

Elizabeth had such simple beliefs. She was naive like a child. She even looked childlike, Ada observed. With the medication for her heart, weakened after a stroke, Elizabeth's blond prettiness was becoming more like that of a 10c doll – round cheeks, a squeezed rosebud mouth, and her once long hair worn in a chignon, now cut and styled in a girlish bob.

It troubled Ada to think how vulnerable Elizabeth had become since Noel died. Ada recalled the time, soon after the move to Geylang, when she returned from school to find Elizabeth wandering aimlessly in the garden, then staring up at the tulip tree as if expecting some mystical truth to emerge from the branches. When Elizabeth started to have panic attacks, there had been no choice but to leave school and help run the boarding house.

"If only I hadn't been so foolish. If only I'd seen through that good-for-nothing," Elizabeth said.

"We were all taken in, Mummy." The good-for-nothing, Hilton Frugneit, was a lanky bald Dutch Burgher introduced to the family by an acquaintance of Noel. He began to be a frequent visitor, welcomed for his cheerful company. "All his talk about being in the import export business." Ada pictured Frugneit selecting a pastel-coloured Sobranie with feline grace from a gold cigarette case engraved with his initials. He had elegance, she conceded, but he was not handsome, not handsome like Noel had been.

"We weren't to know about his drinking and gambling," Ada said.

She shut her eyes against the image of him shouting and striking out like a madman when he wanted money from Elizabeth. "He seemed the most generous man on earth. Flowers, perfume. Jewellery too, for you. And taking Vera and me out." Several times to the racecourse, as it happened, where they'd gorged on fried bananas and watched the card tricksters and the raucous Australians standing on boxes with their slates and chalk. Scoundrels making a packet, Frugneit complained, but he had spent a lot of time with them exchanging dollar notes.

"If I'd told you that he chased the horses, you might not have trusted him."

Ada wondered, not for the first time, if she'd ignored the signs of Frugneit's waywardness because she craved an easier life. She'd welcomed the chance to be free of boarding house duties and to find a job in the Municipal as a Power Samas operator doing the gas, water and electricity bills. The trouble was that having tasted independence, when Frugneit showed his true colours, it was a grave disappointment for her to return to managing the boarding house. Every day Ada felt that life was passing her by.

Elizabeth was tearful.

"Oh, Mummy, please, don't get upset." Ada hated Frugneit. He not only robbed Elizabeth of her money, but also of her health and self-respect. "We must put the past behind us and look forward to a better life," she said, recognising that they each had a different view of what that better life might be.

"Yes, a better life." Elizabeth managed a timorous smile. "We have much to look forward to. You to your marriage, me to my new home. I can't believe how kind Patrick Wood has been." Michael's father had sold her a small house far below market value, so she had money left over from the boarding house sale to buy a flat for renting out.

Ada was grateful for his generosity, but she disliked the sense of being beholden. Not that she believed Patrick would consider that she owed him anything. He was not a petty man. Tall and angular with hawkish features and darkly circled eyes, she found his severe expression rather intimidating at times. But she could cope with Patrick. She liked Patrick.

✼ ✼ ✼

Two days later, when she arrived for a lunch party at the Woods' home, Patrick was waiting to greet her at the top of the verandah steps. She was late and more than flustered. The kitchen had flooded that morning. It had been an ordeal to keep Amah calm while summoning a repairman to unclog the pipe. Ada babbled her apology to Patrick, who smiled, took her hand and bowed slightly.

"You look beautiful, my dear. Beautiful as ever," Patrick said, admiring her dress. "Your mother's work?"

Ada nodded.

"Michael asked me to give you his deepest apology. He has school affairs to attend to, but will be here as soon as he can. Come." With his hand cupped lightly on her elbow he steered her down the wide verandah into a room at the furthest end of the large, rambling bungalow.

They entered through wide-open doors into the spacious dining room used for entertaining. It was a formal room with a big mahogany side-board, high-backed padded chairs, and several portraits of severe-looking men in stiff collars. Guests were seated at the long table beneath steadily beating fans. She recognised a few people from previous gatherings but there were some strange faces. Everyone else seemed to know one another, and the chatter was warm and animated

Ada sat beside an elderly woman wearing black. She smiled at Ada and asked her name. "Oh, so you're Michael's betrothed. I've heard a lot about you. Evaline has…" She looked beyond Ada, and there was Evaline. Ada rose to kiss her.

"I was introducing myself to your future daughter-in-law," the woman was saying. "She's indeed the beauty you said she was, Evaline."

Evaline took a step back to inspect Ada's appearance, smiled approvingly, then looked up at Ada's face, scrutinising it in that judgmental manner Ada had become used to. Evaline was a short woman, rather stout, and with an air of authority, despite the curly grey hair that readily escaped the fixture of hairpins. Ada, conscious that people were looking her way, was pleased to have worn her new dress, a soft pleated white-dotted silk crepe at the new shorter length. She knew from past occasions that the Woods' acquaintances were always well-groomed. As they were polite. And somewhat aloof - as if making it clear that Anglo-Indians were equal to any member of the ruling class. She did not resent this at all. She was fully aware of the superior airs of many Europeans in Singapore.

As Evaline gushed compliments before bustling away to call the servants to begin serving, Ada, seated again, noticed that Michael's sister Charmaine had taken the vacant chair directly opposite. She had her elbows on the table and glared down the white-clothed stretch of it as if she despised the fine patterned china and crystal decanters. Ada felt that Charmaine was deliberately ignoring her and could not help but feel slighted. What had she done to deserve such rudeness? Michael had tried to explain Charmaine's coldness to her by saying that Charmaine was often miserable as she lacked male suitors. Ada fixed her gaze on Charmaine's sullen, dark-complexioned face. Still Charmaine ignored her, even when Patrick stood to welcome his guests.

Wine was poured, water glasses filled, and Evaline entered proudly before a line of white-coated Tamil servants, all of whom carried steaming dishes of food. As Evaline walked up and down behind people's chairs, urging them to sample the lavish array of curries, Ada wondered which was worse: Charmaine's disregard or Evaline's controlling fussiness?

Plates full, the conversation quietened while people ate. The elderly woman at Ada's side said to her in a confiding tone, "It's been a while since I've been to the Woods'. I was in Burma until recently. My husband died there suddenly. The heart. He never complained of anything, so it came as a complete shock. Seeing a loved one suffer a long illness is very distressing, but at least there is time to share the ending, and say goodbye."

"My father died suddenly too," Ada said. "A clot in the brain. My mother has never got over the shock, I think."

There was a patter of applause, a scattering of greetings. Ada glanced up to see Michael enter the room. He raised his hand, smiling acknowledgement. His athletic stride took him swiftly to the vacant chair beside her. He kissed her cheek, and apologised for being late.

"I was late too. I've had a dreadful morning," she began, then, judging that Michael would not be interested in drains, asked, "Have you been busy?"

"More administrative things to do with the head leaving."

"I didn't know he was leaving. Where's he going to? Not back to England surely."

"No. Australia. He's playing it safe. Wise man."

Waiters approached carrying serving dishes. Michael helped himself to food and began to eat hungrily. Ada ate too, tuning into the conversation around her. Patrick was talking to a man at his side, a Chinese man with a birthmark on his cheek. Seeing Ada look in his direction, he stared boldly at her with a lascivious smile. Patrick noticed her too then, and said in a louder voice, "We must congratulate the English. You can't take it away from them. They have grit. The RAF is unbeatable."

Patrick raised his glass to Ada as if she were in some way part of the glory. She guessed he was referring to the Battle of Britain, the months of bombing that had worried her mother, who feared for distant relatives. Ada wished that she had something intelligent to add, as she always did when Patrick talked to her about Britain. Although he always listened attentively to what she had to say, she was embarrassingly aware that his knowledge was far greater than hers. All she could offer was what her parents had told her – the ways of the gentry, fires in Kentish pubs, the blossom foaming in the orchards, frost on the apple trees, which she imagined to be like the shaved ice in kachang. She often thought that one positive fact about living with the Woods would be the chance to learn so many things.

The waiters removed the plates. Guests, replete, waited for the next course, and there was a respectful silence as Patrick spoke more loudly. "It is a great relief to know that a man of Churchill's calibre is in control."

"What do you mean by control?" Michael muttered quietly.

Patrick went on citing examples of Churchill's good sense. "I think we can trust him when he says that Singapore is the Gibraltar of the East. With our naval base complete the Japanese will not be able to attack us from the sea."

"What about from the mainland?" Michael asked in a louder voice.

"They'll never get through the jungle," someone else said. "Hundreds of miles of it. And thousands of Commonwealth troops ready to take them on. Even the Japs know their limitations."

"It is very foolish to underestimate the Japanese, sir," Michael said, leaning forward. Ada glanced at him. There was a heightened colour on his fine-featured face, and she sensed his growing agitation as he continued.

"Tell me, what is the point of a naval base without battleships and submarines, and aircraft carriers? It is war we are talking about. Nasty, brutal war, which we know at this moment is being fought in Europe. Singapore is *not* impregnable."

"Why would the authorities be telling us it is if that wasn't the case?" Patrick asked, frowning. "Why would they want to deceive us?"

"It's more that they need to deceive themselves," Michael replied heatedly. "Convince themselves that they're in control. That they have nothing to fear from little Japanese men."

There was a stirring among the guests. Ada wished Michael would not be so serious. It was not the time or place.

The man with the birthmark said, "Well, I for one am not worried. I've visited the naval base. Singapore is a fortress, surrounded by sea. In my opinion Singapore's never had it so good with the demand for our rubber and tin."

There were murmurs of 'hear, hear', and then a bubbling of excited chatter as mango ices were brought in.

Michael ate his dessert in silence, making little effort to converse with the woman beside him. Ada knew that he was not one for small-talk, but this indifference was more than being uninterested in making polite conversation.

The guests were invited to take coffee on the verandah. Ada went ahead of Michael and expected him to follow her. She was seated on a cane chair talking to the elderly lady again when Michael emerged some time later. There was an angry expression on his face, and his hair, usually combed back smoothly from his wide forehead, now looked as if he'd been raking his fingers through it. He came directly towards her, and hardly glancing at her took her hand. "Come," he said. She began to apologise to the elderly woman, but Michael held her hand firmly and pulled her to her feet. She was surprised at his rudeness.

He led her back into the dining room. His father was standing with the Chinese man. Patrick looked seriously at Michael, and the Chinese man turned his back as they walked through. Ada followed Michael along the back corridor into the library. He stood for a moment without speaking as if trying to control his emotions, then said, "God, how I loathe that man."

The Chinese man, Ada presumed, the one who'd smiled lasciviously at her.

"What did he do?"

"He's been buying up property on the coast. Malay land. And he's boasting about the money he's going to make developing a hotel complex. He refuses to accept that he's robbing the Malays of their livelihood as fishermen and farmers, their traditional way of living. Whole communities are being wrecked. And he had the gall to say the Malays are a lazy bunch. I wanted to hit him."

Ada nodded solemnly, recalling what Michael had told her when he'd first come to the house. They had been on the front verandah watching the Malay children playing on the waste land. "I remember you saying that you admired the Chinese for wanting to get on. But you wished they were more tolerant of the Malays who wanted different things out of life."

She mentioned the feud between Abdul and Amah. Michael had listened to her with a grave attention. She felt closely observed, and this scrutiny, combined with his good looks and quiet authority, had been a little disconcerting. She wondered if there had been a note of spoiled petulance in her remarks – a white woman complaining about the onerous business of managing the servants.

The air in the library was close. Michael took out a laundered handkerchief from the pocket of his trousers and wiped his top lip. She caught the scent of eau-de-cologne. "It's such a pity," she said, "that races can't get on. I'm so pleased that Daddy made sure Vera and I mixed with Singaporeans and sent us to Raffles Girls'. Everyone got on there. Chinese, Eurasians, Indians." Noel thought little of the British tuan besar types who avoided the local markets and shopkeepers, and only shopped at the Cold Storage or Robinsons. "If we have a daughter," she said shyly, "we'll send her to Raffles Girls'."

Michael put his arms around her and kissed her brow. "My darling Ada. From the first time I met you I fell in love with you. I could see that you weren't like other English girls."

She smiled. "And I thought you were a man with strong convictions. And very clever." She paused, then decided to add, "But not so clever losing your temper today. Your father looked a bit upset."

Michael stepped back. "I know. I'll apologise." He looked out the window, his face turned from her. "It's just that I feel a bit frustrated at the moment. I've got a lot on my mind."

"School problems?"

He did not reply immediately, then said, "I'm not going to bore you with all that." He looked at her. "I think we should join the party. I need to make amends and do the chat. Sorry if I embarrassed you at lunch."

She accepted his apology, but as they returned to the party she wondered how she could support Michael, and at the same time persuade him not to work so hard. She admired him for being a man with strong convictions, but he'd lost his temper today, which indicated he was under considerable stress. It was not going to be straightforward, she predicted, being married to Michael.

Chapter 2

Next morning, Ada helped Amah lay the dining tables, and checked the laundry for the dhobi man. When she came out onto the verandah Elizabeth was seated with Mrs Sinathamby, a plump broad-featured Indian woman, who lived in one of the two neighbouring bungalows. She was complaining loudly about the noise and dust from the building works, the general disruption to their once peaceful lives. Ostensibly she was waiting for the hawker, but Ada knew that what she was really waiting for was the chance to talk about the wedding. Her face lit up on seeing Ada, who smiled as radiantly as she could.

"Harry is working hard on his speech" Mrs Sinathamby said, referring to her mild husband who was going to give Ada away. "It will be the proudest moment in his life." Ada had heard this many times before, but she still nodded appreciatively. "He is making sure not to shame you."

"What do you mean *shame*?" Ada asked. "How could he possibly shame me?"

"We know how clever Michael is. And his father." Mrs Sinathamby tilted her head from side to side. "Oh boy, what a family you've married into." Her eyes brightened with curiosity. "And the party?" she asked Ada. "A good time had by all?"

"I think so." Ada hesitated, wondering if she should tell them what Michael had said about the war, and how he'd lost his temper. Both women were waiting expectantly. "The food was delicious, of course. It was in the big dining room."

"Ah, the big dining room." Mrs Sinathamby raised her brows, wanting more. She was familiar with the exterior of the house, having ventured to Serangoon to see for herself where the Woods lived. With its plantation-style rambling structure set on a base of Doric pillars, the house resembled those of the tuan besars in the Tanglin district. She was most impressed by the front staircase, which descended in a spacious inverted Y from a deep verandah. But the elaborately carved barge boards had also been noted - a sure sign that there was plenty of money for detail. She had to depend on Ada to describe the interior.

Ada usually obliged, accepting that material betterment was what the older women wanted for her, and spoke enthusiastically about the blue and white corridor tiles, the many rooms, the library with Michael's piano. Today, however, she was not in the mood to be drawn into talk of grandeur. But aware that the women were looking questioningly at her, she offered, "It's very formal. It reminds me of something out of an English history book. Long table. Chairs with high backs. A huge sideboard. Not my taste at all." She frowned. "I wish Michael and I could have a place of our own. I wouldn't care if it was cramped and ugly." Daring to sound ungrateful she added, "And I wish the wedding was going to be simpler."

"Evaline Wood likes to show off," Mrs Sinathamby said brusquely.

"The Woods have been very generous. We must not criticize, Ada," Elizabeth said.

Of course she must not. The Woods were paying for the string trio, the three-course meal, the four-storied wedding cake from Victoria Confectionary. Only the dresses were the Pendels' responsibility: Elizabeth's to be precise, with Ada's help. Ada suspected that Evaline would have preferred a more elaborate dress than the one she'd chosen – a ground length crepe gown cut on the cross with a yoke of gardenia-patterned lace.

"We are paupers! If not for Patrick Wood where would we be?" Elizabeth exclaimed.

"He can afford to be generous. He's made a fortune from his property deals. And he was left pots by his father from the pineapple preserving business," Mrs Sinathamby said. She had told them this before. It was information gleaned after careful investigation.

Perhaps noticing Ada's troubled expression, Mrs Sinathamby glanced at Elizabeth whose head was bowed as if in shame, and cried, "Chee, they could not have done without your sewing. No tailor can come up to your little finger. Ada and Vera will be the most beautiful girls in Singapore. Melanie too," she added, referring to Ada's friend, who was one of the three bridesmaids. She paused and smiled maliciously. "Their daughter, even, will look nice. Evaline Wood will have nothing to grumble about."

This remark made Ada conscious again of the shadows which loomed over her future. "She is very particular," Ada explained. "Runs the house like a major general. Michael has this quote on the wall of his bedroom." A room stuffed with his schoolboy past, such as his cricket kit and scout memorabilia. "'Dad is the boss of this house and has Mum's permission to say so.'" The women laughed, and Mrs Sinathamby clapped gleefully. Ada smiled, but she was picturing her future mother-in-law. The way she walked with her chest thrust out reminded Ada of a ship's prow cutting a swathe through the water and leaving other vessels to rock in its wake.

"She sets the rules. She set the wedding date, for goodness' sake. There's scarcely been time for the banns to be read."

"She was worried that you might change your mind," Mrs Sinathamby said.

Ada did remember the time she'd visited the Woods' house soon after Michael had told the family about the engagement.

Evaline had led her to the bedroom she and Michael would occupy. Evaline had pressed the thick mattress of the four-poster bed, and pointed out the carved wardrobe doors, all the while holding onto her hand as if she might try to escape.

"And she wants grandchildren. His sister, Charmaine, might not produce for some time."

Ada recalled looking out of the bedroom window and seeing the golden dome of a mosque shimmering in the midday sun. She'd heard the steady beat of a drum, and a muezzin calling people to prayer. Struck by how different her life was going to be, she had failed to register a possible encouragement to procreate.

To prevent Mrs Sinathamby from saying more, Ada spoke with emphasis, smiling reassuringly. "You must tell Mr Sinathamby not to worry about the speech. I know he will do it beautifully."

"You're the daughter he's always wanted." Mrs Sinathamby hung her head. The couple were childless, a state much regretted and demanding sympathy.

Ada was thankfully relieved from making a comforting and grateful remark by the cracked, solemn chant of the hawker.

"Idli...Jalebi..."

Soon he would appear in his grease-stained dhoti, carrying a huge basket filled with sweet pastries and crisp parcels of meat, seeping chilli oil.

"Oh dear. What I would give for a taste. I'm like a beggar living off the smell of salt-fish. I dream of kuey teow," Elizabeth said. And she was off to visit the arcades of her memory for favourite eating houses and stalls selling satay, or chilli prawns, steamed buns, nasi goreng, mah mee.

"Do you want me to buy...?"

"No, Mrs Sinathamby. She cannot eat spicy food," Ada interrupted. The doctor had said not too much salt or fat, not too many spices. Ada had Amah prepare steamed fish and vegetables most days, rewarding her mother with fresh fruit at the end of the meal, and an occasional treat of gula melaka.

"You see, Jem, how she bosses me!" Elizabeth cried as Ada shook her finger in mock severity. "I'm not eating, but I'm still getting fat. Too fat for my clothes." Elizabeth had always been careful to keep her figure, curbing her joyful greed by resisting syrup-drenched Indian sweetmeats.

Ada was worried that Vera would not be firm with Elizabeth about her diet and her rest times and resolved to speak to her sister, when she returned from work next day, about the severity of Elizabeth's illness. Another stroke would kill her.

Ada put the last pin in the hem of Vera's bridesmaid's dress, then sat back on her haunches and compared her reflection with that of her younger sister in the full-length mirror. The dress, like her own in cut but with short puffed sleeves, was the colour of old rose, which suited Vera's white skin and jet-black hair perfectly. She took after Noel with her colouring and had also inherited his slim frame. Ada, with her fair hair and full-breasted shape, was like Elizabeth.

They were different in character, too. According to Michael she was all sense and Vera all sensibility - like the sisters in Jane Austen's novel, the younger impetuous, ruled by her heart, the other level-headed and protective. Ada thought the comparison made her seem dry and staid, like someone's great aunt. Vera was only two and a half years younger, and though she might wear higher heels, paint her nails red rather than pink, and choose the latest dress in fashion instead of simpler styles from the McCall pattern books, Ada considered that she took good care of herself - brushed and curled her thick blond hair, dabbed Vaseline on her lashes, and when she was a working girl went to every tea dance or matinee that she could.

Vera smoothed the dress over her hips. "I don't suppose you'll go dancing much when you're married. I mean you and Michael don't go dancing much now. I must say I can't imagine not being able to dance."

Ada frowned and got to her feet. She disliked the implication that she and Michael were going to surrender youth instantly after marriage. "Michael might not like dancing as much as me, but he readily takes me to the Recreation Club if I want to go," she said defensively, failing to add that he was happy to let his friends partner her. "But we both just prefer going to the pictures. It was one of the first things we discovered about each other." She and Michael had sat under the rambutan tree while Elizabeth was having her nap. Later, in the soft passage of small talk with Elizabeth, Michael had asked if he could take Ada to the Cathay the following week.

Elizabeth had predicted wedding bells as early as then, Ada remembered. It was after Michael had dropped her home. Elizabeth, watching him walk on the moon-washed path to his car, had said something about him being serious, but also very kind, and that he would go somewhere. And although they had different backgrounds, it would not matter if they respected each other. Elizabeth was always saying that Michael was a decent man, and that he reminded her of Noel.

Vera, looking at herself in the mirror, began to practise a dance step as if completely uninterested in what Ada had said. "I haven't told you that Madame has found something vunderfewl for her gearls." Vera was mimicking her dancing teacher, a flamboyant Hungarian who taught ballroom, tap and national dancing, and exhibited her young talent at carefully chaperoned private functions in the city. "I can't wait."

"You know that you can't leave Mummy all the time. I won't be there..."

"I'm not going to leave her *all the time*." The colour rose in Vera's cheeks. "It's all very well for you going off to your nice life."

The nice life that Vera wanted for herself, Ada thought. She remembered Vera accosting Michael one morning after service at

St. Andrew's and inviting him to a tea party. A sing-song, she'd called it. He probably had no idea what a singsong was. He bowed his head but did not smile. Well, he was hardly known to them. He probably only accepted the invitation because Vera had asked him to play the piano. Apparently, she'd heard that he was a brilliant pianist.

Ada remembered Michael turning up at the boarding house in an immaculate white suit and bowtie. You could tell he was forcing a smile. He sat at the old piano and played with intense conce ntration like someone who'd been hired to perform, hardly glancing up when people applauded loudly. She thought he was shy, but Vera said later that it was not shyness. It was disdain for the shabby furniture, the faded cretonne. Of course, she felt put out because he appeared neither impressed nor entertained when she had sidled in wearing one of her dance costumes – gauzy pants caught at the ankle, yashmak, embroidered bolero – and began to move sinuously around the room to the wavering notes of Arabic music on the phonograph. He was seated on the settee and looked down at his feet as if embarrassed. Ada remembered how she'd rescued him by saying the Malay children were playing near his car and could accidentally scratch it. It was then, out on the verandah, that they began talking about serious things.

She was aware that without Vera she would not have got to know him, but she could not forget what Vera had said when she learned that Michael had proposed. She'd said that Michael was marrying for white blood. She actually used the coarse expression 'watering down the stengah'. Ada could understand jealousy, but that comment was unforgivable.

Ada packed the sewing basket. "I don't think your life is that unpleasant, Vera. It's not me who goes off to the Sea View every day, dressed to kill. I'm left here to run the place. Who does all the shopping? Who sews your dance costumes?" Her voice was rising as she tried to quell the image of Evaline inspecting her features and blond hair. "You'll have to sew your own clothes now."

"But I can't. I'm not clever like you with my hands."

Elizabeth had failed to pass down the seamstress skills in the family to her younger, dance-struck daughter. Ada had accepted Elizabeth's lack of insistence that Vera learn to sew, understanding that it made for an easier life. Besides, she, Ada, enjoyed sewing, and had a real sense of achievement in completing a garment according to Elizabeth's high standards.

"It's just practice, Vera. You just get better the more you do it. Like with your dancing."

"I know it takes hard work to be good at something." Vera crossed her arms, contrite. "And I know how hard you work. And that you deserve to have a nice life now." She sighed "It's just that I feel very frustrated sometimes. I don't want to be an old maid, and a hotel receptionist forever. I want to do something good with my life."

Ada softened, aware of the same need to better herself, and that unlike Vera she now had the opportunity to do this.

"You are very talented and beautiful, Vera. You will do something good with your life."

This was not the time to say, as she had often said, that it would have been wiser for Vera to have remained at school. Vera was adamant about leaving after the troubles with Frugneit. It could not be denied that her earnings as a receptionist at the Sea View helped.

"Do you really think so?"

"Yes. If you're determined, you'll get there. It's determination that counts." Ada nodded firmly, although she was thinking about luck. Or fate, as she preferred to call it.

Ada helped Amah clean and tidy following supper that evening, then, as was customary, took out glasses and a jug of iced coffee to share with her mother on the verandah. Elizabeth was on her cot. The darkness was relieved by the light from the tiny glow of a mosquito coil, which had attracted a large furry moth. Ada could not see her mother's face, but she noticed her unusual quietness, and decided not to bring up the subject of Michael at the lunch party.

"You've worked very hard today, Mummy. Too hard. You mustn't push yourself. We'll get everything done. Now that we've finished Melanie's dress there's only Charmaine's to do." From the kampong laughter could be heard, seeming to encourage the bullfrogs to croak more loudly. Still Elizabeth did not say anything. "Are you all right, Mummy?"

"Yes, child."

"You don't need to worry about anything. The dresses are beautiful. You're a genius."

"I love to sew. It's the one thing I can do well. And when you have your baby I'll help you sew the clothes and prepare the cradle."

"Oh, Mummy, that's thinking far ahead!"

"Babies come more quickly than you might like." Elizabeth shifted on the cot. Ada sensed she was about to embark on something of an awkwardly confidential nature, as she had at the time of Ada's approaching menstruation. Elizabeth warned that when Ada got her 'friend' she must be careful not to 'lead men on'. It had been murky talk, and Ada had silenced her by saying she knew it all, though she did not, not about leading men on anyway.

"Don't worry, child," Elizabeth said. A slight pause, and she continued. "On your wedding night you will give your body up. It'll hurt at first. A little blood." Elizabeth hesitated again. "I'm only telling you this to prepare you. My mother left me to find out for myself. She thought I knew it all from seeing the animals, I suppose. I don't want you to have the shock."

"It's when the hymen tears," Ada said briskly. She wanted to silence her mother with superior knowledge, and detach the image of animals humping each other from what everyone knew was an essential biological fact. Did Elizabeth not know that girls talked and giggled?

"It is your duty, you see. It's a wife's duty to give her body up. You'll do it because you love him."

Ada imagined her naked body stretched out on the marriage bed like a corpse, a sacrificial victim. She did not want to think of it like that.

"Michael's a decent man. Like your father. I know he'll be considerate and patient, even if a bit clumsy as it's his first time too. You'll grow to think it's all right. You'll be proud of yourself."

Ada gulped the coffee and wiped her hand roughly across her mouth. She was annoyed with Elizabeth for making her feel anxious - as if it were a trial she was about to undergo. She knew that Michael desired her very much, and not only from the way he eyed her breasts. His goodnight kisses were definitely becoming more insistent, which in fact she did not at all dislike, secretly enjoying the tingling in her vagina – near her hymen, probably. But she feared that although he might be clumsy the first time or two, she would be much clumsier - gauche, completely unattractive.

She thought of the women who never married, spinsters like her school teachers. They did not have to worry about pleasing a man. They appeared happy enough, laughing together in the staff room. But perhaps they went home at night and wished they were with someone clever and handsome who would give them lovely children?

She hugged her knees and stared out into the dark emptiness of the waste ground. The cicadas were deafening. There were so many frantic tickings and whirrings, and the eerie wah-wah of monkeys. The jungle was very close.

Chapter 3

March, 1941

Ada was resting on the bed, propped up on pillows, when Michael came into the room after his shower with a towel wrapped around his waist, and rummaged in a drawer for clothes. He was lightly muscled, the skin of his chest fairer than that of his face which caught the sun despite his diligent wearing of a topee. Although Ada had seen his torso before when they went swimming, she'd never seen him – or any man, for that matter – completely naked, and kept her eyes averted as he began to dress. She would wait to bathe and change into her going-away outfit until he'd left to join the guests already milling in the house, spilling out onto the verandah, gathering their energies for more food, laughter and talk after the reception. Anglo-Indians love to party, Evaline had said when she was planning the snacks for the evening.

"Tired?" he asked, coming to stand beside her, and adjusting his underpants. "You can sleep in the car." He stroked her hand with his thumb, moving it back and forth as he studied her face. Of course, he'd caressed her hand before, but this time he seemed to do it with a searching pressure. "I've told them not to worry about feeding us. We'll get there quite late."

He was referring to the home of two bachelor friends whom he'd not seen for a few years - since they all attended Raffles College and trained as teachers. An over-night stay, to break the journey up-country to the Cameron Highlands for the honeymoon, provided an opportunity to meet again. "They'll understand if we want to have an early night." A room in a small hotel near the friends' house had been booked. Ada felt a mixture of nervousness and excitement at the mention of an early night.

"You were marvellous today, darling. Coping with a horde of strangers. Dad said so as well. And Mum was crowing with pride."

Ada had a clear image of Evaline darting busily between the groups of guests, then scurrying at intervals to twitch the train of the wedding dress, to smooth back the veil. "Show everyone your rings, Ada." A flawless diamond set in a circle of rubies bought with a loan from Patrick, and a broad wedding ring fashioned by Evaline's favourite magician with gold. Everyone, so many strangers, had been very charming, but it had been such an effort to smile endlessly, achingly.

"I felt a bit nervous going down the aisle, in case I tripped. I don't think I've ever been in a room with so many people I didn't know." The place had been filled with the smell of perfume, both from the elaborate flower arrangements and the expensive scent of the fashionably-dressed, immaculately made-up women. She'd wished for the chance to go outside, breathe deeply.

"And you didn't have to give a speech. Think how I felt."

"You sounded very confident." She hesitated. "Did you mean what you said?"

"Of course. And I'll say it again." He straightened. "I have never met a woman more beautiful, more intelligent and sensible, and more loyal. I thank Mrs Pendel from the bottom of my heart for bringing up Ada to be such a fine woman, and I apologise for stealing her daughter."

He bowed, and Ada laughed, and then grew serious, thinking of her mother. During the speeches Ada had noticed Elizabeth seated at the end of an adjacent table close by. There had been a prickling of sweat on her pale brow, and she had stared ahead blankly as the best man addressed the gathering. The speech was clearly very witty, for laughter rippled endlessly along the tables, and faces beamed delightedly at Michael. The teasing seemed to be mainly about his competitiveness in sports, or ambitious pranks that had not always worked out the way he'd wanted. But Ada was only half-listening, her attention on Elizabeth, and as soon as possible she went to her mother, filled a glass with water and made her drink. Elizabeth, despite Ada's urging, had refused to leave and insisted on coming to Serangoon to see the couple depart.

"Everyone's been telling me how beautiful you are," Michael said.

"Do you need to be told?"

Michael looked taken aback for a moment, then seeing her smile, he grinned and patted her cheek. "You're not going to let me get away with anything, are you? I like that." He stepped back and looked into her eyes. "I've told you why I love you. So, may I ask, what is it about me that made you fall at my feet?"

"No, it'll go to your head." She slid off the bed. "And it would take too long." He caught her arms and kissed her on the lips. She rested her cheek against his for a moment, then leaned back. "I must get ready now. And see if Mummy is all right. She's exhausted. I'm a little worried about her." Ada thought guiltily of how hard Elizabeth had worked. Her mother had lost her appetite in the final sprint of finishing the dresses and had refused her evening meals of steamed fish and vegetables. Ada had asked Amah to prepare mild curry and nasi goreng to tempt her palate.

After Michael had left, offering to check on Elizabeth, Ada showered and dressed quickly, then inspected herself critically in the mirror. Noting that with the blue of her dress her eyes appeared more vivid and large, rather too girlish perhaps, she composed her face into what she believed was a mask of self-assurance before going out onto the back verandah.

She was looking about for her friend Melanie amongst the noisy groups of people and white-coated servants handing out drinks and titbits, when she noticed Mrs. Sinathamby seated beside Elizabeth on a deep rattan settee, beckoning to her. As Ada approached Mrs Sinathamby said loudly, "Such a beautiful dress. It does you credit, Elizabeth. Always you do excellent work."

"Not my work. Ada sewed that," Elizabeth said, smiling up at Ada.

Mrs Sinathamby fingered the silk sash that crossed under Ada's breasts and tied at the sides. "Such fine material. And the colour. Oh, my, how the blue suits your eyes. It's Loretta Young you remind me of, I'm thinking."

Michael, who'd been fetching a drink for Elizabeth, appeared at Ada's side.

"Oh my. Your husband puts any actor in all the American pictures to shame." It was strange for Ada to hear 'husband', as if her changed status had been long established.

"Perhaps we should try our luck in Hollywood, Ada," Michael said, his gaze passing admiringly over her dress.

Mrs Sinathamby chortled with delight. "You have not only a beautiful wife, you have a clever one. You heard her mother say it is Ada's work?"

"Talented, beautiful, clever. I am indeed the luckiest man on earth."

A group of children rushed down the steps and headed for the tennis court at the back of the large garden. One of the servants followed them. It would be his duty to supervise ball and marble games and top spinning, while the parents continued to party. Evaline had thought of everything. Ada had made sure to thank and compliment her several times at the reception, but she was not sure if Evaline in her excitement had heard her.

And here she was now, advancing towards them, her chest thrust out like a mother hen. Lighter skinned than Michael, the dark around her eyes, like that of her husband Patrick, had the effect of narrowing the bridge of her nose. The couple resembled birds of prey, or owls, although apart from domestic matters it was Patrick who had the greater share of the wisdom.

Ada was aware that her thoughts were uncharitable, and hardly helpful if she intended to get on with her mother-in-law. She smiled directly at Evaline, who pushed between her and Michael and, turning to each in turn, announced, "Have you ever seen such a pair? Think what their children will be like! Ada's fair beauty and Michael's brains."

"So I have nothing to offer in the way of good looks, Mum?"

Several guests had joined the group, and Evaline's reply was drowned in a burst of laughter which drew others closer. Wanting to escape attention, Ada crouched down beside Elizabeth. "We're going soon. You can leave then. The Sinathambys will take you home. I'm worried that you've overdone it."

"Don't worry. I'm feeling much better out here. Outside. The hall was hot." Elizabeth opened her fan and flapped it briskly.

"Well you must rest, rest, rest. Promise me."

"I promise. I'll be very sensible. You must not worry about me." Elizabeth patted Ada's arm. "Now go and find your husband so you can leave and make a start on your journey. You don't want to get overtired either."

Ada looked up to see that Michael had left the others. She found him in the drawing room. He was talking to Patrick. They were having a serious conversation, it seemed, and Michael was nodding soberly. Then Patrick noticed Ada and indicated with a slight inclination of his head that she follow him out onto the front verandah. Michael turned away with a quick encouraging smile at Ada, and she wondered why Patrick should wish to speak to her alone.

The front of the house was shaded by short, dense palms. Patrick stood beside Ada, and they looked for a few quiet moments out onto the carefully cut lawn and the circular bed of cannas standing rigid like hostages within a ring of white rose bushes. Ada had time to admire the banks of bougainvillea in the side borders and notice that there were several pili nut trees – trees her father had unsuccessfully tried to grow. All was neatly cut, well groomed, unlike the garden – if you could call it that – of the boarding house where Abdul had been hard-pressed to keep back the fast-growing vines and low-lying shaggy plants. What she saw now was in contrast a ruthless taming, a triumph of authority, which somehow made her feel diminished.

Patrick turned to her. "Michael tells me you're worried about your mother. I will make sure our family doctor, Dr. Wong, visits her. He's an excellent physician, one of the best in Singapore."

"That is very kind of you. I am worried, Mr Wood."

"You must call me Patrick. Evaline and Patrick. Now that you are properly one of the family."

"Thank you. Thank you, Patrick."

"It's the least I can do." He looked out onto the garden again and frowned slightly, then continued. "I'm very proud of Michael. Naturally, I am. But I can see that he is also impulsive, and a bit wilful, which comes with having strong beliefs and a desire to do what he feels is right, I think. It relieves me to know that he has found someone who will be a steady influence on him." Patrick paused and glanced at her. She noted the gravity in his tone. "But what's more important is that you appear to have the capacity, the strength of character, to forgive his transgressions."

"As he will forgive mine, I hope." Ada attempted a smile, wondering about the word 'transgression'. It sounded biblical, something much more serious than impulsiveness. She recalled Michael's anger with the property developer at the lunch party, which had disturbed her. Was that what Patrick was talking about?

"God bless you, my dear," he said. She detected a tinge of sadness in his expression. "I'd prefer it if you didn't pass onto Michael what I've just said." He looked towards the garden. "Now. I must not keep you any longer. I know Michael wants to set off."

"Yes, I'd better go and find that impulsive son of yours." She hesitated, wanting Patrick to say that there was nothing to worry about. But he just stood there, so she kissed him lightly on the cheek – an act of reassurance for herself rather than Patrick – before hurrying inside.

At first, filled with confusion, she registered nothing, then noticed Michael in a far corner talking to Vera. Both were standing by a long sideboard covered with ornaments, and trophies won by Michael in tennis tournaments and for scholarship. Michael had made light of these in the face of his mother's lavish praise when Ada first visited the house, as he'd made light of the stern, sallow-skinned man in a black-framed portrait on the wall above. Ada knew this to be Michael's grandfather who had established the family business. Vera was laughing, and Ada wondered if Michael was mocking him, saying something to counteract any sense of the family's importance and wealth. Vera had changed into a flared tea-dance frock that showed off her small waist, and she fussed with her curls, stretching up her long, slender neck. She looked young and free. Ada felt a flash of envy.

Michael looked over his shoulder and saw her. "Time to leave, Ada? We can start saying goodbye to people. I'll pack the car. As soon as they've finished tying the cans to the back. It's going to be a noisy take-off." He gave Vera a jaunty bow. "Thank you for lending such grace to the occasion, Vera." As he passed Ada he said in a low tone, "I hope Dad put your mind at rest about your mother."

The two sisters were left eyeing each other warily. Ada mentioned the doctor, then Vera interrupted her. "You don't need to remind me about looking after Mummy. I'm not as selfish and careless as you think I am."

"I don't think you're selfish or careless."

Vera watched Ada with large, baleful eyes, as if expecting Ada to qualify her statement with a criticism. But perhaps encouraged by Ada's kind expression she said, "I know I say things without thinking. And I'm very sorry."

"You were wonderful today, Vera. I couldn't have asked for a better bridesmaid." Vera had fixed her hair and applied her makeup. "I heard people telling Mummy that she's lucky to have two lovely daughters."

"Oh, Ada, I'm really going to miss you."

Ada put out her arms to Vera and kissed her. "I'm going to miss you and Mummy like anything." Tears pricked her eyes.

"Don't forget to throw the bouquet so I can catch it," Vera said as they drew apart.

Ada nodded, then turned away, not wanting to betray her feelings, and hurried to fetch her bag and posy, as she could hear Patrick marshalling the guests onto the verandah.

When she stepped onto the verandah, Melanie was the first to see her.

"Off now, Ada, off now to your new life?"

Ada grasped Melanie's hand. "Thank you for being my bridesmaid, Melanie."

"I did nothing. Thank you for being my very good friend. I hope you won't forget me."

"How could I possibly forget you, Melanie?" Ada said, thinking that Melanie, more than anyone else, understood how hard it had been for her to leave school. Melanie would visit the boarding house bringing school gossip, and the books she was studying in English class. They'd read *A Midsummer Night's Dream* and *The Merchant of Venice* aloud together, trying to make sense of the strange and beautiful language.

"And we'll be living closer to each other than we were before."

Melanie made it sound as if a line had been crossed, as if life would never be the same again. Naturally it would be different; she had two families now and would have to adjust to the role of wife and in-law; she and Michael had still much to learn about each other. Patrick's remark about forgiving Michael his transgressions had unsettled her, but when she noticed Michael talking to her mother, she could only think how handsome he was and how much she loved him.

She kissed Melanie goodbye, and made her way towards him. He smiled broadly at her. "Ready?" he asked.

"I'll come and visit every day to see Amah and Vera are being strict with you," she said, hugging her mother.

"I'll be all right, child. Especially since I know I have nothing to worry about." She patted Michael's arm and looked at Ada with the composure of someone entirely satisfied, completely trusting.

It was Mrs Sinathamby who appeared flustered. "Promise you'll come and see me. No need to give warning. Harry and I think of you as our daughter," she cried.

Harry, beside her, expanded with pride. He'd walked Ada down the aisle, a thin bent man, trembling with responsibility. Ada thanked him again, praised his speech, and then turned quickly, wanting to be away. It was all too much.

Amid effusive farewells and disconcerting calls of 'good luck', Ada took Michael's hand and descended the stairs. A few feet on towards the car she looked back. There was Melanie, arms folded, refusing to play the game, and Vera with her arms half-raised. Ada turned and threw the posy. There was laughter and applause, and Ada glanced back to see Vera with the bouquet, triumphant and unaware of Charmaine glowering at her side.

By the time the couple reached the home of Michael's friends, the moon was high. Ada could see an old, lattice-windowed Malay house set up on thick wooden posts. When Michael tooted his horn in the weed-ridden driveway, overgrown on either side with a tangle of vines and ferns, two men bounded down some rickety wooden steps, waving their arms jubilantly over their heads. One, Sanjiv, was a lanky Indian, wearing spectacles; the other, Jimmy, a Chinese, short and thick-chested like a wrestler. Ada, having been informed by Michael of their wit and intelligence, was pleased to see their playfulness. But as soon as the two friends were inside the house, after the back-slapping and genial insults, they drew themselves upright as though standing to attention as Michael made the introductions, and looked at Ada with so much respectful caution that she reddened.

To escape further awkwardness, she made a move towards a room adjacent to the entrance space where she could hear classical music playing on a gramophone. The room was messily stuffed with crippled rattan chairs and a large, badly scored mahogany table strewn with books and newspapers. The men seemed to be waiting for some comment.

"What beautiful music," she said.

"You like Mozart?" Jimmy, asked.

If this was Mozart, then yes. She nodded, appreciating the brisk lightness of a French horn, and felt a slight thrill, anticipating the chance of learning more – about music, about everything.

"Are you a musician too?" he asked politely.

Ada presumed the 'too' was referring to Michael. "I always thought I would try and learn to play the piano one day. But Michael is so good." She loved to watch his fingers moving lightly on the keys, seldom faltering.

Michael was behind her. "I'm not, you know. And if you want to learn you must. We have a piano in the house, and we can get a teacher."

"Or you could teach her, Michael," Jimmy said.

"I could, yes." Michael's gaze rested on her face, as if searching her for hidden talents.

Ada felt self-conscious. "My father used to play. But nothing serious," she said quickly. The family, sometimes with guests, would sit around the piano and sing as he played music hall songs in a boisterous, clumsy way.

"Well, I'm tone deaf, I'm afraid," Jimmy said, grimacing.

Michael was sauntering around the room. He picked up a book and examined the cover. "*War and Peace*. Mmm. Interesting reading for our times. I wonder what Tolstoy would write about the war now. And I wonder what will be written about it when it's over. What we missed knowing at our peril."

"What do you mean?" Sanjiv asked, adjusting his spectacles.

"We should know a lot more about what the Japanese think. How they think. Anything that would tell us about their mentality could be useful. Not so very long ago they were allies of the British against the Germans."

"But they modelled their army on the Prussians. They helped themselves to China. I can't understand why the British think they're not a threat. Just look at what they did in Nanking. They're savage beasts." Jimmy spoke fiercely.

"They're a complex race," Michael said, in a slow, contemplative voice. "I've been reading as much as I can. You've heard about *bushido*, I suppose. The way of the warrior. The Japanese are a naturally obedient people. Very orderly and decorous. And they have a strong loyalty to their emperor. A great sense of duty. They're capable of incredible self-sacrifice. They prefer to kill themselves rather than being taken prisoner. *Hara-kiri*, it's called."

His eyes were full of awe, and Ada was reminded again of his intensity, the Michael of strong convictions who worried his father. "Perhaps they kill themselves because they're frightened of what their enemies might do to them," she offered pragmatically.

"It's more than that. Much more." Michael strode out of the room. Ada wondered if he were annoyed by her comment and bit her lip.

Sanjiv followed Michael, and Jimmy glanced at Ada. "We're having suckling pig tonight," he said, as if offering consolation.

She gave him a wan smile. "You shouldn't have waited for us. We didn't expect..."

"It's all ready. We can eat straightaway."

Ada was thinking of something to say when Sanjiv returned. "Michael's gone to the car. He's gone to get a book. He's right. We should know more about the Japanese."

Jimmy muttered something which Ada did not catch, but he looked upset, probably about what was happening in China, Ada guessed. But now he smiled, remembering his duty as a host, and said, "I hope you like suckling pig."

"I do" she said. "Is it hard to prepare?"

He was explaining about rubbing the skin and insides of the pig with salt when Michael came back into the room holding a book.

"I brought this with me." Michael opened it and flicked through the pages. "Listen to this." He began to read. "'We go up to the mountain. We bleach among the mosses. We go down to the sea. We welter in the brine. But whate're betide, Rejoicing I die. For I die for thee.'" He looked up, clearly moved. "It's a folk anthem. What chance have we against men with belief like this? The British and Commonwealth soldiers coming over... many of them are not much more than children thinking they're out for an adventure. You can't imagine them being prepared to commit *hara-kiri*."

"You sound as if you respect the Japs," Jimmy said, his tone resentful.

"I do respect them for their sense of honour," Michael replied. "And it would be wise for the British to do so as well. And stop thinking of them as hopeless fighters. That they can't see to shoot properly because they've got slit eyes."

"It beats me that the British aren't calling in the locals to train in case there's an invasion," Jimmy said, crossing his muscled arms.

"They don't think we're capable," Sanjiv added. "Sometimes, I think the Japs might be better masters than the British. They can't be worse, anyway."

Jimmy snorted.

"For you perhaps, Sanjiv," Michael said. "The Japanese know India wants the end of British rule. But for Jimmy and me, it's a different story."

Ada studied his features to gauge how threatened he felt. Would Michael's Anglo blood count against him? And then he looked at her, and his expression made her suddenly realise that should the Japanese invade she would have more to fear than Michael had. It was such a distressing thought that she dismissed it instantly.

The pig had been roasted over a pit, and they ate the succulent meat wrapped up in naan bread with spicy pickles. After a few beers Michael appeared to put aside his worries about the Japanese and relaxed with his friends. Sanjiv and Jimmy lost their previous inhibitions in her company and began to speak freely. Ada was pleased to see Michael boyishly enjoying himself as the men traded memories with one another, and swapped old jokes which had them laughing loudly. She wondered if Michael's 'transgressions' were simply pranks, the ones the best man had spoken about in his speech. Seated on the trunk of a fallen tree in the light of a yellow moon and candles set in jars, she was reminded of beach picnics, the carefree and privileged life she'd enjoyed as a child. She had been quite a mischief, too. She remembered how she and Vera would run away from Amah, ducking behind the baskets on the five-foot way, or try and steal the tin of condensed milk that Amah strung up out of their reach.

"You look tired, Ada," Michael said.

"I was just dreaming."

He stood and reached down for her hand. "It's been a long day." He drew her to her feet. "It's time we left. And I'm still sober enough to drive us to the hotel."

The others rose too, and shook Michael's hand, then shook Ada's. She thought they looked a little disappointed that Michael was leaving, yet at the same time they did not try and dissuade him. In their quiet manner and respectful nods to her they seemed to be acknowledging that she'd been patient in allowing them their merriment, and that this was her wedding night.

Chapter 4

HE WAS AS PATIENT WITH her as Elizabeth had predicted. He lifted her nightdress and caressed her, told her how beautiful she was, taking his time, not at all clumsy - but she felt stiff and awkward. The pain was sharp and quick, and when his breathing, which she heard coming fast in her ear, ended in a small moan, she let out a tiny accompanying whimper. She regretted this instantly, because as he drew away from her she looked up to see his frown. "I'm sorry," he apologised. "I was trying to be gentle. I hope you're not too hurt." She murmured that she was not - the emotional turmoil she was experiencing helped to dull the soreness. He held her gently and kissed her cheek, and then got up from the bed. She watched him pause for a moment and look at himself in the mirror set above a cabinet. He turned his head as if to view the sharp planes of his cheek and confirm something about his appearance. She wanted to tell him how handsome he was, but he seemed caught up in his own thoughts. She resisted the urge to say, "I'm sorry, Michael, it will be better next time, I'll know what to expect."

A crowing rooster woke Ada at dawn. She lay watching a mottled lizard fastened like a filigree silver brooch on the patchy wall, and listened to the incessant shrill hiccups and whooping of jungle birds. Michael was lying with his back to her, snoring quietly. Contentedly? Had it been all right for him last night, she wondered. Had her nervousness shown?

She rose now, put on her new lemon silk kimono, and opened the door onto a small balcony. The garden was neatly kept – the Malay manager and his wife were tidying the borders before the heat of the day. The woman, seeing Ada, waved, and indicated she would bring up the breakfast tray.

Michael was awake when Ada returned from her shower, and was sitting on the side of the bed rubbing his head. "Had too much of Jimmy's home-brew."

"I had a sip. A bit bitter for me. But the pork was delicious." She slipped off her kimono and self-consciously began to dress. He'd seen everything, but she still felt shy. "I enjoyed the evening. I liked Jimmy and Sanjiv. They're very witty. I can understand why you were good friends at school. You've got a lot in common."

"It's good to see them again. We used to do a lot together. They were scout leaders at college too. I was Yellow Bear, and Jimmy was Running Bear. And Sanjiv was Tiger Cub, I think. We had a lot of laughs." Michael had told her of the Rover scouts, his days in the jungle, the tribes in their tree houses playing their nose pipes.

"And you all chose to become teachers."

"Yes. That's true. It might've been because we all loved doing the scouting." Ada looked enquiringly at him.

"It's very rewarding being with young people who are really eager to learn," he continued. "Teaching them how to fend for themselves and work together as a team, even something as simple as digging a latrine. Real survival skills which they wouldn't have had a chance of getting otherwise."

"I expect your pupils love you. I loved all my teachers." She had especially loved beautiful Miss de Silva, who always told the girls to take their lessons seriously, so they could go far in a man's world. When she gave her rousing lectures, her eyes would scan the class impartially but come to rest on Melanie Chow and Ada, as if silently encouraging them.

"I cried buckets when I had to leave them. I went around the school sobbing."

Miss de Silva had cried, too. "You don't need to go to school to keep on learning, Ada," she had said. "Keep up with your reading." Ada had been top of the class in English every year. She always wanted to be a teacher, as did Melanie, who now taught at a school in Outram Road. Ada wished that she could have taken her exams.

"It must've been a real blow," Michael said. He knew that she'd been forced to leave school after her father's death.

"My father would've turned in his grave if he'd known," Ada said. "He had such ambitions for me. He always used to say I was a clever girl, and to go after what I wanted, like he did." It was her, not Vera, whom he'd take on his trips to Boat Quay, as though grooming her for responsibility. No wonder she was 'sense' to Vera's 'sensibility'. She pictured him sniffing the air, relishing the aroma of sizzling garlic and chilli, the scent of lacquered chicken, the pungent tang of drying fish. It was only durian that made him hold his nose. He could even ignore the stench of the river. Not for him the enclosed world of a Kentish village.

"I wish you could've met my father," Ada said. "You both would've got on well together."

"I really wish I could've met him too."

Michael had heard a lot about Noel – his coming out to Singapore with the Straits Trading Company and working as an overseer of cargo-handling on the docks. Noel had hoped to become a planter, but not having either the capital or the connections he decided to go into the hotel trade and put into practice what he'd learned in his days of service. He had no qualms about serving others, and turned his back on the English community who disapproved of his friendship with the locals, becoming what they called 'native', so native that he accepted Asian guests. Michael said that it took courage to have done that.

"He was very clever. Not educated like you," Ada said, "but he knew a lot of different things. He liked to talk to the guests. He was a wonderful husband and father. I've often thought that Mummy got taken in by Frugneit because she only knew what was good. And believed all men were like that."

"I suppose that if you've been lucky enough only to have known a good relationship, then you might not be on your guard," Michael said, stepping away from her and looking out of the window.

"Mummy says that if you marry well the first time you should be content and not try again. So, don't die, Michael. I don't want to end up as a lonely widow."

"I'll try not to." He did not turn to her, but she could see from his profile that he was serious. "And I'll try my level best to measure up to your father."

"Mummy said that you reminded her of him. She said right from the beginning that you were a decent man."

Michael looked at her now, and his smile seemed bashful, as if he did not deserve such a compliment. "We'll set off as soon as we can if that's all right. We don't want to get there too late."

They left the hotel immediately after breakfast to continue their journey to the Highlands. The road was flanked on both sides by dense green. Here and there trees rose above the canopy, their thin trunks bare until the light-seeking branches sprouted at their crests like opened parasols. Then they drove out onto a wide plain with rubber trees on one side of the road, and acres of palms on the other. Ada gazed in wonder at the butterscotch rivers and the bright green algae-covered lagoons; admired the grace of the women walking in the heat, straight-backed, carrying firewood on their heads; laughed at the naked children chasing the scampering chickens while the young men, spears at their sides, idled in the shade, and the elders squatted in front of smoky log fires.

When they began to climb upwards again through forest, a fine drizzle began to fall, and a mist hung over the hills. This was the English coolness that she had been promised. "It's so different here. It's wonderful," she said.

"Our scout camp wasn't far from here. I wanted you to see where we used to come."

"The air's so much fresher. It's a relief. I feel that I've got more energy already. Daddy used to say that he'd forgotten how to walk briskly like he used to do in England. You had to. To keep warm. I'm not sure I'd like to live in such a cold country." Her voice faltered. "Mummy says she'd never be able to survive there now."

Michael glanced at her. "What's the matter? You look sad."

"I told Vera about Dr. Wong seeing to Mummy. I hope she took it all in."

"I'm sure she did. She'll manage, now that you're not there and she can't leave it up to you." He patted her knee. "We'll take lots of photos and your mother will see you smiling happily in every one, instead of looking as if you're carrying the world on your shoulders."

"Not like you then."

"What do you mean by that?"

"I've never known anyone who was more concerned about the welfare of others," she said, thinking of his anger with the Chinese property developer.

"Well, you've been keeping the wrong company."

She realised that he was being flippant, disowning the suggestion that he was especially caring, but after a moment's silence, she said, "Not the wrong company, just a different one. The one that has to think of what's for dinner, or if the clothes are washed." Reminded of the duties of running the boarding house, she wondered how she'd ever managed.

"Perhaps one day it won't be like that. Men will have to think about all those things and women will be the ones saving the world."

"But we're already doing that, aren't we? Without your meals you'd be good for nothing, Michael." She smiled, watching him laugh.

"You'll have more time for yourself now," he said, seeming to understand what lay behind her remarks, the regret for her abbreviated education.

"I want to do my share. I hope your mother asks me."

"She will. But she does have everything under control."

Ada made no reply to this.

"Don't worry. We won't have to live with my parents for long. I'm going to apply for married quarters. Though I'll have to wait my turn. Unless I get promotion. But I'll never be a headmaster, I'm afraid. Except if all the Brits do a bunk from here."

"But if the British do a bunk then the Japanese will take over, and what you were saying yesterday, that anyone with white blood…" She stopped. She did not want to talk about the war now.

Michael squeezed her hand, and perhaps sensing her apprehension said, "Let's not think about that. We're on our honeymoon, darling."

Yes, they were on their honeymoon. Besides, what was the point in worrying about something that would probably never happen? It was in the papers nearly every day that the Japanese had better things to do than invade Singapore. And if by some horrible turn of events it should happen, then there was even more reason to treasure every moment of happiness. Live in the present. Gather ye rosebuds. Goodness, she would never have another honeymoon.

The land had now become terraced for market gardens. Workers in wide straw hats bent over the rows, and on the roadside there were stalls heaped with glossy fruit and vegetables.

"Look, let's buy some bananas," Michael said, slowing the car.

As soon as it came to a halt, curvaceous smooth-skinned women in bajus and sarongs swayed gracefully towards them and smilingly offered spider bananas for a few cents. There was a knowing sensuality in their every move, it seemed to Ada. Reminded of her sexual inexperience, she only half-listened to Michael when he pointed at the grey scars on the slopes and talked about the slump years of tin mining, the difficult time for the workers.

They stopped to eat at a roadside house. Satiated by the meal of beef rendang, both were quiet as they travelled on over hillsides thickly quilted with tea bushes. Through a light mist, Ada could see the pickers with baskets on their backs, and in the distance the large white houses of the European bosses, which made her think of her parents, how they'd left England to make a better life together, and how her mother was now on her own, and still missing Noel.

The sound of a nose-flute echoed dolefully in the lush valley. Ada looked at Michael. She could not bear the thought of losing him.

By late afternoon the clouds were swimming fast together and darkening as they collected. They looked threatening, doom-laden.

"It's going to rain cats and dogs. There's going to be a storm and a half," she said.

Michael smiled. "Sometimes I think you sound more Eurasian than I do, Ada. But if you want to be really correct it's *bulls* and *bisons*. We should be there before they stampede." He pointed to a large white building, striped with black, at the top of a jungle-covered hill. "That's the hotel. It's mock Tudor." He said this with satisfaction. Critical of the British he might be, but Ada considered that there was a great deal of respect as well. It was a strange mixture of love and hate.

As they drew nearer, Ada saw golfers striding with purpose across an expanse of smooth green, no doubt aiming to complete their game before the storm broke.

There was a clap of thunder, and a seam of gold pressed out on the purple sky. It was raining by the time they reached the entrance. Leaving the car to be parked and the luggage to be brought in, Ada ran quickly up the steps while Michael tipped the attendant.

She blotted her face with her handkerchief and gave her name to a smiling blond woman at the desk.

"Ah, yes, Mr and Mrs Wood. It's your honeymoon, isn't it? Well I hope you have a wonderful time! We'll do everything to make your stay with us as perfect as we can!" Michael appeared and stood beside Ada. "You don't mind if I see to this gentleman here while we're waiting for your husband?"

"He is my husband." Ada expected the woman to beam another welcome, toss around words of delight, but detected instead a tightening of the lips. Was that disapproval beneath the finished smile and effusive wish for their stay to be most pleasant? Ada looked at Michael to see if he'd noticed that the woman was put out to find Mr Wood was not blond and blue-eyed like his bride. To her relief he showed no sign of doing so.

But she felt annoyed, insulted, and again later that night when they entered the beamed dining room, and people looked up at them with an affronted curiosity.

She told herself that she should not be shocked, should have guessed, should have been prepared. Hadn't her father, because of his friendship with the locals, been cold-shouldered? In Singapore, she and Michael did not go to the haunts of the British, which was the reason perhaps they'd not experienced such rudeness. So was it to be like this whenever they ventured as a couple to places the British thought belonged exclusively to themselves?

The waiter brought a watery mulligatawny soup. Michael immediately began to eat in a determined way, as if he were trying to ignore the staring, to demonstrate his indifference. Ada lifted her spoon, sipped, then abruptly stopped and glanced boldly around her until heads turned and eyes lowered. She put out her foot to touch Michael's. "It's the first time I've seen a fire *inside* a building. I've seen them in pictures, of course, but not like this."

"I thought you might like a taste of Old England," he said.

"It's different, yes."

She must have sounded half-hearted because he looked carefully at her, then leaned forward and said quietly, "Take no notice of bigots. They want you to share in their wretched insecurity." He smiled, and spoke in a normal voice. "Perhaps I should've taken you to Penang. But you've been there. And I wanted to show you a part of the world I've had lots of adventures in. I'm a kid really. Men never grow up, as you probably know."

Ada looked about the room again. No one was staring now, but the confident English voices sounded strident, hostile. She studied Michael as he checked the menu for his beloved desserts. He did have a boyish face, vulnerable too, and she felt a surge of protectiveness towards him. He raised his head, and his gaze rested on her for a moment, then he reached out for her hand and squeezed it as if in gratitude.

The rain was beating down hard when they went upstairs to the bedroom, and occasional gusts of wind drove it dramatically against the shutters. Ada was reminded of the man who used to play for the silent movies at the Cathay, increasing the tempo and pounding the keys whenever something dangerous was about to happen. After a shower she put on another crepe-de-chine nightgown with her mother's carefully drawn threadwork, then slipped into bed while Michael was in the bathroom. When he emerged, she turned to look at him and smiled. She would not allow him to see her nervousness.

He was as gentle with her as the night before, and only as he felt her relax did he see to his own pleasure. She heard his quickened breathing, responded to his growing excitement, and although when he made that moaning sound again she cried out too, this time it was from pleasure, and the relief of having felt it. But he seemed to become immediately aware of her, and she sensed his caution, a withdrawal of spirit.

"It didn't hurt at all," she whispered.

"You must tell me if I ever do. I want you to enjoy it, really enjoy it."

"I did," she said.

"Are you sure?" he asked, a trace of doubt on his face. She smiled, and he stroked her neck, examining her features in the light of the bedside lamp as if trying to detect how honest she was being. "I love you with all my heart, Ada," he said, kissing her again.

Chapter 5

May, 1941

Ada was aware of a long tailed mynah observing her from the feathery branches of a large angsana tree, its head cocked to one side as if bemused by the madness of an English woman out in the full sun. The asphalt was baking; heat came up through the soles of her sandals, and the fire, which Amah had made in the centre of the tennis court, roasted her face. It was like being in Hell, but she welcomed the suffering as a form of penance and waited patiently for Amah to throw another wad of paper money onto the blaze. Ada had often mocked the old woman for her superstitions, but now she envied her. How consoling it would be to believe that Elizabeth would have an afterlife in which she would want for nothing.

In the morning of the funeral Amah had beaten her chest and wailed before a beautiful paper house and motor car for Elizabeth to enjoy in the next world.

"In next life your mother have everything she want," Amah had said. It had been comforting to think of that during the funeral service as the congregation knelt and prayed, formal and quiet. At the graveyard, when Michael put his arm around her, Ada had cried silently, but the grief seemed to go more deeply inside her. Sometimes she felt that there were ashes in the pit of her stomach. It was guilt, of course. She knew that Elizabeth had become very over-tired sewing for the wedding. And then there was the move from Geylang to Corbett Road.

Ada cursed herself again for having left the hospital bed where Elizabeth lay, hung around with tubes and wires. She was unconscious, but at the last moment might have opened her eyes and seen that she'd been abandoned. It was dreadful to think that she died alone. Ada remembered the last time she was with her mother. It was only a month ago, here in Serangoon, before the journey upcountry. She said goodbye to Elizabeth then, but it was not a proper goodbye, not enough gratitude. She'd been thinking about herself; how she would fare on the honeymoon.

Ada looked towards the forest beyond the tennis court. Michael had said that he used to go into the deep woods with his sling and satchel and pretend he was Tarzan, take a pot shot at the monkeys and birds. Once he found a dead snake and chased a screaming Evaline around the garden. It was hard to imagine Evaline being frightened of anything.

Ada looked down at Amah. She was sweating profusely. "Come, Amah. It's time we went inside. You've done enough."

Amah remained squatting and squinted at the notes in her hand like a card shark assessing the deal, then glanced up at Ada. "Go." Amah gestured with her head towards the house. "You rest now. Must rest."

"I am going to lie down for a while." She did feel tired, but what she wanted most of all was the solitude; time to mourn.

In the quietness of her bedroom beneath the beating fan she sat upright by the shuttered window, placed her hands in her lap, closed her eyes and conjured an image of Elizabeth hovering above, her face serene because she was at peace. There was no sign of any hurt for her daughter's impatience with naïve remarks. She did not blame Ada at all for the sewing she had to do. Instead, she fondly recalled those times they'd sat together and worked. Ada pictured Elizabeth seated with a tape measure around her neck, her legs folded under her, the arch of one slender bare foot resting on the sole of the other, the toes flat and straight, the instep high. She could sit like that for hours and sew, little finger crooked, lips pursed in concentration. "Invisible stitches, Ada, or you'll have to unpick."

Ada opened her eyes. This was not what she wanted to remember, a mother wearing herself out with sewing. Quickly she sought another memory. It was the rainy season, so humid. All the teachers were on edge and waiting to pounce. In maths class, the compass kept slipping in her hand, and she could not concentrate. A shrill voice rang out and she stumbled to her feet. She'd never been scolded like that before. She was feeling very downcast when Amah came to fetch Vera and her.

As soon as she had reached home, Elizabeth, seeing her drawn face, hugged her and stroked her back. She'd cried noisily, pressing her face into a soft neck scented with Pears soap, while Vera kept asking what the matter was, and complained that the floor felt sticky. That kitchen with Elizabeth had been the safest place, and Ada yearned for it now. It hurt so much to think she would never talk to her mother again.

Ada had showered and dressed and was seated at her dressing table combing her hair, readying herself for the evening meal, when Michael returned home later than usual from afternoon games. He kissed her neck, then threw some marbles confiscated from his pupils onto the bed.

"What a day. Everyone excited about something. Not sure what. The juniors were impossible," he said. Ada watched him in the mirror. There was a brightness in his eyes, as if he'd been affected by the mysterious restlessness. "And how are you, darling?"

His tone was as compassionate as ever, but Ada sensed that he was distracted.

"Perhaps it's someone's party today?" she suggested. Michael shrugged.

"You look tired," she remarked, inviting him to talk about himself. He'd been so patient and understanding about Elizabeth.

"No, not tired. I just feel filthy. It's sweltering. I need to have a shower. And then you can tell me about your day."

He was aware that Ada had not settled in the household yet. She'd told Michael that she felt like one of the ornaments on Evaline's sideboard. Although she might have wished for release from the duties of the boarding house, she found herself lost with Evaline in such superb control of the home, family and servants. She realised that work gave her a sense of having some worth. She tried to busy herself with sewing, but found that sewing made her miss Elizabeth all the more. As for reading, her one-time love, she'd become stuck on a book, *After Leaving Mr Mackenzie* by Jean Rhys, which someone had given Melanie. Apart from her mind being clouded by sorrow, Ada had little sympathy for the heroine who behaved like a rebel, yet was prepared to be a kept woman, and was pathetically dependent on men.

Michael was intoning something in the shower, as he often did – lines from a poem or a play. When he emerged from the bathroom she asked, "What was that you were reciting?"

He ran his fingers through his damp hair and picked up a comb from the dressing table. "It's a far, far better thing that I do, than I have ever done" he said, combing his hair. "It is a far, far better rest that I go to than I have ever known." He stopped, comb poised, and looked thoughtful as if taking in the significance of the lines.

"What's it from?"

"*The Tale of Two Cities.* Charles Dickens. It's about a man who goes to the scaffold to save his friend."

"Were you reading the book at school today?"

"No." He looked excited, and she waited for him to say more, but he was clearly thinking of something else, something he was not intending to share with her. She did not believe it was the pupils' unrest that was preoccupying him, and recalled the Woods' lunch party a month ago when he'd claimed to have a lot on his mind. He was not angry this time, but this was the Michael who was strange to her.

★　★　★

Two Tamil servants brought in dishes of lamb cutlets and vegetables. The family ate English food in the evenings, Indian or Chinese midday. Ada wondered if this was a way of trying to keep a balance between the Anglo and the Asian parts of themselves. She preferred the spicy curries, the fragrant dhal, the succulent brinjal, but had not regained her appetite lost after Elizabeth's death, and indeed in the past couple of days had felt quite nauseous at meal times.

"Still no appetite, Ada? You're looking pale. Isn't she Michael? Look at your wife," Evaline said.

"I'm looking, and she seems as beautiful as ever."

"I've thought of buying tickets for *The Mikado* next Saturday," said Patrick. "Have you seen it, Ada?"

She shook her head.

"Saw it the first time when I was a young man, fancy free in London." He liked to reminisce about his business trips to England on behalf of his ailing father, and seemed to do this whenever Ada was around lately, as if offering her a link with Elizabeth. He was a kind and insightful man. He seemed to understand that she felt like a stranger in the household.

"I don't want to go," Charmaine said.

"No one is forcing you," Patrick replied.

"I'm going to a dance at the Club. I'm going with some of the girls I met on my shorthand typing course."

Ada was reminded of Charmaine's latest boast – her swift promotion in the office since passing her exams. It was difficult not to feel envious.

"You must make sure that you give Priti time to get your dress ready. Last time…"

Michael spoke over his mother. "Sanjiv's got a headship."

"He's younger than you." Evaline sounded offended.

"He's at an Indian school, Evaline. Michael's is a different establishment entirely," Patrick said, a note of warning in his tone.

Evaline ignored him. "You should've gone to England, to Cambridge, like your father wanted you to, and come back top dog."

"And where would that have got me?" Michael said. He had told Ada his reasons for not going. A cousin had been very lonely there, experiencing not only isolation but sometimes downright rudeness. Michael had not wanted his predictable anger at similar treatment to taint the pleasure of his studies. Patrick had given way, allowing him to attend Raffles College until he would hopefully mature and see the use of going onto Cambridge. He'd lacked any inclination to do this, however, and instead had trained to be a teacher.

"You could've worked for your father, but no, you had to help others out," Evaline went on, then turned to Ada and spoke forcibly, pushing her coarse grey hair behind her ears. "What Michael says is true, you know. The British have always kept the top jobs for themselves. They've treated us better than Asians, but never thought us good enough to be treated like equals. It makes me wild to think that they used to encourage their men to marry Indian women." She threw up her hands in a gesture of disgust. "And then, oh lordy, the Indians did not want to know these women. Or their children. Are you surprised that we stick together? If not for our ancestors learning to speak English and building themselves up, we would be eating dirt today. It is a sin."

With Charmaine having mentioned the Club – the Recreation Club – Ada pictured the manicured sward that divided it from the all-white Cricket Club at the opposite end of the Padang. She saw it as a symbol of the distance between the two races. The British might have permitted the Eurasians to be in eyeshot and in a prime position, thus granting them superiority over the Asians, yet still did not allow them equality. Indeed, it was a sin.

She was about to say that not all British people felt superior to Asians, her own father for instance, when Patrick spoke.

"Education is everything."

"But what if there are no jobs?" Michael asked. "We train the boys to be clerks. Thousands qualify, and because the country has no need for so many, the pay is a pittance."

"Our day will come," Patrick said quietly. Michael's face was flushed. Was he on the verge of becoming angry? Ada anxiously fingered the silver condiment set – a scrawny coolie pulling a rickshaw – and glanced up at a portrait of a Victorian gentleman, proud of having built himself up.

"If not for the Asians then at least for us," Patrick continued, straightening his back. "At every critical point in the development of the British Raj, Anglo-Indians have fought and helped win battles. The Khyber Rifles, the Shekhawati Brigade, so many gave their lives."

"And where has that got us? Look at our son." Evaline stretched out her arm and flapped her hand at Michael. "He's the best teacher in his school."

"You don't know that," Michael said.

"You've told me how the headmaster relies on you. The children love you. They worship you. You must speak up. You must demand to go higher up."

"Mum, you just don't know how it works."

"I think you're frightened of tipping the boat." Evaline looked boldly at Ada. "You must get behind Michael. Push him to speak up. What is the point of working hard every day, all the time, and getting nothing for it? He must demand what they owe him."

Ada glanced at Michael. She could see his annoyance, and she disliked Evaline's glare. "I'm sure Michael knows how to go about these things."

Evaline tossed her head. "You can't let people walk over you, my boy."

"Evaline, Ada's right," Patrick began.

"What does she know? She's British. She hasn't had to suffer like we have."

"I'm not saying that you haven't been treated unfairly, Evaline. All I'm saying is I think we should leave it up to Michael to do what he thinks is best," Ada said, both surprised and emboldened by her firmness. Evaline opened her mouth; Ada spoke more loudly. "Michael has enough to think about without me nagging him."

Michael's gaze met hers. "I think you do look pale, Ada. How about we take a drive to the beach?"

The sparks of the twin poles of a trolley bus against the dark sky seemed to Ada like a celebration of her release. She took in deep thankful breaths of the hibiscus-scented air as the car left the city and sped along the lush verges of the road, then past the moonlit pineapple plantations.

"Better?" Michael asked, glancing at her. "Mum can be a bit overbearing. She likes to make her point."

Ada made no comment.

"Still very sad, aren't you?"

"It'll take time, I suppose. Time heals. Mummy used to say that." Ada sighed. "But she never got over losing Daddy. He adored her." Ada remembered how he used to watch Elizabeth comb her hair on the verandah with the silver-backed brush given to her by a kind mistress for a wedding present. He'd stand there and smile, full of pride. Perhaps Elizabeth was deceived by Frugneit because she was blinded by her need to be loved like that again?

Aware of Michael's anxious glance, she said, "I hope your mother didn't think I was being rude."

"She probably did. But it does her good to be challenged from time to time. Dad doesn't much because he wants an easy life."

"Still, I'm only the daughter-in-law."

"You're my wife. That's what's more important. When you spoke up for me I could've leapt across the table and kissed you." He smiled.

"I wish you had," she replied, feeling warmed by his remark, although she knew that Michael was quite able to stand up to his mother, and often did. "But then again you might have injured yourself, so we wouldn't be coming out here."

The moon was higher when they reached the sea, and shone down on the flat darkness like a spotlight picking out the fishermen hauling in their nets on the cigar-shaped boats beyond the pagar. There was no evidence of the barbed wire fences that had been erected on other beaches – as some sort of pathetic hindrance to invaders, Michael had said. Ada slipped off her sandals and dug her toes in the sugary sand. She could smell wood smoke. It was here, she could well recall, that Michael had proposed to her. A romantic spot, with the palms silhouetted against the sky and the sea ruffling gently.

"Do you remember what you asked me here, Michael?" It had been one afternoon when they drove to Katong for some sea air. Japanese women were paddling in the water, holding parasols to protect their alabaster complexions. A group of boys appeared with a paper kite. It caught the wind, and Ada, looking up and hearing Michael, believed that she'd never seen anything more graceful and free as it soared above the beach. But had she heard him correctly?

He took her hesitation as a rejection perhaps, because he'd stared at a spot over her shoulder. She'd heard the slight defensiveness in his tone. "You know my background," he had said. "Would you like to think about it?"

She realised what he was hinting at. Once he'd pointed to a portrait of his grandmother and said that people thought she was Spanish, and that he resembled her. He'd seemed relieved when Ada agreed.

Her heart had increased its beat, but she tried to sound as light-hearted as she could. "And you know my background. Wouldn't you like to think about it more?"

"Why would I want to do that? Why would any man want to?"

"Well, no one's come forward before." Her tone was playful, but in fact, not counting the eager partners at the tea dances from whom she'd accepted invitations for group picnics, and who had visited the house until she made clear her lack of interest, Michael was her first serious boyfriend. "I don't need to think about it, Michael. Yes. I would like to marry you."

"Of course I remember," Michael said now, putting an arm around her waist. "It was one of the most nerve-racking moments of my life."

"*One* of the most. I see. Not *the* most," she said, pretending to be offended. He laughed, and she caught his hand. "Take off your shoes, Michael. We can paddle."

The warm sea slapped gently on the shore, retreated and slapped again, a laconic melody that soothed her, made her feel she could say what was on her mind. Michael removed his shoes and they walked in the water. A few yards on, Ada said, "I feel I'd get over Mummy more easily if I could get out more. I've too much time to think about her, and I can't settle to anything. My mind keeps wandering off when I read."

"No one is preventing you from going out, anywhere you choose." He put his arm around her waist again.

"It's not about gadding. I need something to *do*. I'm used to feeling useful." She hesitated. "I thought of going back to the Municipal. There might be work for me. I remember Violet de Sousa getting married and coming back to fill in for people when they got ill. She said it worked well."

To her surprise Michael answered, "I think that would be a very good idea. I was wondering if you would do something like that."

"Perhaps I could do a shorthand typing course as well."

"Yes, yes. Or think about finding a tutor so you can carry on where you left off."

"Do my exams, you mean?" She looked up at him, wondering if he were serious, and felt a rush of delight.

"Why not? I really think you should."

She detected an urgency in his tone, which made her suddenly feel anxious. "It's been years since I did any studying. I might not manage…"

"You'll soon get used to it. You were a very good student." He paused, then said slowly, as if he did not want to alarm her in any way, "I've been asked to do a little bit of extra tuition for the older boys. I'll be busier than I have been. Home late sometimes. I don't want you to feel lonely."

"So better if I was occupied?"

He said nothing.

"I envy you going off each day. You've got a real sense of purpose."

"Well, I've got to save up for us, so we can live on our own."

"But it's not just that. You also do work for which you're not paid, Michael." She was thinking of the scouting, and free extra music tuition he gave the boys who could not afford the fees. "You don't just say how terrible it is that there's so many poor people, for instance: you give generously of your time to help them." She sighed. "I would love to be as useful as you are in the world."

"Lots of people do much more than me."

"Do you think one day they'll let married women teach?"

"I think that day is on the horizon. More women want to use their education, and to stop them because they're married is absurd. It's wasting a lot of potential. Not to mention money, when you think how much education and training costs."

"It'll cost a lot for me to have private tuition. Do you think we can afford it?"

"Of course."

"I wish I had your concentration. I watch you when you're with your books. You don't let anything distract you."

"Look." He led her out of the water. They reached the far end of the beach, and he picked up a palm frond and drew a circle on the sand, then divided this in half with a curved line. "You've seen this, haven't you? You know about Yin and Yang, don't you?"

"Opposites. Good and bad. Strong and weak. That sort of thing?"

"It's a bit more complex." He pointed to the two halves in turn. "One side is Yang, male. The other side is Yin, female. And the two are always striving towards harmony, because the ideal is to have a balance. You don't want a hot desert, and you don't want bitter cold, for instance. Now imagine this half. It's black. The other half is white." He drew two smaller circles in the larger part of each half. "In the black one, there's a small white circle. In the white one a small black circle."

"Which means what?"

"Each side has the seed of the other. See, as this side grows, the seed of the other appears. It's a cyclical process. A constant striving to gain something the other half has."

"So what are you trying to say?"

"Everyone has the potential to find what they believe they lack. You haven't had the chance to recognise your full worth, all your strengths."

"Or the chance to recognise all my weaknesses."

"I think you do enough of that, Ada."

"You don't have as many weaknesses as I do."

"That's not true, I'm afraid," he said quietly, his tone serious.

She sensed that he was preparing to say more. He took her hand, and they turned to face the sea. A soft breeze carried the smell of salt. The water was a glossy velvet. It was a beautiful evening, and Ada decided that she wanted it to remain that way.

"Well, it's good to hear that we might be equals as far as weaknesses go, Michael. But let's not list them now. Let's enjoy being here. It's such a lovely evening. Everyone has weaknesses. But remember, we can change. You just have to work on what you lack."

Michael put his arm around her and kissed her brow. They stood in silence. The fishermen began to crease the surface as they paddled their boat steadily towards the shore. Michael drew her closer. She felt calmer and more content than she had for a long time.

Chapter 6

Only Charmaine was in the dining room when Ada came in for breakfast. Ada had overslept after having woken at dawn, feeling a lurch of nausea. Returning from the bathroom, she had noticed that Michael was not in bed.

"Has Michael already left for school?" Ada asked Charmaine, who was was hungrily eating a bowl of creamy porridge. Ada grimaced slightly, feeling sickened by the smell of the food.

"I don't know," Charmaine replied abruptly, as if offended.

Ada suspected that Charmaine had interpreted her expression of distaste as a criticism. Evaline was constantly cautioning Charmaine not to spoil her figure – somewhat on the ample side – and Ada had heard Michael recently teasing her with a thoughtless chant, possibly from childhood days, 'fatty fatty boom-ba-latti, ate up all the ghee chapatti'.

Apart from the time she'd been chosen as a bridesmaid and chattered with excitement during her dress fittings at the boarding house, Charmaine had remained as aloof from Ada as she'd ever been. Ada hoped that in time this would change when Charmaine saw her position in the family was not threatened by a sister-in-law whose looks Evaline continued to praise. Ada had noticed that Charmaine, although spoiled materially, did not enjoy the attention which Michael, clever and articulate, received from his father, or the admiration of his ambitious mother.

Evaline was also growing more impatient with Charmaine for not attracting the right suitor – any suitor, to be precise – who would enable her to achieve some status in the Anglo-Indian community. Evaline did not seem to place much value on Charmaine having a good job.

Ada followed Charmaine's gaze, and saw Amah shuffling along the path that led from the servants' quarters, her face grim with displeasure. Ada hoped that it was not Abdul who had caused this. Ada had reminded Amah, since she'd arrived in Serangoon after Elizabeth's death and Vera's move to the flat of a work friend, that there was to be no more quarrelling. Patrick and Evaline would not like it, and she might not be welcome in the household.

Ada was about to go outside and call Amah when Charmaine stood up and said, "I've told her to iron my dress. And she hasn't done it yet."

"Perhaps if you asked her nicely, Charmaine. She doesn't like being ordered about. She's an old woman."

"She's a servant."

"I believe that you get the best from people when you treat them well."

"She's very rude. She answers me back."

Ada had heard this, and had scolded Amah, but knew the old woman was stubborn and had a lot of pride. "You want elephant ivory grow out of dog mouth?" she'd said to Ada. Pleased with her remark, Amah had pulled back her lips, and her gold tooth – for the rainy days of advanced age – gleamed triumphantly.

Charmaine pushed past Ada and stomped out onto the verandah. At least a quarrel with Abdul would be forestalled, Ada thought as she heard Charmaine making her demand, and went to search for Michael. If he had not already left for work, he'd be in the library. He liked to play the piano before school, and he did his marking in there.

He was at his desk.

"What are you doing, Michael?" She peered at the book in front of him, a page of oriental script. "Japanese!" She'd been told by his proud parents that he'd always been keen to learn native languages and was fluent in several. "Is that why you got up early? To study this? Why?"

"Because I think the best way to understand a people, other cultures, is to try and learn their language."

She remembered what he'd said to Sanjiv and Jimmy about the advisability of understanding how the Japanese thought. She was about to ask if he had the time for studying since he was so busy at school, when she felt nauseous again, and covered her mouth.

"What's the matter, darling?"

"Just a bit squeamish. Probably something I ate. I was sick this morning."

"Do you want to go back to bed?"

Ada shook her head.

"Speak to Mum. She has a cure for everything."

"I'm sure she has," Ada said sharply, thinking of Evaline pestering the servants, bustling continually, unless she had her friends over for an endless game of cards or mah-jong. But Ada was also annoyed with herself. As Michael had warned her, he was absent more with his teaching duties, and she was still underemployed and had not done anything to further her plans discussed on the beach a couple of weeks before. It was simply that she felt inexplicably tired. Perhaps she was still suffering from the shocking loss of Elizabeth? But after talking about the future, her opportunity to study again, she had felt quite buoyant.

Michael looked mildly puzzled, and she was sorry for snapping. Since the evening at the beach she'd felt closer to him than ever before. Their love-making was surely proof of that – although, she thought, her breasts had begun to feel uncomfortably sensitive.

"I really must see about Mr. Moses today." This was the name Michael had given her of a retired school teacher who tutored privately. "If you're sure we can afford it. I don't want to think that Patrick…"

"Of course we can. Go ahead." Michael began packing his satchel. "I'll try to be home as early as I can this evening. You've been very understanding." He kissed her cheek. "Take things easy today."

After he left, she returned to the bedroom and sat on the bed. Ahead was a picture of a sampan on a fiery sea. The sails were lifeless, the boat becalmed. She stared morosely at it for a moment, then imagined herself diving from the deck into the smooth warm water as she used to do with Noel at the beach parties he arranged for his guests. They'd swim together out to the anchored boats. She had done that with Michael too, she recalled, and pictured them competing to reach the pagar first. He would win, but not by much. They had not swum together since their marriage, she realised.

"Ada, Ada." Evaline was calling her, tapping at the door. The instant Ada replied, Evaline burst inside. "Michael tells me you're not feeling well."

"I'm all right."

"You look out of sorts. I've said this. And you have no appetite to speak of. It's not surprising. You've had a lot of sadness. It takes time to heal. But too much time with your thoughts only adds to misery."

Surprised and mollified by Evaline's understanding, Ada decided to speak up. Evaline was not a mind-reader.

"I'm used to being busy, Evaline."

Evaline nodded emphatically. "Then it's time to teach you how to run a home. See everything is done properly. Come with me."

Ada realised that there was no use saying she did not need to be taught, and followed Evaline as she bustled down the hallway towards the kitchen. A florid Indian cook, slicing onions at the bench, barely glanced at them, as if needing to show the utmost diligence. Evaline stood, hands on hips.

"To it all, there is a key. Time. No matter what it is, take your time. Don't let any of the servants do things hurry-scurry." She pointed at the onions. "See how wafer thin the slices are. This helps them to brown quickly in the oil. Hot oil. Hot. Must be hot." She beckoned Ada to the fridge and held open the door, so Ada could view the slabs of meat. "Make sure you buy the best ingredients." She reached for a plate of red flesh and lifted it under Ada's nose. Gagging, Ada took a step back and placed her hand over her mouth. Evaline surveyed Ada's body.

"How long has this been going on?"

Before Ada could reply, Evaline, glancing guardedly at the cook, clasped Ada's arm and ushered her out onto the verandah. "Your breasts hurt, do they?" Ada blushed. Evaline's face lit up. "You could be pregnant, Ada. You must see our Dr. Wong straightaway."

Ada looked out onto the lush garden, and tried to absorb what had been said. She had not thought to be 'caught', as Elizabeth would put it, quite so soon, and though she smiled at Evaline, who was clearly delighted, she felt nothing but confusion.

"It's good the nausea is only really bad in the mornings. A girl at work said she felt terrible all day," Vera said. "So glad you could come out. I thought we should celebrate."

Ada smiled agreement and tried to look as animated as she could. The air in the amusement park was heavy with the smells of coconut milk, grilled meat, ripe fruit, and sweat.

She felt quite overwhelmed with the noise of dance band music and shooting galleries. She did not recall the Great World being so frenetic. There was an underlying current of hysteria, which she believed must be to do with the behaviour of men away from home, parents, anyone who might disapprove of their desire to have a good time. Across from her in an open-sided bar with a billiard table in the centre, soldiers were lounging back in their rattan chairs, beers in their hands, raucously singing 'run Hitler, run Hitler, run, run, run' while the doll-like taxi girls lolled coyly around them in their tight cheongsams, looking sleek and available. It saddened Ada to see them earning their money in this way, many of them fleeing the war in Indo-China. But without education or training what else could they do?

"The doctor said at the end of December," she had told Michael when she returned from the surgery. She saw a shadow cross his face, so fleeting she wondered if it had been her imagination.

He'd taken her in his arms and kissed her, then noticed her expression. "Aren't you thrilled?"

"I'm not really used to the idea yet. And what about my studies?"

"Once you're properly over the morning sickness there's no reason why you can't start, and then carry on until you get too tired. And after the baby is born you can continue when you feel up to it. Amah will be here for you to have time for studying. And Evaline."

"I can't wait."

"For the baby?"

"To not vomit in the mornings."

Bright lights exploded and a sabre-toothed tiger sprung across the navy sheet of the sky. The words, 'Tiger Balm' flicked out before trickling down onto the blanched leaves of a palm. She looked at Michael who was standing a short distance ahead in front of a wooden platform supported on trestles. Next to it was a makeshift tent, beside which stood three Chinese - a woman and two men. Their faces were thickly painted in white, and their brows, marked out heavily in black, slanted upwards like bird wings. All wore high, beaded hats that resembled the roofs of Chinese temples. Two bright blobs of pink highlighted their cheeks.

At the sound of a gong the three actors climbed onto the dais. Immediately, to the beat of drums interspersed with a clash of symbols, the men gripped the hilts of their swords, stood aggressively with their legs apart in their long, heavily embroidered gowns, and began to gesture at each other exaggeratedly, twitching long steel fingernails. The woman held her tasselled head on one side and watched them with a sorrowful fascination.

"Have you ever seen so much passion conveyed with so much restraint?" Michael said, turning to the sisters. "It's all there. Hatred, love, jealousy, loyalty. It's most definitely opera. Wonderful."

"But not like the opera you listen to?"

"The language is different. The music. But the intention is the same."

"What's that?"

"To stir the blood."

Ada wanted him to continue. His eyes were bright as they often were when he spoke about music or great literature. He was clearly moved - as he had been, she recalled, when reading the Japanese folk anthem to Jimmy and Sanjiv.

Vera was not listening. Excitedly, she pointed towards a hall where band music was playing loudly. "Do you fancy a little trot around? The exercise will do you good, Ada."

Ada was about to refuse, knowing that Michael did not like dancing, when Michael took her arm and ushered her forward. "She's right," he said.

They found a table close to the floor, and as soon as Vera was asked to dance by one of the soldiers at a nearby table, Michael rose.

"How about a trot, then? I think trot is the right word for what I'm capable of."

"You're a good dancer," Ada remarked as they began to circle the floor. Michael grimaced. "I think you set yourself such high standards in everything that you're not happy unless you excel."

"Are you saying that I'm a competitive killjoy?"

"No. I'm just saying that you can just enjoy yourself and not worry if you're not as good as you think you should be. I saw you with Jimmy and Sanjiv. I know you can be very light-hearted and playful. I like that. I like seeing that side of you. Not the Michael always working hard. Or studying Japanese."

"I take what you're saying very seriously indeed," he said, smiling.

She smiled too, recognising the jest. She was pleased to have spoken openly, and without offending him.

They passed a group of soldiers swigging from bottles. Conscious they were staring at her and Michael, she was reminded of the time in the Cameron Highlands' hotel, the hostile looks of the guests.

When the music stopped Michael ushered her before him, and as they began towards their table a cheery voice asked, "Can I have the next dance?" A soldier, a moon-faced blond youngster, appeared at her side. He was no doubt boldly confident after an evening's drinking, and believed that all women in the room were as easily accessible as the taxi girls. Michael stepped forward between her and the soldier.

"No cutting in. No cutting in," the soldier drawled.

Michael held Ada's hand and began to move on.

"You go for coloureds, do you?" the soldier said.

Ada turned to face him. "Are you referring to my husband?" The soldier took a step back. "I don't know what you mean by 'coloured.' But I do know that I definitely prefer men who can hold their drink and don't behave like ignorant louts."

Michael gripped her arm and walked on. "Ignore him," he said. "He's a fool."

Vera was at the table. "What was that about?"

"He was pestering me to dance."

Michael leaned forward, blocking her view of Vera, and asked a waiter to bring them a jug of cold beer and another of fruit juice. When he sat back his smile was tight and Ada could sense he was trying to contain his anger. They would not go yet. They must pretend indifference. A mere soldier boy was not going to drive Michael Wood away.

Vera noticed a friend from work, who beckoned her over to a nearby table, and Ada was left sipping her juice beside a brooding Michael. She looked about the room. The boy had disappeared. Not all of the soldiers were drunk. Most of them looked to be enjoying themselves in a sensible fashion.

"Don't be upset, Michael. As you said, he's just an idiot. He's had too much to drink."

Michael said nothing, and she thought again of the time in the Cameron Highlands. It was sobering to think that she and Michael would continue to face prejudice. As adults, they would cope. But what about a child? Their child? How could they protect it from being hurt?

Chapter 7

September, 1941

Ada was writing, seated at the dining table, when Evaline hurried into the room from the front verandah where she'd been resting.

"Why is it that I must see to everything? Where is Ahmad? My plants are crying out for water," she said, her voice agitated.

"Shall I look for him?" Ada asked, imagining the old Malay was hiding somewhere in the depths of the grounds with Abdul. They both worked hard, keeping the garden tidy and diligently carrying cans of water from the storage tank to the plants, but they kept in rhythm with the sun and avoided it when it was at its searing peak. It was unusual for Evaline to be interfering with them, especially as plant watering was an evening job.

"No. No. It is too hot." And with this Evaline grabbed her handbag lying on the dresser, then barged onto the verandah and down the steps.

Ada watched her head towards the servants' quarters, glancing back towards the driveway as if waiting for someone to emerge. When an Indian woman appeared and began to follow Evaline down the path, Ada realised that Evaline had only used the search for Ahmad as an excuse, and wondered about the need for pretext. The woman was very dark-skinned, possibly a Tamil, and wearing old-fashioned European clothes – an ankle-length, high-waisted mauve dress, long-sleeved, very demure. She glanced back at the house as if on the look-out for someone. Ada could see that she was young and pretty. Evaline stopped, her features severe, and called sharply to her. The woman tossed her head defiantly, but then obeyed. The two women disappeared around the side of the building.

Ada, wondering what Evaline could be doing, waited for a while, then was about to go to her room when she saw the Indian woman returning quickly up the path. Before she cut off to the side of the house, she paused and stared up at the window opening. On seeing Ada, her expression was one of intense curiosity. Evaline now reappeared, her face thunderous, and shouted, "Off you go." The woman hurried away, clutching what looked like dollar notes.

"Who was that?" Ada asked when Evaline came puffing up the steps.

"A servant. A bad girl. I had to kick her out."

"What did she want?"

"Money, of course. Wages I kept back for deceiving me." Evaline's sallow skin was dark with blood stirred up from some inner turmoil, and she avoided Ada's eye. "But this time is the last. You must always be careful to stop servants taking advantage of you."

Ada followed Evaline inside, wanting to ask more. The girl was delicate-looking, thin-shouldered.

Evaline hurried to the back of the house. Ada heard her in the kitchen speaking loudly, stridently, like someone under stress, but as soon as Ada entered the room Evaline made an effort to calm herself, drawing up her body and holding her head erect. When Ada began to question her, she cut her off. "I am busy, Ada. I don't want to waste time talking about a chit of a girl." She turned her back and began speaking rapidly to the cook, clearly upset by the arrival of the Indian woman.

Ada decided that she would ask Michael about this servant. When his car drew up in the driveway she left her book to greet him, her spirits rising as they usually did when he returned home after work.

As soon as she stepped out onto the verandah, Evaline appeared beside her. Ada sensed her impatience as Michael climbed out of the car. Evaline called sharply, "I want to speak to you, Michael. Come into your father's study immediately."

Evaline might show frustration at Michael's refusal to push himself forward for promotion, but Ada had never heard her talk like this to her beloved son. Ada looked questioningly at him when he'd mounted the steps, and he raised his eyebrows as if equally mystified, then bent down and kissed the top of her head before following his mother. Ada felt annoyed at being excluded, but went into the bedroom to wait for him, wondering at Evaline's behaviour.

She was trying to concentrate on her book when the door opened and Michael strode into the room. He said nothing, and immediately sat on the dressing table chair and began unlacing his shoes.

"What's the matter?" Ada asked anxiously.

"I really don't want to talk about it. It's not important."

"What do you mean, not important?" She did not like being brushed off like this. Michael pulled off his socks, then stood with his back to her and took off his shirt, preparing for his shower. "Your mother's been in a bad mood since a servant you used to have came for her wages this morning. Evaline said she had to kick her out. That she'd been deceitful. How was she deceitful?"

"I don't know." He sat down on the bed, his arms resting on his knees, his body slumped. He looked dejected and weary – probably weary of his mother, Ada thought.

"She didn't look deceitful. Perhaps she didn't like the way she'd been treated. Charmaine speaks rudely to the servants. To Amah in particular. And then she wonders why Amah won't obey her. I've warned Amah that she could get kicked out."

Michael did not look up. Ada felt a spurt of resentment. He was bored with household matters? She very much hoped that their baby would be a boy and would not have to cope with domestic worries.

"But if Amah is kicked out, then I'll have to go with her," she said.

Michael looked up now, and his frown gave way to a tired smile. He put out his arm for her to sit beside him. "Can I come too?"

He pulled her close. His sweat smelled of pepper, not at all unpleasant.

"I can't wait to get a place of our own, Michael. I don't care how small it is, or how dirty and shabby. We'll paint it and clean it."

"Or get a servant to. Whom we'll ask very nicely, of course."

Ada heard the quiet jest in Michael's tone, but continued seriously, "I felt sorry for that girl. She didn't look like a wicked person at all."

"Deceitful doesn't mean wicked. And you know how particular Mum can be about cleanliness and dust. The girl might just have slipped up."

"When did she leave?"

"A while ago."

"It must've been before I met you. Because I've never seen her before. In fact, apart from Priti, and Amah of course, I haven't seen any female servants." Ada creased her brow as she visualised the staff of the household. "Do you remember her at all?"

"I…" He stopped. Ada looked at him. He seemed worried, downcast even.

"Do you remember her?"

Michael leant forward so she could not see his face, but his voice was subdued. "I taught her for a while. She told me she wanted to learn English. She wanted to better herself, which I quite understood."

"So did you get to know her quite well?"

He remained quiet for a moment then gave a faint sigh. "As well as a teacher knows a pupil."

"Did you like her?"

Michael pinched his nose, and looked to be considering the question carefully, then said slowly, "I thought she was clever, and she seemed keen to learn. What teacher wouldn't appreciate a pupil keen to learn? I was new to teaching at the time. Not long out of college. I was pretty enthusiastic about imparting knowledge."

"Evaline wouldn't have liked that at all. Perhaps that was the reason she got rid of her. The English lessons meant she wasn't doing her work?"

Michael said nothing, and shook his head sadly, bewildered perhaps by his mother's behaviour.

"I wonder why she's just coming back for her wages now. If you say she left a while ago."

He was rubbing his forehead in a worried way.

"So what were you talking about with your mother? Were you talking about the servant woman?"

Michael sighed. "You know when Mum's upset about something she has to off-load at once to either Dad or me."

"The woman turning up really bothered her, I think."

"Look, just don't think about it anymore," Michael said impatiently. "It's really nothing to worry about. Let's talk about something else."

"Yes. About how we're going to find a place of our own as soon as possible."

"We'll find a place of our own soon. I promise," said Michael, stroking her back consolingly.

Indeed, Ada did not think more of the matter, and tried to fill her time with crocheting a baby shawl and reading over the notes on the Shakespeare plays which she and Melanie had discussed together in Geylang. Now that she was over the morning sickness, Mr Moses, the tutor, was due to come to the house shortly.

Then, about a week later, a letter arrived addressed to 'Michael's wife'. Both Patrick and Evaline were staying with friends upcountry, and Ada sorted the mail not expecting anything for herself. Surprised, she ripped open the envelope to read, 'Your husband has a black woman'. The message was made up of letters cut from a newspaper. Her heart thudded as she stared at the words.

Michael was at his desk in the library. Before him was a page of diagrams. She placed the note on the book. "This came in the post, Michael. What does it mean for heaven's sake?"

He read it, then rose, tight-lipped. "It's someone trying to make trouble."

"Why?" Her throat was dry. "Why, Michael?"

"They want to make you turn against me. It's jealousy. They're jealous of me." He flushed darkly and placed his hand on the desk as if needing to support himself.

"Jealous? Who is jealous of you?" Incredulous, she took a step back.

He shook his head, appearing as bewildered as she was. "I know many people. In the scouting world, the schools, the Club."

"But who could be *so* jealous to write to me like this?" She waited for an answer, and when he did not reply repeated her question. Still he was silent. Was that flush a sign of guilt? Her gut tightened. He did not look as indignant as she might have expected of someone who had been so badly wronged.

"Why do they think a black woman could come between us, Michael? Why not a white woman?"

He frowned, then said, with an expression of distaste, "Because it sounds more plausible for someone like me, I suppose."

"You mean a white woman wouldn't look at you?"

"Something like that."

"But *I* did."

"Yes, you did, darling. And I don't stop thinking how lucky I am."

She studied his face. He looked very sad. "Why are people jealous of you?" she asked quietly.

"For getting on. Having money behind me. For marrying you." He raked his fingers through his hair.

"It's such a horrible thing to do."

"That's the way the world is, Ada." He looked directly into her eyes. "Ada, I know it's been a shock to you. It's a cruel and nasty thing for someone to have done. I'm really sorry." He gave a deep sigh. "I don't want you to think about this anymore. It's not good for you to feel so agitated." She allowed him to put his arms around her. "I love you, Ada. I wouldn't hurt you."

"Why do you love me?" she whispered.

"For all the reasons I've told you many a time. But I'll tell you again."

She watched his face carefully for a sign of guilt, and though he looked dejected, the sincerity of his tone and the imploring directness of his gaze anchored her in the soothing balm of his praise.

She carried the words through the day and used them as bulwarks against the ugly message. She comforted herself with them before she fell asleep. But the next morning when she woke to find the bed empty beside her, she heard the dhobis talking in Tamil on the pathway beneath the verandah, and without invitation the young Indian woman entered her thoughts. The woman was pretty and very dark-skinned. Was she the black woman? Was she the one who'd sent the letter? Suspicions flooded into Ada's mind so quickly that she sat bolt upright. If the Indian woman had been sacked a while ago, surely she would not wait and only come now for her wages? So did she come because Michael had been more involved with her than he'd said? Was she blackmailing Evaline? Perhaps Michael was still seeing the woman? My God, was this Michael's transgression?

Ada realised that she'd never eaten out with Mrs. Sinathamby before. Mrs. Sinathamby had been more her mother's friend. But with Melanie on holiday in Penang with her parents, Ada had contacted someone else she knew who might offer a sensible view of things - unlike Vera.

The curry shop was in Market Street. She washed her hands in a greasy sink beside a glass showcase housing orange Indian cakes. It was smeared with finger prints, and she remembered this was the sort of place Michael would never visit and told her to avoid, as he also schooled her (quite ineffectually) never to touch hawker food. He was quite particular, what with his immaculate suits, his eau-de-cologne soaked handkerchiefs. No doubt people were envious of him. But to be jealous, that jealous?

She waited until the food arrived – curries, yoghurt and rice daubed like artist's colours on a banana leaf palette – to begin talking about the message and the connection she'd made between it and the Indian servant woman. Mrs Sinathamby began to eat greedily, deftly scooping up the food with two fingers and thumb. Ada dipped in a finger, tasted, and reached for her glass of iced water.

"Don't drink. It'll burn more," her companion warned her.

Ada knew this, but what was the pain of chilli sealed into the tongue to the confusion she felt, and the fear that Michael was deceiving her? She noticed a group of men at the opposite table watching her. One smiled when she caught his eye. She looked away quickly. She was an oddity here, a white woman eating in a cheap curry house with her fingers.

As Ada spoke Mrs. Sinathamby glanced up from time to time, but contemplated the food more, and Ada wondered if

Mrs Sinathamby realised how disturbed she was. At last Mrs. Sinathamby sat back, greased fingers poised, and said, "Such a story you have been telling me. You are very troubled, I am seeing this. But Ada, your husband has told you that people are jealous and want to make trouble. Why let them? They will only succeed if you let them."

"But the woman coming to the house, and Evaline giving her money?" Ada leaned forward and searched the older woman's broad, sweating face. Was it easy comfort she was being given, or was it good sense?

"There are wicked servants, you know. Not all are like Amah and my girl Menon. You know she has married, and is well on the way like you?"

"Evaline called Michael into the study as soon as he got home."

"So?" Mrs. Sinathamby waggled her head.

Ada shrugged. "He said she was upset about the servant coming and wanted to get it off her chest. She's very emotional like that. When she feels there's been some wrongdoing." Ada remembered Evaline haranguing Michael about going for promotion. "I wish we had a place of our own."

"That is quite understandable. I had a strong longing not to live with my mother-in-law. And she was a quiet woman. Not at all bossy. But women like to be the mistress of their own home. And especially when they are to be mothers. As you know, that was sadly not what I had to look forward to."

"Michael agrees with me that we need to find place of our own soon."

"He is saving his money, I hope. Some young men live way beyond their means."

"Michael does not spend."

"Then he is a good boy. And you must trust him."

"But the message!"

"People are jealous. How much must you be told that?" Ada looked down at her food. "If you are being a good wife then there is nothing to fear."

"What is a good wife?" Ada asked, her voice sounding hard and bitter even to herself.

Mrs Sinathamby glanced over her shoulder as if checking that no one would hear. The room was filled with the babble of voices. She turned her head again but did not look at Ada and directed her comments over Ada's shoulder. "As your mother's friend it is my duty to make you understand that men have appetites. Some are hot-blooded and do stray. But few leave."

"Frugneit left," Ada said.

"Ah." Now Mrs Sinathamby looked fully into Ada's face. "There you see. You judge Michael, a clever educated boy, by what a good-for-nothing wicked man did. Remember there are good men as well as bad men. Your father, was he a bad man?"

"So I should just be grateful that Michael doesn't leave?"

Mrs. Sinathamby shut her eyes for an instant, then opened them to give Ada a hard, brown stare. "Think what would happen to you, Ada, if he did. Be content. He doesn't beat you, does he? He doesn't use bad language, eh?"

"And I should be grateful for that! But if I have no trust..."

"Chee. You must find it then." Mrs Sinathamby reached across the table and laid her large warm hand over Ada's. "You must try very hard. It is for your own good. Your dear mother would say the same if she was here."

A hunched paanwalla man, in a vermilion shirt which complemented his paan-stained mouth, shuffled between the tables. He was laughing as he handed out the wares - betel nut leaves wrapped around betel nuts and lime. He said something to Mrs Sinathamby, who translated for Ada. "He's says he's a Rajput. It's a secret recipe to make breaths sweet for lovers." She winked slyly.

Ada, annoyed by her companion's insinuation and talk of being a 'good wife', which reminded her of Elizabeth's 'giving her body up', pushed away from the table.

"Thank you for your advice, Mrs. Sinathamby. Please give my best wishes to Mr Sinathamby. Tell him I still remember the speech he gave."

"You've not eaten much, Ada. I hope you've not taken offence by what I am saying." Ada stood, shook her head in denial, offered tiredness as an excuse for wanting to return home, and forced a smile. Mrs Sinathamby did not look convinced, and said, "Wait, Ada. Let us go together. I am thinking we will stop on the way to see the astrologer so you can put your mind at rest. You don't have to rely only on me."

Ada protested at the need for this – it was all ridiculous superstition, like Amah's offerings of paper money. But Mrs. Sinathamby was overbearing in her persuasion, and took Ada's wrist to lead her down the busy street.

Most of the doorways were open, and glancing inside one narrow room Ada was startled to see, beneath a tinselled statue of a goddess, a near-naked male figure lying on a bed and fondling his penis. Shocked, she averted her eyes quickly, and looked at her companion, wondering if she'd seen the man, but Mrs Sinathamby appeared oblivious. Ada felt irritated with her for insisting that they should make this trip to the astrologer, but at the same time she recognised how ignorant she was of the ways of men.

At last, they stopped and entered behind a beaded curtain into a dark space. The air was stifling, and as Ada's eyes became accustomed to the darkness she could see a man breathing life, with a thin pipe, into a sheet of gold melted over a charcoal brazier. Across from him an old man sat cross-legged before a large, cloth-covered book. He was naked except for a loin cloth, and a garland of fresh flowers was looped on his glistening chest. He inclined his head at Mrs. Sinathamby's request, and gravely opened his text. Curry stung the back of Ada's throat, and, feeling nauseous, she fought the urge to run into the street as the old man began to chant through the netting of his white beard.

Mrs. Sinathamby translated, but Ada was only half listening, and once they were outside again asked for the prophecy to be repeated.

"Ayee. It is not all bad. You have no need to worry. At first you will have troubles when outside forces come."

"The Indian woman!" Ada's heart skipped.

"Oh no. It is the war."

"The war. It's going to come, then?"

"Chee! Who knows? But you must be prepared. Take things carefully. Be strong for those who are close to you. I am glad not to be living in the middle of the city in these times."

Ada thought of the baby she was carrying, and the words revolved in her head. So many words, so much advice. And yet there was a single message. To cope with what was to come, she must try to put aside all her doubts. She must not allow herself to imagine there was something more to the relationship between Michael and the servant woman than that of a conscientious teacher with a keen pupil. She must not allow the spite of other people to spoil her marriage. She must not forget that Michael was a clever and considerate husband, encouraging, kind. Equally importantly, he would be an excellent father.

Chapter 8

OCTOBER, 1941

ADA RETURNED TO THE HOUSE with Evaline after shopping, and found Patrick in a troubled state. He was seated at the dining table facing the wireless, his hands flat on the table with fingers spread. Evaline, upset by an argument she'd had with her magician jeweller, was oblivious of his mood.

"How does he think he can get away with being uppity with me?" she said for the umpteenth time. "For years I've been a good and faithful customer. For years. Never will I go back there again. It makes my blood boil." The Indian jeweller had been short with her insistence that he melt down some bangles to make a necklace for Charmaine. The design was too intricate, and when Evaline would not accept this, he shrugged, pulled a face and turned away. What was the world coming to, Evaline had exclaimed as they trudged home through the sultry heat? Asians were getting above themselves, she'd said with Anglo-Indian superiority. They were showing their heads because they stupidly believed that the Japanese would come in and allow them to be top dogs.

Patrick pushed back his chair.

"I must visit the Hume Pipe Company immediately."

This announcement was insufficient to catch Evaline's attention. She was flapping a handkerchief in front of her face as though signalling for help.

"We'll have to get the garden dug up."

At this Evaline stopped and stared at him with her mouth open.

"Thomas has just said we must take care of our own bomb shelters. We will have to build above ground because of the high water table. Concrete pipes will be best. With granite over the top, then turf for camouflage."

"But my flowers," Evaline cried.

"You won't need flowers. If the Japs think to attack us we'll need shelters and gas masks. And we'll need to grow our own vegetables."

"But this is not England. We are not having the war here. You said."

"There's no need to be unnecessarily alarmed. But it's always best to be on the safe side, that's all." With this, Patrick stalked out of the room.

"Oh Lordy, what is the world coming to." Evaline pushed her plump, bejewelled fingers into her hair and shook her head in dismay.

Ada made her sit down and went to fetch cold drinks for them both. That morning she'd seen a group of Eurasian men practising rescue duties, running through the streets with stretchers. She knew from Michael that volunteers were training as air raid wardens and fire fighters. Michael himself had joined the Medical Auxiliary Services, and the Eurasian Defence Corps. Although troubled that Michael might be called upon to fight, she allowed herself to be reassured by the government's repeated claim that there was nothing to worry about, and, like Patrick, viewed the exercises as a way of being on the safe side.

Not wanting a conversation now with Evaline about the war, Ada returned from the kitchen with a glass of lemon barley water for her mother-in-law, then escaped with her own glass to the sewing room.

Her lessons with Mr. Moses had only just begun when he became ill and was persuaded by his daughter to retire properly and move to her home in Kuala Lumpur. Ada was determined to find another teacher as soon as possible after the baby was born and spent some time most days reading from the history books he'd left her, completing *Great Expectations* and *Hamlet* and doing what algebra and geometry exercises she could with Michael's intermittent tuition. But she was becoming increasingly aware of the life in her womb and wanted to prepare for her baby. She spent more time sewing baby clothes, smocking the bodices and edging the little puffed sleeves with lace. She loved the delicate work, and was pleased to be busy – had insisted, when Evaline spoke of having the baby things made by a Chinese seamstress, that she would do all the sewing for the child. She could now well understand her mother's vehement wish to sew the wedding clothes.

Although the room was on the cooler side of the house, and the fan was whirring at top speed, the needle kept slipping in her fingers. When she heard the muezzin calling from the mosque she wiped her damp hands on a towel, stood and stretched. She must not sit still for long. Her legs were swelling, and Dr. Wong had told her to take frequent and gentle exercise. Wandering into the corridor she noticed Evaline carrying a large box into a spare room used for storage. Ada stood in the doorway, and Evaline pushed the box hastily into a cupboard with a startled, guilty expression.

"Clothes and toys for the orphanage. The poor little things," she said, placing her hand on her chest as if to emphasise her concern. There was something overly theatrical in her gesture, yet it was not uncommon for Evaline to display her compassion for the underdog. When passing a ragged child beggar on the street she would toss some coins and mutter, 'suffer the little children to come unto me'.

"I could sew some little dresses and romper suits for them," Ada said.

Evaline shook her head. She seemed embarrassed by the offer. "It really is not necessary."

"I'd like to. It wouldn't take me long at all."

"No," Evaline said. Her tone was sharp, but she reached out and grasped Ada's arm as if in apology, then made some excuse about needing to check on something in the kitchen.

Ada sensed the older woman's agitation. Mystified as to what lay behind it, she decided to relate the incident to Michael when he came home. After his shower that evening, she described what had occurred. "She seemed quite anxious," Ada concluded.

Michael listened, his expression grave. "You know that she likes to do things her own way." He paused, thoughtful, even moved, and said, "She loves children."

"Your mother does have a kind heart."

Michael sat on the bed. His face was drawn. "She does have a kind heart," he said quietly. "Like you." He reached for her, pulled her to sit on his knee, and rested his head on her shoulder.

She stroked his hair, feeling protective of him. "You're looking very tired. You're working too hard," she said gently. "But you must be relieved we're being advised to prepare for the worst. It's the best way of avoiding it. Yes?"

"I hope so."

A few days later, to Ada's surprise, Charmaine came to the sewing room. She'd never sought out Ada's company before. When learning of the pregnancy she had offered only a subdued congratulation. This had not concerned Ada as she'd understood Charmaine was reacting to her mother's ecstatic response and was possibly anticipating Ada's elevation in the household as the bearer of a longed-for grandchild.

More surprising was the compliment, "You're looking very well, Ada."

"Thank you. On the whole, I'm feeling very well."

Charmaine sat on the floor and began to fiddle with the hem of her skirt without speaking for a few moments, then said, "I can't imagine having a baby."

"Why not?"

"I have to get married first." She paused, and tugged at a loose thread before continuing. "I met someone at the Club. He was very nice. He said he'd call, but he hasn't. I keep waiting and waiting. I haven't said anything to Mumma. She'd start feeling sorry for me, and I couldn't bear that. I know where he lives. I thought to call on him. But I know that would be wrong." She looked up at Ada, perhaps hoping for an encouragement to go ahead anyway.

"Yes, I don't think that would be a good thing to do."

"So what can I do?"

"Wait. And in the meantime, go out and mix with as many people as you can."

"Is that what you did? Is that how you met Michael?"

"No. Michael came to our house. My sister invited him to her party. I wouldn't have met him otherwise."

"You were lucky."

"I was very lucky," Ada said, reminded of Elizabeth saying, 'You don't know how lucky you are, Ada'. It used to get on her nerves.

"I bet you can't wait for the baby."

Ada smiled in agreement.

"A woman at work just had a baby, and her husband did the bunk."

"Poor woman. That's very sad."

"I know Michael would never do that," Charmaine continued. "He's too responsible." There was another pause. "Do you mind him working hard all the time? He's looking haggard."

Ada sighed. "I've told him he's working too hard." Evaline had remarked that morning, "He can't stand back, that boy. Too high thinking for his own good."

Charmaine continued. "The trouble with Michael is that he wants everyone to think the best of him all the time. I've never worried about that. I do what I like." Ada looked unconvinced by this statement, and Charmaine added, "Anyway, I'm definitely not like Michael who thinks he always has to be the perfect son."

Perfect son. Decent man. A good boy. Yes, Ada thought, how believable was it that Michael could betray her? As Mrs Sinathamby had said, why let the jealousy of others poison her mind? Why fret when he did not come home until late? But even as she told herself how foolish she was not to trust him, the image of the Indian woman staring up at the house, her expression so intensely curious, intruded into Ada's mind.

When Charmaine left, Ada could not return to her sewing. She went to her bedroom, sat down in front of the mirror, and stared at herself critically. Her face was fuller, pink-cheeked. Perhaps she'd reached the 'blooming stage' much talked about by Evaline and her friends? She forced a smile. She was a healthy mother-to-be. Michael was always telling her how beautiful she looked these days. He probably thought she was perfectly content sewing and studying; that she was not interested in what he was doing. But if she knew more, she would imagine less. So why not ask him for a bit more of his time, more of his company?

The car inched behind rickshaws and bicycles, and hawkers with loads balanced across their shoulders. On the pavement – the five-foot way – the shop-keepers were doing brisk trade from their crammed, open-fronted shops. Chinatown at night was not a safer world, Ada knew it would be foolish to think that, but darkness masked the squalor of the day. You could only smell the cabbages rotting in the drains, the putrid fish floating in the canal. Washing poles were drawn in, and families – the menfolk with their singlets rolled up, bellies on show – crowded between the open shutters, the rooms behind them lit by dim electric bulbs the colour of weak tea. Through the open window she could hear the frenetic click of abacuses, the chirp of infant voices, the plucking of a Chinese lute, a fire-cracker's explosion – all marked out against the rise and fall of a loudly spoken, multi-inflected language. This was life; this was what Noel had loved, and what he always said England could not match. "Why would anyone want to live anywhere else than Singapore?" she recalled him saying. Why indeed?

Michael parked the car outside a temple. An old man was scrubbing the steps. Long red banners, marked with Chinese characters, fluttered at the entrance. Through the open door she glimpsed a gigantic Buddha. He was unlike the laughing, rotund Buddhas seen in most temples. Slender and long-bodied, with elongated ear-lobes nearly reaching his shoulders, his sage expression reminded Ada of Patrick, whose small kindnesses belied his somewhat aloof manner. Once or twice lately she'd caught him watching her with a grave face. Perhaps he understood how lonely she felt sometimes, with Michael so busy.

"You haven't changed your mind? You still want steamboat?" Michael asked, opening her door. "There's a good Szechuan around here as well."

"I'd prefer a steamboat. Haven't had one since..." Since Frugneit, she realized, and thrust the memory away.

Michael took her hand and they walked in and out of the shadows of the five-foot way. There was a light breeze and the swaying paper lanterns slapped light on the deep glaze of porcelain tiles, catching two pig trotters offered for sale by a withered old woman, then the painted face of a street walker, next a young mother's lap filled with child. Three women coping with poverty, and possibly loneliness too, Ada thought. What right had she to complain of anything?

"In here, Ada." Michael ushered her into a brightly-lit room. Roasted pigs, dyed red, hung from hooks along the wall. Apart from themselves everyone was Chinese. A slight woman ushered them to a small round table, and as soon as they settled brought a rusting gas-burner and lit it under a bowl of clear broth.

"What a treat," Ada said. "It could be the last one for some time. I don't expect we'll get much chance for a while once the baby is born." Michael nodded, his lips pressed together, seeming to deliberate on the significance of this. She continued, "I can't wait." She paused, anticipating a smile, some remark that he too was impatient for their baby, but he stared seriously at her. "We haven't done this for ages, have we, Michael? Been on our own together. It's like old times." She wondered if he realised how much she missed him. "I've hardly seen you lately."

"I'm sorry. But since the Head left I've got everything on my shoulders."

"And all your work for the medical service and the volunteers. Do you need to do so much, Michael?"

"Well, since I've been saying for a long time that the locals should be called as volunteers I have to put my money where my mouth is."

The waitress brought dishes of raw meat, fish and diced crisp vegetables to dip into the simmering stock, and then into small bowls of different sauces, dark brown to deep red, sweet and sour. Michael lifted his chopsticks. Ada tapped the ends of hers on the table and watched him pick up a sliver of fish. "Do you think there is anything I could join? Like the M.A.S.?" she asked. "I think it would be sensible for me to know some first aid. And you never know with children what accidents might happen."

"I'm not sure that they would take you on at your stage. But I could teach you the basics. Yes, you should know some first aid." He put down his chopsticks, looked carefully at her, then said slowly in a gentle voice, "But it would be wiser if you left Singapore." She sat back, and stared at him, wondering if she'd heard him correctly. He looked very serious. "If the Japanese invade the British will have a hard time of it." He paused, then said hastily, "I think you should leave. Go to Australia."

"Australia!" She opened her eyes wide. "We don't know anyone there. Would you be able to get a job? What about your parents?"

He put down his chopsticks. "I wouldn't be going with you, Ada."

"You wouldn't be going with me! You can't mean that. We've just got married. We're having a baby." She looked incredulously at him.

He reached for her hand. "I'm not in the same danger as you."

"But you have white blood," she protested, drawing away her hand. "You told your friends when we were on honeymoon that Anglo-Indians could be in trouble if the Japanese invade."

"But not in as much trouble as you, Ada." He looked down at his fists on the table. "And I can't abandon my pupils. Or the volunteers. I'm needed here."

"But what about me?" she said angrily. "I need you. You must come with me. How can you push me out to cope on my own with a baby?" Did he want her out of the way so he could be with the Indian woman? She felt sick with anxiety.

As if he'd not heard her, Michael looked up and said, "Our friends, the d'Aranjos, have decided to leave. They say they'd be very happy for you to go with them."

"You didn't tell me you were going to do that. I can't believe you did that without speaking to me first." Ada felt betrayed, and said, her voice fierce, "I'm *not* going to go with the d'Aranjos. I know I'm not needed here like you are, Michael, but I'm not leaving Singapore without you." She glared at him. He looked away. "And what about Vera? I can't leave her. And your family? Are they going?"

"Charmaine might. I've tried talking to Mum and Dad, but they won't budge."

Ada shook her head. "Well, I'm not going either. Singapore is my home."

Michael leant forward and looked directly into her eyes. "Do you want to live in a country where you'll be punished for being British? The Japanese will see you as their enemy."

"You said *if* they invade. They might not come..."

"Even the authorities are changing their minds about that, Ada."

"I'm not leaving without you. I'd die from worrying about you. And I couldn't bear to be in a foreign country, having the baby on my own. Our child will know both of us right from the start. Surely you want that too?"

"Oh, Ada, Ada, Ada. You must realise what danger you could be in."

She hated the word 'danger'.

"*Could be*. You don't know, really know what the Japanese will do."

"Just think what they're doing now, in China."

"But they hate the Chinese."

"They hate all their enemies. They can't afford not to."

"Then you'll be in danger as well. You must leave too. You must come with me. And Evaline and Patrick. We must all go."

Michael frowned. He clearly did not agree. She flushed with anger.

"If no one else leaves then I'm not going to. How do you think I'd feel being miles away worrying about you all?"

He began to speak. She cut him off. "Please let's not talk about this anymore. Let's not ruin our evening with an argument." Her mouth was dry. She swallowed hard and reached for a glass of water. Hand trembling slightly, she sipped a few times, then picked up a slice of raw beef with her chopsticks and dipped it into the steaming broth. Michael also ate, and there was silence between them until Ada said as firmly as she could, "So. When do the lessons start?"

What better way to show that she could be of use if the war came?

"When will you be free to give me lessons?"

He looked wearily at her. She avoided his gaze. He remained quiet for a while, then said in a reluctant tone, "I don't have M.A.S or the volunteers on Friday. I'll have to finish off at school first, but next Friday would…." He stopped. There was a commotion outside: a woman was screaming and men were shouting. Michael pushed back his chair. "Stay here," he ordered.

"Michael, where are you going? Please be careful," she called as he vanished onto the five-foot way.

The screams grew louder, becoming high-pitched screeches of despair. She headed for the doorway. People jostled for space, pressing back against the sacks and boxes lining the alley. They were looking in one direction, towards the noise of weeping and the shrill cries of children. When she stepped forward to see more clearly, someone shoved hard against her, and she clutched onto the door frame for support. Righting herself, she was aware of bodies rushing towards her. Three Chinese youths in red shirts and bandannas charged past. One held a knife smeared with blood above his head. She looked back from where the boys had come to see a girl beating her chest with her fists. Someone picked up a greasy bicycle chain and hurled it into the drain. Something terrible had happened. Now another figure pushed through the crowd - a young man in whites. It was clear that he was in pursuit of the boys, and people stepped back to let him through. She called to him as he raced by. It was Michael.

"I was angry with him. I shouted at him."

Vera looked surprised, perhaps because it was the first time Ada had criticised Michael to her. "You can tell me all about it after I've had my photo taken. We can go on and have a soda." Vera led the way, stepping out like a show pony, which made Ada feel ungainly and heavy-footed.

On Middle Road a huge billboard displayed a gigantic bottle of Haig whisky. On the corner was the Colonial Bar, its sides open, the male occupants propped up on stools, appearing aloof from the sweltering crowd. The street was lined with 10c stalls and shops dealing in silk items and porcelain. Ada could smell the ammonia tipped into the drains, and the sweat, but there was also the faint scent of attar of roses for sale in large, curvaceous flasks. The Japanese shopkeepers were doing fast trade with a group of women buying up lacquer trays, and lengths of silk that caught the light and shimmered like oil on water. Prices were astonishingly low. Michael had told her that the Japanese were selling up and moving back to Japan. "You know what that means, don't you?"he said, giving her a keen look which she pretended not to notice.

When they entered the studio, the Japanese photographer smiled broadly and bowed. "Do you remember me, Mr Tanaka?" Vera asked.

"Ah so! Madame Varga and her Oriental Jewels," Mr Tanaka replied.

Vera explained to Ada, "Mr Tanaka took publicity photos of us. I'm surprised he remembers me."

"You have a very good memory Mr Tanaka," Vera said.

When Mr Tanaka smiled and bowed again, Ada reflected on how scrupulously polite Japanese people were. It was hard to believe they would ever be transformed into the fierce warriors Michael had spoken about.

"I haven't come for a publicity photo this time, Mr Tanaka. I need a passport photo," Vera said. He nodded and smiled again. "I'm going to Australia. Like Madame Varga. She left a month ago."

Ada, who was thinking how charming Mr Tanaka was, and how dapper in his well-cut dark suit, silver tie and shiny shoes, saw him frown slightly.

As if sensing Mr Tanaka's discomfort, Vera continued, in an unnaturally cheerful voice, "I am going with a friend from work. It'll be an adventure!"

Mr Tanaka nervously fingered his silver tie. Ada noticed the tight skin of a scar on his white hand. It had a silver sheen, like his tie, and she had the nonsensical thought that he had chosen his tie to match his scar.

Mr Tanaka turned to Ada. "You leaving Singapore with your sister?" he asked.

"I'm married," she replied. "To a local person."

"Not British?"

"No. An Anglo-Indian."

"He does not want start new life in Australia?"

"He's a teacher. He loves his pupils."

"Where he teach?"

"Raffles Institution."

"Ah so. My son is pupil there. Husband name?" When Ada told him, he dipped his head respectfully. "A very good man. Very patient. My son has great respect for him."

"He is very patient. He loves all the boys. He would not leave them."

"And you do not leave him." The photographer dipped his head again. "You loyal wife." When he looked up his expression was grave, and his lips tight as if holding back something he dared not say.

Outside the studio again, Ada said, "That was very awkward, Vera. I don't know why you chose a Japanese to take your photo."

Vera shrugged. "He's a good photographer, and he has to make a living. He is not responsible for what's going on at the moment."

When they reached the ice-cream parlour and settled with relief in a booth, Ada continued to tell Vera about the incident in Chinatown.

"To be honest I wanted to hit him. I felt really bad about it afterwards. I was stupid and hysterical."

"But you were frightened." Vera said. "People say things they don't mean when they're scared. And you're pregnant. That's what makes you feel more scared, I suppose." Vera dipped the long spoon into her ice-cream soda. "Thank God they got away before Michael caught them up. He could've been stabbed as well. I've never heard of the Red Blood Brigade. You wouldn't believe school kids could do something like that."

"There's a boycott on Japanese goods." Ada said. "The man was selling Japanese goods. In Chinatown, for goodness' sake. You can't blame the boys in a way. Just think what the Japanese are doing in China."

"Just think what the Japs will do if they get here." Vera fixed her wide blue-eyed gaze on Ada. "Why don't you come with me, Ada? Michael is all for it."

Ada had rightly anticipated that Michael would put more pressure on her to go after Vera had announced her intention to leave, and the invitation from Vera to accompany her to get a passport photo taken had been his idea. He had hoped that she would change her mind and have her own photo taken as well.

She fished for the ice-cream at the bottom of her glass and avoided Vera's question with one of her own. "How are you for money?"

"I've scraped up enough for the trip, and now that Mummy's house and flat have been sold at last, I'll have enough with my share of the money to keep me going if I don't get work straightaway."

"I'm in no hurry for my share. Keep it until you're settled."

"That's very generous of you, Ada. But I don't think it will be too difficult to get a job. I've got a contact in Sydney from an Australian soldier I met. He says I could get a job working in one of the hotels."

"Can you trust him?"

"I'm not marrying him. I can trust him enough about that I think." Ada looked up, expecting to see Vera smile, but her face was serious. "Why don't you join me, Ada? You could easily get a place on the ship. It's only half-full."

"If things get worse, I might. And if Michael agreed to come as well."

"You loyal wife. Is not so?" Vera nodded her head, imitating Mr Tanaka.

Wanting to change the subject, Ada looked about the parlour. "Do you remember Amah bringing us here after school?"

"How could I forget?"

The ice-cream parlour did the best raspberry sodas in the city. Those days of simple treats seemed to Ada now like a glorious time of peace and blissful ignorance.

"I'm going to learn first aid," Ada said, injecting her voice with optimism. "Michael's going to teach me. We were going to start last Friday, but he didn't get home in time."

She had rung the school and they said he was not there. While waiting for his return, she felt crippled with suspicion. "I'm sorry, darling," he'd said. "It just slipped my mind. I had to see a parent about his son. They invited me to eat with them. I felt I couldn't refuse."

She knew that it would drive her insane not to believe him. For a moment she thought to confide in Vera, to tell her of the letter she had received, but dismissed the temptation to do so, knowing that Vera would be only too ready to offer sympathy, which would not be at all helpful.

"He's just so busy. And when he's home he spends all his time learning Japanese or radio mechanics."

"Do you feel neglected?" Vera was looking at Ada closely. Ada said nothing.

"You knew he was the studious type. You liked that once, him studying, knowing everything." Vera put down her spoon.

"Perhaps he wouldn't take you for granted if you left. Came with me. We could find a nice place to live."

Ada shook her head.

"I don't want to think of you here if the war comes, Ada."

"Please, Vera. You're not going to make me change my mind."

Vera sighed, and looked helplessly at Ada, her eyes filling with tears. "I feel terrible about leaving you behind. And I'm going to be very worried about you all the time." She blew her nose. "I wish I could be here when your baby is born. Make sure that you give it a big, big kiss for me. I hope it'll have Michael's looks and your brains."

Ada smiled.

"I know that you don't mind if it's a boy or a girl."

"Yes. We don't mind. Though we haven't thought of a boy's name yet. If it's a girl we're going to call her Beth. Short for Elizabeth." It hurt to say this. She added quickly, "Thank you for Mummy's brooches."

"She didn't have very much jewellery," Vera said. "I suppose she sold most of it over the years with Frugneit and everything. It must've been hard."

Ada did not want to think of this now. She thought too much of the past. She knew that she must try and live in the present, no matter how difficult it was.

"Perhaps Mummy died at a good time. Who knows what's going to happen now?" Vera said.

Ada recalled Michael pacing the room that morning, saying how outrageous it was that the Air Force had to cope with First World War planes, and that the Fire Brigade would be unable to help if there were incendiary bombs.

Ada did not share this with Vera, and said, "I'm sure Churchill will get the Americans to help us out."

"How do you know that?" Vera scoffed. "Don't tell me you read it in the papers. It's just propaganda."

Chapter 9

December, 1941

"What a darling. I can see Michael in her," one of Evaline's mahjong friends, Elsie, remarked.

"The nose and the shape of the face," Evaline said, her head cocked to one side as she gazed proudly at little Beth in Ada's arms. "But she has Ada's blue eyes. Black hair, blue eyes. She will be a beauty. Long fingers. Like Michael. She'll be a pianist."

"So tiny. Look at the little feet," someone cooed.

"Two weeks early. But she'll catch up." Evaline smiled reassuringly at Ada.

"I'm not surprised she came early. The fright." Elsie shuddered, miming horror and alarm.

Ada had been half-asleep when Michael dragged her from the bed. Patrick was shouting at them to get into the shelter, and someone was yelling in the road that the Japanese had attacked. Servants and family were packed in together; there were women with sleep in their eyes, men in crumpled pyjamas. There had been no warning; no siren call, and the street lights were still on. The planes had flown over, but thankfully it was in the distance that they delivered their bombs. You could hear the distant boom and crash followed moments later by the plaintive sound of ack ack guns. The sirens had sounded then, and people came out into the street, danced and hugged one another as if they were having a party. They believed that the danger was over; that the two battle-cruisers, berthed in the harbour a few days before, would be after the bombers and would forestall an invasion fleet. Ada had rejoiced as well, ignoring Michael's worries that the battleships had no air cover. She'd not thought of herself as frightened, just bewildered, but perhaps she had conveyed some terror to the child in her womb, for Beth arrived prematurely three days later - slowly, reluctantly, despite the concentrated pushing and the encouraging cries of the nurses. What a relief when it was over, what joy to hold the child, and then to see Michael's proud face.

"I was more frightened when I heard about the damage," Ada said. The rapidly decaying bodies laid out like dead fish along Boat Quay; the yawning holes where buildings once stood, and shattered glass in piles inches deep in Raffles Place. Michael had said that the Japanese were aiming for the Chinese and Europeans. He was not facing her, but she heard the severe warning in his tone and had hurried from the room.

"It was terrible, dear. Just terrible." Elsie's carefully painted face drew closer to Ada's. The woman reeked of perfume. "But there's no need to worry. With the Americans in the war now everything will be over and done with before the New Year."

Evaline nodded vigorously in agreement. "It's important never to say die. To keep up spirits."

Ada kissed Beth's brow, and watched Evaline from the verandah doorway as she began to move around her guests. You had to admire her, Ada thought. The party was an act of defiance, as were all the decorations in the house, and the crib with the Nativity statues arranged around it. But it was bewildering, all the shopping for dresses and new shoes for the Woods' annual Christmas party – earlier than usual to be on the safe side – while stepping over rubble around derelict buildings. And with the fresh food still available in the markets, the fishermen still bringing in bountiful catches, who might you want to believe

– the doom-mongers like Michael, or those like Elsie with their trust in the Americans?

"Ada." Ada turned to see Melanie. "Can I have one more cuddle before I go?" Melanie removed the baby from Ada's arms.

"Must you go so soon? We haven't had much chance to talk yet."

"I promised Mummy that I wouldn't be too long. She's very nervy at the moment. My brothers aren't around much these days."

Ada knew they were involved with the Chinese Relief Fund – a fund set up to help refugees in China after the Japanese invasion. "Like Michael," she said.

He had excused himself to his mother for not attending the party because of volunteer duties. In private he told Ada that he had more important things to do than behave like a demented ostrich. The school year had finished, and he spent a lot of his time as an auxiliary worker at the hospital. Most days he would not return home until around midnight, looking hollowed out, eyes circled black. She no longer believed he could be betraying her with another woman, but she had been annoyed with him for not attending the party and had to remind herself that his sense of duty was one of the qualities she admired in him. Still, it saddened her that he saw so little of his child and could not rejoice more in the infant's gradual awakening to the world. It was clear he loved her so much. She could see it on his face when he cradled Beth, smiled and talked to her with the utmost patience and gentleness despite his tiredness, despite the terrible anxiety that rippled beneath the surface calm he showed to others.

"And she's got both my grandparents to see to. They're very frail," Melanie continued. "My brothers are trying to get her and me to leave Singapore. They say that if the Japs invade the Chinese will get it in the neck. Eddie should've stayed in England, even if it is being bombed." This was the brother who'd been studying at Cambridge. "Mummy would never desert the old folk though. And she doesn't want to leave the house either." It was a large and handsome house on Balmoral Road quite near the German Embassy. Ada used to love going there as a child, enjoying the well-kept garden, and the gentle humour of Melanie's father, a wealthy businessman. Ada would return home with tasty things to eat that the cooks had made, and books that Melanie was happy to lend her – in the early days all the Alcotts, and L.M. Montgomerys.

"The house is her one security now she's on her own without Daddy." Melanie's father had died suddenly a couple of years previously. Melanie shook her head sadly.

"It's not that easy to abandon everyone, everything you love." Not looking at Ada, she said, "And I suppose that goes for you too." As if avoiding an answer that would underline her own decision to put love and loyalty before safety, Melanie added quickly, "It's been wonderful seeing you again." She returned Beth to Ada's arms, kissed her, smoothed a finger across Beth's cheek, then, promising to visit again soon, descended the stairs. She waved, her smile forced, before disappearing around the side of the house.

To distract herself from the upsetting thought of the danger she and Melanie could face if the Japanese did invade, Ada moved towards the elaborately dressed Christmas tree in the corner of the verandah.

"Look at all the balls, little one," she whispered, gazing down on the small heart-shaped face with its quiff of black hair. Beth closed her eyes sleepily and raised a tiny fist.

A child shouted. Three little boys were chasing one another along the paths between the vegetable beds. Since the back garden had been emptied of flowers and shrubs, tapioca, spinach, papayas and yams were flourishing with the help of night soil. Sometimes the stench was unbearable. "It's like Lavender Street," Patrick joked, after a fresh laying of excrement, referring to the

Chinese market garden area where you had to hold your nose when passing from the railway station.

The root vegetables were being stored under the house. Evaline had bought large quantities of tinned sardines, powdered milk, condensed milk, biscuits, flour and limed rice, which Ada knew could keep for a year. If there was a siege the family would not go hungry. Patrick had also installed a huge concrete pipe for a bomb shelter, which had fans and a ventilator, as well as benches with flaps that could convert into beds.

Now a servant appeared with a tray of cordials. Ada placed Beth back in her pram and seated herself to sip her drink. She heard a couple of elderly men talking nearby and recognised them as Patrick's cronies. Normally jovial, upright gentlemen, today they slumped dejectedly in the rattan chairs. One leaned forward and clasped his brow. She heard the name of the battleship *Prince of Wales*, and knew they were mourning its sinking and that of the cruiser *Repulse*, when in pursuit of the bombers only two days after the first Japanese attack. Michael had been right to worry about the lack of air cover. Patrick, hunched before the wireless, had leapt to his feet after the broadcast. "Good God! The Japanese have got control of the air and sea."

Ada had used that as her argument for not leaving. "I prefer to die on dry land," she had said to Michael when he pestered her again in between his bouts of angry frustration at the lack of government foresight. She felt sheer panic whenever she pictured herself clutching Beth and floundering in swirling waters, struggling to keep their heads above the surface until exhausted and weak she could do no more, and they slid beneath the waves. What a dreadful choice to make – death on land or at sea – but she had family in Singapore, and if anything happened to her there were others who would love Beth and shield her with their lives. And, for God's sake, she had Michael.

She thought of him now, working in the hospital, and wished, as she often did, that she could work beside him, use some of the skills he had taught her to help the wounded. There were thousands of them, a neighbour had told Patrick. But she accepted that her first duty, the most important one she had ever had, was the care of Beth. And perhaps it was this sense of responsibility, she reflected, which made her more tolerant of Evaline. The flow of advice and eagerness to help might become an irritation, but at the present it was a comfort to have this - to know that there was someone who was as concerned for Beth's welfare as herself.

A car drove up by the side of the house. More guests? She turned, and then stood up smiling. It was Michael. She had not expected him home until late as usual. She waited to greet him at the top of the steps, but he barely glanced at her and strode into the house. Surprised to be ignored, for he never failed to greet her immediately on his return home, she remained where she was for a moment, then, wondering at his behaviour, followed him inside.

He was surrounded by a group of men. Huddled together, they appeared to be guarding a secret, one that made their faces drawn and angry. The women glanced at them, but kept their distance. Only Ada drew near. Patrick turned and saw her, and, taking her arm, ushered her back out onto the verandah. "Michael has just returned from the station with a colleague who's got relatives in Penang. It capitulated yesterday, but the papers have been instructed to keep quiet about it." He frowned and shook his head. "It's utterly shameful. There wasn't a single non-European on the train. There was room for whites only. The local population have been left to the mercy of the Japanese." He looked severely at her. "And the truth is the Japanese have no mercy. I know your answers to Michael when he's told you to leave, Ada. But it would seem the Japanese have the upper hand whether or not the Americans are in the war. They're coming fast overland down the peninsula."

Ada recalled Michael saying that the Japanese would do this as early as the day they had watched the stilted bungalows on the south-west coast at Pasir Panjang bend their long legs and fall into the water. They had been dynamited so the machine guns on the beach would have clear targets. It was a pointless exercise, in his opinion, because the Japanese were too smart to do what was expected of them and attack the coast there.

Patrick's voice was strained with anxiety. "They could arrive here any day. And they are slaughtering as they come. Murdering babies, even. Raping the women. You must go. The ships are still not full, but the numbers of refugees are growing. You must take Beth and leave for Australia. I will give you money."

"Ada." Michael appeared at her side. "Come, I need to talk to you."

"I've been trying to tell her, Michael," said Patrick, pressing Ada's arm. "Go, I'll keep an eye on Beth," he said.

Anxiously, Ada followed Michael into the bedroom and watched him pace back and forth.

"You wouldn't believe it. It's the grossest example of discrimination that I've seen yet," he said angrily. "And it won't be the last. It's an absolute scandal. Not one non-European face to be seen on that train. Of course, we shouldn't be surprised. What do you expect from a bunch of stuck-up imperialists?" He stopped and looked hard at her, and said in a subdued voice, "I know you won't like this, Ada, but I've been asked to supervise the building of defences in the north. Although it's probably too late..."

"Are you going away?" she asked, alarmed, hands clasped tightly together.

"I'll have to, for a while, I'm afraid. We're up against it. They know I can speak the languages. And the men they're sending upcountry know nothing about surviving in the jungle. And are against men who do and have got the help of the locals." He came towards her, his arms outstretched to embrace her. "I'm really very sorry, darling," he said.

She stepped back from him. "Why can't someone else supervise? They know that you've just become a father, don't they? How can you think to risk your life? You know that you'll be in more danger up there." She stopped, aware that her voice was rising, that she was on the verge of sounding hysterical, as she had been that night in Chinatown when Michael had dashed after the Chinese youths.

By the anguish on his face and the severity of his gaze she knew what he would say next, and braced herself.

"Ada, listen to me. This is your last chance to leave."

"But we could be bombed at sea, Michael!" He looked dumbly at her. Seizing on his doubt, she continued, "Here at least we have the shelter, and if anything should happen to you, or me, the family will care for Beth."

Michael groaned. "Oh, God, you should've gone earlier. With Vera. I should've dragged you on that ship."

"And I would've made you go with me. I can't understand why you want to help a bunch of stuck-up imperialists."

"It's not them. It's the people. The poor people of Singapore. It's my duty."

She wanted to ask: what about your duty to us, your family? Instead, she pressed her lips together to seal in the resentment she felt. Michael was not going to change his mind. "If you're going to do your duty no matter how dangerous it is, Michael, then I'm going to do mine. I might have white skin, but I'm a Singaporean, and I want to help, do what I can. I'm not going to run away and leave everyone behind. Look at Evaline. She refuses to leave." In fact, she was showing a sense of duty beyond her duty to the family. Not only was she taking clothes and toys to the orphanage, but tinned food, milk powder and bottled water.

"Oh, Ada, Ada." He shook his head, his expression that of weary resignation.

"You must promise me not to do anything dangerous, take any silly risks, Michael. Like you did that night in Chinatown."

He raised his brows and gave a semblance of a smile. "You're not to worry about me. I'm a sensible chap deep down. I won't do anything stupid."

"If you do I'll never forgive you." She spoke with force, and frowned at him, but noticing him look away as if searching for a suitable response, one that would lead them back to an argument, she said, "Come, come now and be with your little girl."

"Ada. Wait. There's something I need to say."

"Not now, Michael. Please let's not talk anymore." She went determinedly ahead into the corridor, ignoring Michael's tired plea to remain.

On the veranda Charmaine was bending over the pram. Sighting Ada, she said, "Please may I have a little cuddle now? Dad wouldn't let me pick her up in case she started to cry, as if I was a monster or something."

"It's time for her feed, but she looks happy enough at the moment. Go ahead." It touched Ada to see how much Charmaine loved the child. She came to see Beth each morning before work and again after work, sometimes bringing sweets for when the child got older, along with rattles, a stuffed elephant, and yesterday a red frock with a heart-shaped bodice.

"When will your Mummy let you wear your red dress?" Charmaine asked, lifting the baby carefully. Beth's eyes roamed upwards and sideways, and her lips twitched. "Do you think she can see properly yet?" Charmaine carried the infant towards the steps. "Can you see, little one? Would you like to see all the lovely vegetables?" She began to walk down the steps.

Michael said something to Patrick and they both went inside, possibly to discuss Michael's next move. Evaline appeared with a large plate of iced Christmas cake. "I can't give this away. Too much devil curry. Everyone's stomach is two inches above the table. We'll be eating cake..." She stopped speaking. She noticed Charmaine walking between the rows. "What are you doing, my girl?" she called out. "It's too hot. The child will burn. Keep out of the sun."

"It's all right, Evaline," Ada said. "She's only been out there for a few seconds."

"Come in now, Charmaine," Evaline demanded, and turned to Ada. "It's not good to let the child be in the sun. She has the Wood skin."

"So she won't burn," Ada said.

"She'll colour fast, though. You must be careful. Black hair, blue eyes and a light skin are the signs of great beauty."

Ada was pleased that Charmaine could not hear this remark. Only yesterday she confessed woefully to Ada that no one would marry her because she was dark. She never got the leads in school plays, these being taken by girls with light skin. To think that Beth would face similar rejection upset Ada, and she said, her tone severe, "Beth will be beautiful no matter how dark she gets. Brown skin is much better than white."

Evaline glared at Ada. "How would you know, my girl? You wait and see. But I warn you. You'll cry blood when your child suffers."

Ada understood that the fierceness of her mother-in-law's reply came from a strong protective instinct, but there was an anxiety showing as well. She had not urged Ada to leave Singapore, as her husband had done, perhaps because she too was stubbornly refusing to escape. Ada suspected that beneath her hostess' bravado, Evaline was a nervous and worried woman.

Contritely, Charmaine came up the steps. Ada smiled at her and, ignoring Evaline, said, "Come with me. I'll feed her in the bedroom, and then you can have your cuddle."

Beth fed hungrily and briefly. Evaline said she had never seen a baby so easily satisfied, which was probably the reason she rarely suffered from wind. Ada placed the infant over her shoulder and patted her back, then laid her carefully on the bed. "See, Charmaine. Mrs. Sinathamby taught me this." She clasped the baby's feet, stretched the legs then folded them back onto the stomach. "It's like being in the womb again. She likes that."

"She's beautiful. The most beautiful baby in the world," Charmaine said, kneeling and gazing down with rapture.

Beth closed her eyes, replete and content. A fly buzzed into the room, and a lizard appeared from behind a picture, then, as if evading attention, clung immobile to the wall. The baby stretched in her sleep and flung back her arms. She was perfect, yes, perfect. Surely no one, not even a Japanese soldier would want to hurt her, Ada thought. Better to remain in Singapore than risk the child's and her own life at sea. Better to remain in a country she knew, with people she loved, and try to be as strong and calm as possible.

Chapter 10

JANUARY, 1942

THE SHELTER WAS A CYLINDER of stifling heat. Ada, soaked with sweat, longed for water. She and Charmaine had been about to fill the empty bottles from the broken standpipe in the road when the sirens had blared. They were slaves to the sirens.

Amah was shoved up hard against Ada's side, the press of flesh nearly unbearable, but Ada did not push the old woman away. She was grief-stricken, and half out of her wits. "What do now? Only two left," she wept the previous day after learning that two of her fellow amahs had been killed during a bombing raid. Ada knew how close the women had been. They would giggle together in the servants' quarters while they drank endless cups of tea and played cards. All born in China, they'd come to Singapore as single women escaping a life of enslavement to a rich family or a brothel keeper and, after becoming friends, had sworn an oath of sisterhood, as was customary for female servants.

Ada remembered the time Amah had taken her to see the room the women rented as a haven for when they were ill, or too old to work, which was not uncommon for servants to do. It was on the top floor of a tenement near the death houses of Sago Lane with its clutter of coffins and candle shops, beggars and stray dogs. Ada had suspected Amah was attempting to remind her how lucky she was, and thought it to be unfair that Vera had not gone as well. The stench, as she climbed the dark staircase, was dense and rancid with fermenting rice, stale garlic and excrement. On the first floor, narrow recesses, screened only by thin cloths, lined either side of a corridor. She glimpsed an iron cooking pot, and ragged clothes hanging from blackened struts; a rat had scuttled across the floor. To her relief, the amahs' large square room on the top storey had the benefit of a skylight, and it was clean and tidy, with a low table and some cushions. One day they would live there all the time and care for one another. They did not want charity.

Reminded of their fierce independence, Ada felt sick with guilt to think of her stubborn refusal to escape from Singapore when there was still a chance - before the ceaseless bombing of recent days and the strafing of the wharves. Oh yes, she had answered Michael's claim that he was not leaving Singapore because he wanted to help the people with her own wish to help, but that was not the real reason. The real reason, she told herself, was that she, who prided herself for being an independent person when she ran the boarding house, had chosen to risk Beth's life for fear of not being able to cope on her own in a strange land. On top of that, she was now giving Michael more to worry about than he already had.

There had only been one call from him before the lines went down, but she could not allow herself to think that he was dead. She had to believe Patrick when he assured her that the authorities would have informed them if the worst had happened. The words he used – 'authorities, informed, family of the deceased, government protocol' – were comforting in a way. It seemed that there was still some order in the world.

Beth had fallen asleep and Ada's head was drooping when she heard a menacing screeching noise beneath the familiar roar of aircraft passing overhead in the direction of the docks. She had barely time to work out what it could be, when there was a thunderous explosion, right above the shelter, it seemed, and the pipe shook and tilted. Beth, startled, began to cry loudly, tossing her head from side to side. Ada hushed and rocked her, but, unable to calm her, pressed the child to her breast. Beth sucked hard, as though trying to hold onto the woman whose heart pounded as she thought frantically of escape.

"Oh, Lordy, we're done for," Evaline cried out. Amah moaned and muttered while Charmaine sobbed noisily. Ahmad, the only other remaining servant, the rest having chosen to return to their families, kept his eyes closed and pressed his hands together, his lips moving rapidly in silent prayer. Ada began to pray too, her mouth filled with the bitterness of fear.

It seemed an eternity before the grumpy blaring of the all-clear wrenched the air. Patrick stood up, his face gaunt and bloodless, and pushed open the door. With dread, Ada waited for an outburst of despair, but then heard him shout, "My God. We haven't been touched. Thank God Almighty." Incredulous, she joined Patrick outside, and yes, there stood the house, the wide back verandah miraculously solid as ever, the big rear windows of the dining room facing serenely onto the garden.

Evaline fell to her knees and gave thanks. Charmaine pushed past Ada and ran to follow Patrick into the house. Ada, tearful with relief, was halfway up the back verandah steps, ushering Amah before her, when she heard Charmaine scream and Patrick shout, "We've been hit. The front's been hit."

The house was filled with smoke. Ada clutched Beth tightly and stumbled forward. The front doors lay splintered and broken on the tiled floor of the reception room, the framed ancestral portraits had fallen on their faces, ornaments lay shattered, and the heavy chairs had been tipped over by the force of the blast. Patrick staggered towards the opening, his arms outstretched before him as though to ward off a violent intruder.

"They've got us! We've lost our steps," he called hoarsely. The grand outside staircase that led up to the front verandah was a heaped and broken mass of wood. In place of the central bed of cannas and roses there remained a large smoking pit where the shell had landed. He turned around, staring down at the floor as if expecting it to collapse beneath him.

"Michael. We must find Michael," Evaline cried.

"Why isn't Michael here?" Charmaine demanded. "I can't believe he's left us to cope on our own."

"He's where he's needed most," Ada said, trying to sound reasonable in the face of Charmaine's anger, but she too felt abandoned. She remembered Michael on the evening that he left Serangoon. They had been in the library, and he had rested one hand on the piano's polished top as if laying claim to a past life. "Look after Beth for me. Tell her I love her," he'd said. And she had replied, "You make sure that you come back and tell her yourself."

The light in the morning, due to the raging fires, was burnt-orange. It was as if a child with dirty hands had smudged a picture of a sunset and drawn lamp-posts leaning in all directions. The air stank of cordite, and was thickened with exhaust fumes and smoke, making it difficult to breathe. Patrick, driving with the utmost concentration, slowed the Vauxhall as they passed a cemetery. Ada could make out vultures circling over piles of corpses. With the explosion of bombs drowning out the irrelevant screech of the sirens, it all seemed so unreal to her that she felt detachment rather than fear. This was surely a nightmare from which she would soon awake.

The car came to an abrupt stop. Patrick cursed loudly. In front was a deep crater measuring the width of the road. He began to back the car, sweat coursing down his face. Ada predicted that at any moment he would throw up his hands and refuse to go further. His spirit was at breaking point. The shelling of the house – which, thank God, had only damaged the steps and not the pillars – would have been enough to shake him, but then had come the message from Michael brought by a puny Malay boy while Ahmad was boarding up the front doorway. It said that the Causeway had been breached by retreating Commonwealth soldiers from the mainland to hamper the advance of the Japanese. 'The Japanese are unstoppable,' Michael wrote. 'They will be in Singapore within days. You must leave the house and find shelter in the Selwyn Building. There is safety in crowds. No one can vouch for the behaviour of peasant soldiers drunk on victory. I will meet you there. Come as quickly as you can.'

"What, what is happening? Go on." Evaline punched Patrick's arm. "We cannot keep going back. This is madness."

"Do you want me to fly, woman?" Patrick snapped.

All around were buildings with their fronts missing like dolls' houses. You could see the remnants of normal life – a shattered table, a legless cot, a broken chair. It was as if a hungry monster had been on a rampage. And everywhere there was the foetid smell of death.

An Indian man appeared at the window of the car and peered through the grimy glass. He looked angry and contemptuous, but then saw Patrick and instantly retreated to join a motley crew of Indian soldiers. Ada remembered the leaflets that had come pouring down from the sky a few days ago. They showed a picture of a fat British soldier stuffing his greedy mouth while a scrawny Indian looked on with drooling lips. The message was clear: it was time to rise up against the white imperialists. It occurred to her that Patrick might be relieved for once to be recognised as an Asian, rather than an Anglo-Indian who considered himself superior to Asians.

"We must go back home," Charmaine shouted.

"Do you want to be slaughtered?" Evaline turned to glare at her daughter.

"We should've all left Singapore weeks ago. The d'Aranjos are in Australia now." Charmaine shook her father's shoulder.

"It was you who would not leave. You could've gone with them. I told you to." Patrick's voice was strained with exhaustion.

"We can't go on," Charmaine wailed.

"Stop that noise at once. I can't think," Patrick said angrily.

"You see, you see. You're sending your father mad." Evaline slapped Charmaine's wrist. "And a mad man cannot drive us to safety." Her voice rose shrilly. "We will be killed."

Ada, cradling a crying Beth, leaned forward and touched Evaline's shoulder. "We'll find a way soon. We must be patient. Look, look at all those people. They're walking. If we have to, we must walk." There were Europeans from upcountry - women in soiled dresses dragging their children, men in dirty whites. A large family of Indians carried a table and chairs. A Chinese couple stumbled beneath the weight of a coffin.

"I can't walk. I want to go home. I want to go back. I prefer to die in my own home." Charmaine began to weep noisily, and Beth to cry more loudly, but Ada coaxed her to feed again as Patrick took a side turning past the wrecked shop houses on Kim Seng Road. The car zigzagged around mounds of rubble, fallen trees, and a dead cow, then stopped for a group of Sam Sui women dragging corpses from a pile of rubble. It seemed to Ada that their red headscarves were emblems of courage, and she took a deep breath, willing herself to remain calm.

The car moved on and they came to the canal. On the black, oily water, swelled by three weeks of rain, mutilated bodies jostled against one another, then bumped onwards with the rigid mutiny of logs. Through the thick black smoke that filled the air, Ada caught sight of some British soldiers, their clothes and faces smeared with soot. They were seated on the edge of a monsoon drain and swigging from bottles. Shrouded in smoke, they looked unreal, like phantoms - until one of them rose and staggered into the middle of the road in front of the car. Patrick tooted his horn. The soldier did not move. He was holding a pistol. The car jolted to a halt. Patrick clambered out. "What the bloody hell are you doing, man?"

"Patrick. Patrick. Get back here," Evaline shouted.

The soldier stared at Patrick, then lifted the pistol. Charmaine screamed, and Beth cried shrilly. The soldier laughed and lowered his arm. "Old man go home," he shouted in a drunken voice, then turned and lurched away into the crowd.

"You fool. Get back into the car," Evaline called to Patrick. He stood transfixed, but when she called again, slumped back into the driver's seat. "You can do nothing against drunk men with guns, Patrick."

A police car drew up alongside. For a moment Ada believed that the city still had law and order, and this was the reason the soldier had departed so swiftly. But there was a loud honking for people to get out of the way. She glimpsed men with cases on their knees, like travellers about to go on a journey. The car moved on.

"They're running away. The cowards," she exclaimed.

"They're all cowards. We're doomed. They're all hooligans." Evaline threw up her arms in disgust.

As if to emphasise Evaline's words, there was a burst of gunfire and the sound of splintering glass. A few yards ahead, two soldiers were shooting bottles in a liquor store as if at a rifle range in the Great World.

"Scorched earth policy," Patrick said. "Stop the Japanese from getting hold of it. Nothing worse than a drunk Jap." His words were clipped, the precision of his speech attempting perhaps to pass for self-control. Ada wondered what might be worse than the filthy, unruly soldiers she saw now looming out of the smoke. They staggered past, baying like crazed animals. Patrick slapped the steering wheel. "The world has gone mad. I cannot go on. It's impossible."

Ada could see the road was clogged with people. "Then we must walk. Get out and walk," she said fiercely. "We have no choice. We can't go back." She pushed open the door and, clutching Beth tightly, stepped onto the road and began to walk. She feared to look back, expecting to see them all still in the car. If no one joined her then she would have to return and think of something else. But what else? She had to reach the Selwyn Building and find Michael.

She heard Amah calling her. She glanced behind. There was Evaline, mouth open in a perfect O of astonishment, arm in arm with a startled Charmaine, and Patrick, thin-lipped, supporting a frail Amah. Ada's legs felt weak, but she knew that she must appear strong, so she faced ahead and kept on walking.

Michael seemed miraculously to appear in front of Ada as soon as she stepped inside the Selwyn Building. His eyes were red, his face unshaven, his hair matted. He stank of stale sweat. He wore khaki instead of whites. But he was Michael. He hugged them all. "I didn't think you were going to get here. I've been watching that door for hours," he said. "Go and get some food and water." He gestured to a long trestle table at the end of the crowded room and, when his parents with Charmaine and Amah headed towards it, gave Ada and Beth another suffocating hug.

"It was terrible," Ada said. "The bombers flew right over us. So many people are dead, Michael. And the fires! The buildings! What's going to happen to us? The soldiers are drunk, the policemen are running away." She could not pretend to be strong and sensible any longer. "It was terrible." Tears filled her eyes and ran down her cheeks. Michael cupped her face and wiped it with his thumbs. "What's going to happen now, Michael?"

Charmaine returned. "You should hurry, Ada, there's hardly anything left."

"Get some food for Ada, Charmaine," Michael said. "Give Beth to Charmaine, Ada. I need to talk to you."

Ada did not want to let the child go, yet she heard the agitation in Michael's tone, and obeyed. He grasped her arm and led her to the side of the room, turning her shoulders so she faced him, and spoke urgently over the noise in the building.

"Listen to me, Ada. The Japs are going to get here very soon. You'll need to be very careful. You're a beautiful woman. And the Japs are hungry in every way. You must stay here until you're told by the authorities that you can return home. And when you do, keep yourself out of sight. Stay indoors. Bolt the door." He stopped, bit his lip, then stared directly into her eyes. "I know what a devoted mother you are. You're the best mother any child could have."

She looked down, hiding her shame. He had pleaded for her to leave Singapore. She had not gone; she had not put Beth's safety first.

She was still thinking this when he continued, and his next words did not register immediately. "But if you're interned...you must leave Beth with my parents."

"What did you say?"

"The Japanese will be the new masters of Singapore. They will wreak vengeance on the old rulers. All the British. They will make you a prisoner. You must leave Beth with my parents." Around them was the noise of people jabbering and children wailing, but she was conscious only of Michael's serious gaze.

"Why do you say leave Beth with your parents? You'll be there." Michael said nothing. "Won't you?"

"Not for the time being."

"Why?"

"I've still work to do."

"What work?" She gripped his arm, digging her nails into his flesh. "There's no point in building defences now. What work?"

He looked helplessly at her as she glared at him with fury. "I'm very sorry, darling. I can't help it. I have duties..."

"I can't believe you're still putting your duties," she spat the words, "before Beth and me, before your family." He tried to put his arms around her. She pulled sharply away from him.

He stepped up to her and held her arms by the side of her body, trapping her, compelling her to listen to words she did not want to hear. "I love you and Beth with all my heart. I'm not abandoning you. I'll come back as soon as I can." He removed his hands and nodded, trying to reassure her. "You are very strong, Ada. And I know that you'll be very sensible."

The word 'sensible' - it pained Ada to hear that, thinking again how stupid she had been in her refusal to leave Singapore believing that she would have the support of the family should anything happen to her. Not for one moment had she really thought what it would mean to part from Beth, God knows for how long.

She stood there in a daze. Michael tilted her chin and kissed her on the lips, then hugged her tightly. Ada could feel his body shuddering. When he released her and stood back his face was awash with tears. He tried to say something, but choked.

"Oh, Michael," she said tearfully, "please be careful. Please come back to us as soon as you can. I love you. We all love you."

He shook his head, unable to speak, cupped her face and kissed her again, then turned away and walked towards his parents. Numbly, she watched him hug his family, clasp Amah's hand, and bend his head to kiss Beth.

He turned to look at Ada, his expression full of sorrow. Overwhelmed with shock and despair, she did not move towards him immediately, and when she did stumble forward he was caught up in a crowd of soldiers heading for the doorway. She could only guess that the arm raised in a half, forlorn salute of farewell was his, and by the time she forced her way through the jostling crowd streaming out of the building, and looked around for him, he was gone. Gone, before she was able to tell him that she would do everything she could to make sure Beth came to no harm. Gone, before she could say that she would pray for his safe return.

She stood there distressed and confused, until Charmaine approached with a crying Beth. "We've been searching for you, Ada. Come inside now. Patrick wants to talk about what we must do." Ada took the child in her arms, held her close and wept.

Chapter 11

FEBRUARY, 1942

THREE MEN, BRITISH SOLDIERS, WERE standing on the vegetable path. They looked surprised to see Patrick emerge from inside the house with Ahmad. They must have been asleep in the abandoned shelter when the family had returned home. Their uniforms were filthy and torn, their faces blackened with dirt. One stooped and picked up a sweet potato. Ada, coming out onto the verandah with Charmaine, heard him say, "I've got an allotment at home. Love my veggies." Charmaine beside her began to cry. Exhaustion affected them all. It had been a slow journey back to Serangoon along roads packed with cars and lorries. There was no fear of bomber planes, but the listless groups of soldiers, the deserted streets, and the eerie silence of a city under a pall of oily smoke kept them on strenuous alert, expecting trouble.

The soldiers moved closer to the house. Ada could see by their expressions that they were not expecting to find a white woman living with Eurasians. The allotment owner now inclined his head in sympathy to Charmaine. "Don't worry, luv. We've surrendered. You've made it so far. All you have to do now is obey orders." He came forward to shake Patrick's hand. Then his mates joined him, shaking hands as if something worthwhile had been achieved.

Patrick invited the three inside and showed them the boarded-up front of the house, the shrouded furniture. "Ahmad, our old gardener, stayed behind. He said he preferred to die in Serangoon than in town. I don't blame him. It was Hell there. We're lucky he did stay. He managed to fire off shots with an old rifle of mine and scared away the looters. Damned lucky too that our car wasn't stolen."

In the dining room they sat around the big table – dusty and chipped but otherwise undamaged. The soldiers spoke of hand-to-hand fighting in the swamps, how the Japanese had swarmed in on the north-west corner and not the east of the island where the majority of the Commonwealth troops were assembled. It was a losing battle, they said, a hopeless business, nothing left to do but retreat. Ada pictured the drunk British soldiers shrouded in smoke with the burning shophouses around them.

She gave Beth to Charmaine and asked a dazed Evaline to search out some biscuits while she made coffee. The soldiers' description of what they had experienced filled her with fear and anxiety, and her hand shook as she measured out the bottled water. Yet, returning to the dining room, she was struck at how strangely convivial it was, and she smiled at the soldiers, imitating a former self. The vegetable grower, a stocky sandy-haired man, answered her smile with a freckle-drenched grin, then looked seriously at her. "You're English, aren't you?" Ada gave a scant nod, anticipating being told what danger she was in. "Not sure what they've got in store for you, but in the meantime be careful and keep your head down." He glanced at Charmaine. "And you too."

His friend, a dark-haired, handsome boy, perhaps to distract Charmaine from her obvious terror, gestured towards the piano which had been removed from the library at the front of the house by Ahmad and Patrick before the journey to the Selwyn. The instrument, standing in the corner, and diminished by the size of the big dining room, seemed like a symbol of loss and defeat. "Who plays?" the soldier asked.

"My brother," Charmaine said quietly.

"Your brother? Is he here?" The boy coloured. Had he asked after a dead man?

Patrick said, "He's a volunteer. I expect he'll be back as soon as he can."

Ada looked at Patrick. He appeared to be avoiding her gaze. Was he hiding something? What did he know about Michael?

"If I clean these do you think I could have a tinkle?" asked the third soldier, lifting his big hands apologetically. Patrick tiredly waved him towards the piano.

The soldier soaked a dirty handkerchief with bottled water and wiped his fingers, then sat to play. His touch was heavy, and Ada was reminded of how lightly and faultlessly Michael's hands would pass over the keys. Missing him desperately, her eyes filling with tears, she forced herself to think of the advantage he had in being able to speak some Japanese. Not only did this show he respected the language, but he would be able to argue his way out of a difficult situation, and tell the Japanese that he admired them for their courage, and loyalty to their country and emperor. Flattery was an invaluable weapon of defence.

The soldiers started singing 'Rule Britannia', at first under their breaths, then louder until the others joined in, Patrick dragging himself to his feet, and Evaline mouthing the words with her coarse hair stiffly awry and her eyes wide in bafflement. The men sang on and on, the musical hall songs Ada recognised as her father's hummed favourites; they sang until they were hoarse, before Patrick led with 'Jerusalem' while she and Charmaine went to concoct a broth of rice, carrots and dried mushrooms on an old wood stove which had been resurrected for use.

Patrick went into the garden and dug up one of his buried whisky bottles. He filled the glasses. The men toasted one another. "To King and us", they shouted. Then, perhaps overcome with dread of the future, everyone grew quiet, and it was on this note of sadness that the soldiers shook hands. Advising them all to stay inside the house, they stepped out into the pitch darkness.

As soon as they left, Patrick advised the women to go to their rooms. Ada saw him in the garden after she fed and settled Beth. He lit a fire and began tossing papers onto it. Ada guessed that he was trying to rid himself of anything that might cause him trouble with the Japanese.

She stood in front of the wardrobe and riffled through Michael's clothes. "Oh Michael," she whispered, "where are you? Please, God, keep him safe." She buried her face in one of his white jackets – it smelled of him, pepper mixed with talc and cologne – then removed it from the hanger. She hugged it as she lay on her bed beside Beth in her cot and fell into a restless sleep.

Next morning, the family were together in the dining room when they were startled by a loud knocking on the back door. Someone called out for Patrick. It was their Chinese friend, Dr. Wong. "Drunken savages," he shouted, staggering into the room. He mopped his brow and described the Japanese driving through the city in trucks still covered with palm leaves and branches torn from the jungle, waving their flags, honking horns. "Brutes. But they're not fools. Look how quick they were to repair the Causeway. Then coming on their bicycles like it was a *picnic*. Nothing whatsoever to stop them. Who could've believed it? And you should see the support they're getting. Not just the Malays and Indians, but Straits Chinese as well. All of them waving the bloody Rising Sun." The doctor stood with his knees turned in like a horse baulking at a jump. "And where are the bloody British soldiers? Packed like sardines. Prisoners now of the Japanese. Hundreds, hundreds of them on the Padang and Esplanade." Patrick put his arm around the man's shoulders to calm him, and led him outside.

Ada watched the two men in a huddle on the back verandah. They muttered together for some time, the doctor throwing up his arms from time to time in a gesture of angry disgust. When he left, Patrick came inside, shaking his head.

"It's too easy to blame the British. Only a few ruffians are giving them a bad name. It's the British soldier who was doing his duty and dying for us who will end up with his head on a block. It's sad to think how the mighty have fallen." Ada could see he was genuinely upset. For all his criticism of the British and their high-handed ways, he respected them. Even aped them with his 'frightfuls' and 'straight bats'. He would click his fingers at the waiters like a tuan besar when they dined at the Recreation Club. It used to annoy Michael. Of course they were in the heart of tuan besar country - St. Andrew's spire rising above the trees, the cricketers on the Padang, the clock with its trustworthy chime in the tower of the Victoria. A world of privilege, gone forever perhaps, and best gone, but could the Japanese be trusted with their promise of a better life for the non-Europeans? It occurred to her that it did not matter now that she had always thought the people of Singapore deserved better treatment from the British, and that she had felt closer to her Asian friends than any white person she knew - apart from her parents, of course. The colour of her skin, rather than her beliefs and loyalties, was going to determine her future.

That night, after Patrick had lit some candles – the electricity wires had long been hanging like useless vines from the telegraph posts – Ada sat with the family at one end of the dining table and nursed a sleeping Beth. The child appeared indifferent to the noise, perhaps having become accustomed to it. Japanese soldiers were celebrating victory in the streets, their drunken shouts and laughter sounding unnervingly close. A shot rang out, then another. Charmaine whimpered; Patrick drummed his fingers on the table and fixed his eye on Ada as if forbidding her to show her fear. "Looters," he pronounced with disdain. "This is what war does. Turns ordinary people into criminals." Evaline flicked through pages of the Bible, muttering passages at random, then pushed it aside and pressed her hands to her cheeks. Her face was drained of colour, which made the dark skin around her eyes more pronounced. She could pass as fully Indian now, Ada thought, and anxiously studied Beth's face. What would happen to her? Would she be seen as English or Asian? Would she be allowed to remain with the family, as Michael wished, if her mother were made a prisoner? But the thought of leaving Beth behind was intolerable.

Evaline suddenly burst out, "I cannot do everything. Always it is my duty to watch the servants."

"Do you mean Amah? I saw her go into the servants' quarters," Ada said.

"She must stay with us. It's too dangerous out there. Someone must fetch her," Patrick ordered.

Ada rose to do his bidding, but as she handed Beth to Charmaine she heard the sound of boots crunching the gravel on the driveway, then pounding up the back verandah steps. Next, there was a demented banging on the bolted door. Beth woke, and cried loudly. No one moved. The door shook with the thumping, and Japanese voices shouted in Malay for them to open immediately. Slowly, Patrick got to his feet, then as the hammering began again whispered urgently to the frightened women, "Go to your room, all of you. Lock yourself inside." He looked at Ada, appearing critical of her appearance. "Make yourself as modest as you can. Hide your beauty."

Although she recalled Michael and the British soldier giving her the same advice, Ada hesitated, wanting to avoid isolation, as her room was at the opposite end of the house from Evaline's and Charmaine's.

"Go, go," Patrick hissed at Ada. Was he angry that her nationality would make it more difficult for them all? Ada held Beth against her chest and ran to her room. Ignoring the child's crying, she dumped Beth on the bed, then hurled clothes from the chest of drawers until she found a long-sleeved blouse. With trembling hands, she struggled into it and fastened the buttons to the neck. Next she put on a long skirt used for beach picnics, and then there was only her hair to cover. Quick. Quick. Beth cried more loudly. Ada picked her up and put her on the breast as rough voices echoed down the corridor and furniture scraped across the tiled floor. With Beth sucking frenziedly, Ada, scarcely daring to breathe, watched the bedroom door, expecting at any moment to have the heavy boots kicking it down.

But then the back door slammed, and the sound of voices came from the verandah. She could hear men laughing, then the familiar low-pitched grumble of Patrick's car being driven along the driveway.

"They've gone," Patrick called. "They've gone." She stood up and flung open the door. Patrick was in the hallway beckoning to her. "They wanted the car." She joined him in the dining room. He pointed to the sideboard. It had been cleared of the jade ornaments and silverware, including Michael's trophies. "They asked if we had any Chinese servants. Amah must come inside."

Evaline ran into the room. "They've gone?"

"For the time being. But they'll be back. They said that they want our house to use for officers. I think someone has told them our house would be suitable. They've not wasted any time in coming here," Patrick said.

"Oh, Lordy, what is going to happen to us now? Oh, Lordy, we are to lose our home. That is not right. How can that be right?"

"Right or wrong. It makes no difference. That is the case, Evaline. The Japanese are our new masters, and we shall have to obey. We will move into the servants' quarters."

Charmaine appeared, and stood in the middle of the room clutching at her skirt. "Why doesn't Michael come back? We need Michael now. We can't manage without him. He would know what to do."

Patrick said nothing and wiped both hands over his face like a diver coming up from the deep. Again, Ada wondered if he were hiding something about Michael, but, aware she could not confront him now, summoned an assurance she did not feel. "We have to manage without Michael. He'll be back eventually. It must be impossible to get through. In the meantime, we need to lock up." She placed Beth in Charmaine's arms then strode purposefully to the door. "I'll get Amah."

She was on the back verandah when something moved in the smoky darkness. She stood motionless, but then as a figure drew towards her she ran back inside and shouted at Patrick to lock the door. He walked too slowly, he fumbled, oh so stupidly fumbled with the keys. Terrified, she yelled at him to hurry, but before he could reach her the door flew open and a stocky Japanese soldier strode into the room with a drawn sword. He was wearing his cap pulled low on his forehead. He stank of whisky and sweat. He marched about shouting, then with one sweep of his hand cleared the sideboard of a remaining condiment set and crystal bowl. They crashed to the floor, and Beth began to howl.

Ada rushed forward to take the child, but the soldier stood in front of her. He grinned at her and, as she tried to skirt him to reach the baby, grabbed her arm. She pulled away, but he gripped more tightly and dragged her towards the settee. He threw her down, then marched to Charmaine, slapped her face and tugged a gold chain from her neck. It was the one piece of jewellery that had not been buried in the garden. Charmaine stumbled, nearly dropping Beth. Ada leaped up to rescue her, but the soldier barred her way. As if in slow motion he lifted his sword with one arm and pointed at the baby with the other. Ada recalled what Patrick had said when he tried to persuade her to leave Singapore after the invasion of Malaya. Japanese soldiers had slaughtered babies. She fell on her knees and held out her arms. "Please, please don't hurt my baby. Take me," she sobbed.

The soldier laughed at her. He gestured with his head towards Beth. "Haafu," he said, repeating the word as Ada sobbed. With a savage leer, stooping over her, he ran his sticky fingers down her neck and clutched her breast. Angry now, and without any sense of caution, she grabbed his hand and bit hard on his thumb. He reeled back, letting out a guttural cry. Freed from his grasp she struggled to her feet and ran for the door.

To her horror, two Japanese soldiers appeared, blocking her way. "Why you run?" one asked. "Why you frighten?" She looked wildly at them, and then behind at her attacker. His arm was across his face as if trying to hide from the newcomers, but they noticed him and shouted in Japanese. Immediately he rushed past Ada and out the door.

"No worry. He give himself up to our men now." The two arrivals were both middle-aged. "You English? Yes?" one said, nodding at her. Through the haze of fear she noted the civility of the man, his neat uniform, his shiny boots.

"My daughter-in-law," Patrick said, coming forward.

The soldier bowed stiffly. "You very lucky we come in time. We have shame for what happen and offer our apology. Our men fight long and hard, but no excuse for bad behaviour. We punish him. But not possible to protect more. Tomorrow all Europeans must register for internment in Changi prison, and Eurasians with direct European parent." He turned to Ada. "Tomorrow morning truck come for you. Take you to Padang to register." Pointing to Beth, he asked, "This your child?"

"Yes," Ada whispered, taking Beth from Charmaine's arms.

He turned to the other soldier. "Haafu," he said, and gestured at Beth. "Where father?" he asked Ada.

Patrick's voice was high-pitched with tension. "He's at the hospital. He's been working as a medical attendant."

"Eurasian child with English mother. We make exception for very young. The child better with father. It have good food when we live here." He turned to Evaline. "You cook for us." He addressed the room. "We masters now. We fair if you work hard and obey us. No longer you running dogs of British Imperialism." He gestured at the piano. "Next time I come I play Schubert for you. I take great care of your instrument. All your belongings." The men bowed stiffly again, before turning sharply on their heels and marching out the door.

No one spoke. No one moved. Then Charmaine ran into her mother's arms, and Patrick croaked, "Officers. Quite different from the warrior class. Well educated. He spoke quite good English. It's wrong to judge a whole race by the deeds of a few. We're lucky to have such people take over our home." Evaline cried out, a wild animal yelp of protest. Patrick put up his hand to silence her. "We must adapt ourselves. Those species that adapted well, those were the ones that survived. We must be crafty and cautious."

"Crafty and cautious! Crafty and cautious!" Ada's voice rasped with indignation. "Is that what it takes to stop being raped!" She clenched her fists and shook her head in angry dismay; Patrick bowed his as if ashamed. It was Charmaine who was the first to move towards her, then Evaline came, and they hugged Ada as well as they could with the baby between them. Ada wanted to cry, and then she wanted to hit something. Caught between the impulses of fear and anger she stood immobilised, her mouth working around words she could not utter.

Patrick shuffled aimlessly around the room, not looking at her. Ada began to cry noisily.

"You must be brave, Ada," Patrick said.

"I cannot leave Beth." Her voice was thick with tears. "How will she feed? Good food is my milk."

"You needn't worry about the milk. Dr Wong will find us a good wet nurse. My mother had one for me. It's not unusual. Don't look like that, Ada. Beth will be better off left with us. And it will only be for a short time," Patrick said.

Evaline took Beth from her. "Go and wash. You must feel dirty. It was a terrible thing that nearly happened."

Ada's hands trembled as she washed her face, spilling the precious water. Her breasts felt heavy, the milk ready. The milk made only for her baby. She could not bear the thought of another woman feeding Beth. And it was impossible to believe that a stranger could replace a mother's love. No one could. Not Evaline or Charmaine, or even Amah. Only a mother would watch out for Beth's welfare every second of the day, anticipate her needs, and interpret her cries.

She slumped to the floor, burying her face in her hands, and imagined what awaited her - the cramped and filthy conditions of a prison, the bad food, the cruelty of soldiers. How could she condemn a baby to that? Michael had insisted Beth be left behind. Ada's gut churned with confusion and fear.

When she returned to the room, only Patrick was there, standing at the window and looking out into the darkness. He turned to her, his face grave. Ada waited. He pinched the loose skin of his throat. "Patrick. Do you know something about Michael that I don't? Tell me."

Patrick sighed deeply and turned to face her. "Michael said nothing more to me than that he would keep low if the Japanese took over."

"Because of his work for the volunteers?"

"I don't know." Patrick hesitated, then said in a quiet voice, "he wanted me to tell you that you and Beth are dearer to him than his own life, and that he loves you."

She groaned. "What's he doing, Patrick?" Patrick did not catch her eye. "He's been doing something more, hasn't he, than working in the hospital and building defences?"

"Oh, Ada, he never confided anything to us."

"But you guessed didn't you? Why didn't you try to stop him? He would've listened to you."

"He was always an independent boy. Very clever. He could pick up languages like drinking water."

The same old stories, how could she listen to them? "You don't know how much it hurts me to think that he's chosen to do something that's taken him away from us. Surely his first duty is to the family."

"Ada," Patrick whispered. "He's doing what he thinks is right."

"What he thinks! What he thinks!" She struck her hand against her chest. "What about me? What about his child? What does he *feel* for us?"

"Think, Ada, when you saw the soldiers behaving like animals, and giving up on their duty to protect us. Remember what you said? What cowards they were."

She did remember. She took a deep breath, trying to calm herself and use reason to overcome her hurt. Didn't she love Michael for his fearless sense of justice? Didn't she, not so long ago, regret not being of more use in the world at such a terrible time? She opened her mouth to speak, but suddenly a deep weariness came over her. In utter despair, she heard a baby crying.

Chapter 12

ADA PACKED A SMALL SUITCASE. Patrick told her to travel light because soon she would be back home. In went four of her plainest frocks, a few changes of underclothes, a mosquito net, a packet of Alka Seltzer, a torch, a tin flask of water, Dettol, quinine, aspirins, and a toilet bag stuffed with soap and toothpaste - but no make-up. Patrick had also told her that she should cut her hair, for she must remain as unattractive as possible.

She fingered her long hair and thought of how she had refused to have Charmaine cut it the previous evening. To have done so would have meant admitting defeat. She remembered the time when Frugneit, in a drunken fit, had taken a carving knife and brandished it in her face. He shouted like a maniac because she had hidden the key to Elizabeth's desk where the accounts and petty cash were stored. He grabbed the long plait that hung down her back and pressed the blade against the thick strand, ignoring her cries of pain and anger. She managed to pull away and flee to her room, to lock the door and amass her hate. She planned to kill him one day, drive Amah's heavy knife into his heart and gloat over his squealing body.

Anger revisited, she felt drained, and sat abruptly on the bed. Beth was asleep in her cot. How long would it be, Ada wondered as she gazed at the child, before I hold you again? Dear God, please protect Beth. Please protect me so that I will return and be a good mother. Please let Beth forgive me when she's older and knows that I left her.

"Ada. It's Charmaine. Can I come in?" Without waiting for an answer Charmaine entered, her expression sober. "Mumma said you should take your sewing." Ada pressed a finger against her lips and glanced at Beth. Charmaine whispered, "You know how much you like to sew. It will help you take your mind off things."

Ada pointed at the sewing bag on her pillow. She had already thought to pack it. And a book. There was only room for one. She picked up *Rebecca* from the dressing table and tucked it under her clothes in the suitcase. The novel was one Melanie had lent to her before her wedding. She had only read a few chapters but remembered now that it was a story of a woman coming into a household where there were secrets. She frowned as she thought of Michael. What had he been hiding from her? What danger was he in? Where was he?

"Don't worry, Ada," Charmaine said, putting an arm around Ada's shoulders. "You don't have to worry about Beth. We'll take good care of her. We'll..." She stopped. "But what if that soldier comes back?"

Ada led Charmaine into the corridor where they would not wake Beth. "He won't. He'll be strung up like a pig by now. And you'll have the officers here. The soldier who attacked me was a peasant." Patrick had said that thanks to the educated officer class arriving at the Fall there had been fewer examples of atrocities in Singapore than up-country.

"You don't need to worry, Charmaine. Just don't catch anyone's eye, and never be on your own. And try not to make yourself too pretty." Charmaine glanced at Ada quizzically, her expression lightening, perhaps because she was seldom referred to as pretty.

"Charmaine, I'm depending on you. Amah could be interned as well." The Chinese had been called to register the following day. "There'll be a wet nurse, but you might have to be mainly responsible for Beth. Your parents are old. And they'll have enough to worry about. You must make sure everything is done properly. Her feeds. Her baths..."

"And keep her out of the sun."

"I'm relying on you, Charmaine."

"You can rely on me. I'll guard Beth with my life."

"I only hope Amah isn't interned." Ada glanced at her watch. The truck which would take her to the Padang for registration could arrive any time. "Please, stay here with Beth. I must say goodbye to Amah."

She found the old woman in the servants' quarters seated on her iron bedstead, her worn hands clasped in her lap, her expression downcast. When Ada knelt before her she looked startled.

"I'm sorry, Amah. I didn't mean to shock you."

Amah stared fearfully at Ada.

"What's the matter?" Ada said gently.

"Cut off head. Soldier cut off head." A neighbour had told the family of the heads nailed to posts on Anderson Bridge, the bloodied scalps a warning to all Chinese.

"Not *your* head, Amah. No one's going to cut off your head. They're not interested in a little old lady like you. It's the men they're after." She sat beside Amah and felt a thin arm encircling her waist. She was propelled back in time, to the boarding house – Amah rushing to protect her against a drunken Frugneit. "I don't want to leave, Amah. I don't want to leave."

"You no cry now. You come back soon." Amah's voice was stern. Ada understood. Amah would not show her sadness. It would make the parting more painful. "Beth safe here. Go. You must be strong mother."

Evaline said the same. It was approaching noon when they heard the shouts in the street, and the sound of a truck approaching. Patrick went to fetch the suitcase from the bedroom while Ada stared down at Beth in her arms and tried to make a mental imprint of her features. The child had the most beautiful face.

"She looks so much like Michael. I'm going to miss her so much. Oh, God, I've lost them both. I don't know what do."

"You'll come back soon. You must be strong, my girl," Evaline said, raising a clenched fist. "And you've packed your sewing things? It will help you to keep busy."

Ada nodded, striving to hold onto her grief. "When is the wet nurse coming?"

"I will fetch her as soon as you leave."

Ada had met the woman the night before, a plump Eurasian beauty with her own satin-skinned baby. It was unbearable to think of another woman feeding Beth. It was unnatural.

"I'm not leaving."

"You have no choice, Ada. They will drag you out," Patrick said behind her.

"There'll be a hullabaloo, and Beth will get frightened. You don't want that do you? Here, Ada, give her to me," Evaline said.

Ada held Beth more tightly, trying to embed the shape of the small form in her body's memory before Evaline lifted the baby from her arms. She would have the snaps of Beth that Michael had taken, promising a studio photo when life was back to normal, but these could not replace the touch of warm, soft flesh.

"She'll forget me," Ada said, starting to cry.

"You'll be back soon. She won't have time to forget you, my girl."

Ada studied Evaline's face for a sign that she believed what she had said and noticed with alarm how much her mother-in-law had aged; her hair was unkempt, her complexion grey. How could she care for the child on her own if something happened to Amah, and Charmaine were not there? Ada shook her head in dismay. How stupid she was not to have left Singapore. She would never forgive herself if anything should happen to Beth.

Patrick clasped her arm.

"The truck is outside now. You must go, Ada."

Ada stepped forward to take Beth. Patrick's grip tightened. "The child will have a better life here with us, Ada. You must leave her now." He picked up the kapok-stuffed bedding roll and the suitcase. "Come."

Numbly, Ada allowed Patrick to steer her towards the door. "You must not let anything happen to her," she said.

"I will do my level best to look after your baby as you would," Evaline replied gently. "And we will pray for you. You do credit to the Wood name. We love you dearly, Ada."

Ada forced a smile of gratitude. "Don't come to the front with me. I don't want them to see Beth."

So Evaline and Charmaine remained on the back verandah, and Ada felt their pity as she walked down the steps. Without looking up she followed Patrick along the back path and around the corner of the house.

When they reached the gate, Patrick bent to kiss her wet cheek. "Beth will be safe with us. You mustn't worry. Just remember to do as you're told. And guard your mosquito net."

Someone hauled her up onto the back of the lorry. A voice shouted in Japanese, and the truck jerked forwards, its gears graunching. Ada kept her eyes on Patrick's tall stooped form standing in the road. He raised an arm in farewell. Slowly, she raised hers, seeing an old man who might not survive the war, who might not be there to lead and protect the family.

The sun drove down into Ada's skull, bored a hole to let in the flaming heat. Half blinded by the cruel light from the glittering metal of stolen cars dumped on the Padang, where the women prisoners were assembled for registration, she looked away into the distance beyond the Esplanade. The sea was crowded with native craft - parahus and junks. They filled the spaces between the funnels of sunken vessels, and it struck her that everything solid and British had gone.

There was a stench of rotting flesh. It came from the corpses in the uncovered trenches that had churned up the once smooth green of the Cricket Club. Bile rose in Ada's throat as the guard, reeking of stale sweat, paced up and down between the rows of women, his long sword dangling at his side. "Tenko, tenko," he barked. The women bowed again from the waist as they had been schooled to do. Scuffed boots paused in front of her. She remained bent. The boots passed on. She righted herself, but soon the soldier returned, this time with another, and one by one the women bowed low again.

The second soldier – taller, thinner – shouted at them in English. "Gold. Money. Where keep?"

Disgusted, for no one replied, he drew his sword and sliced the air. A woman cried out in terror. "Why you in Singapore?" he bellowed at her, but before she could answer he turned abruptly and stomped to the end of the line towards a pile of coconuts, grabbed a coarse shell and sliced off the top. Lifting the gaping incision to his lips he returned to prowl before the parched internees. It was supposedly a form of torture, along with the merciless sun. The woman beside Ada swayed dangerously. You were slapped for swaying, falling, not bowing. Ada kept her eyes to the front, praying the woman would not fall, and saw a thick-set Japanese climb a dais. He began to speak, and the throbbing in her head grew. It was hard to concentrate, to take in the lesson that the Japanese were the faithful subjects of an emperor who had descended from the all-powerful sun god, while the British were the descendants of monkeys.

★ ★ ★

Ada's limbs ached, nearly as much as her head. She craved water and wondered when she might open her suitcase and drink, sparingly, very sparingly from the tin flask, because it was a long walk to Katong where they would stay before going on to Changi. She must not show her discomfort or fear. She must be like the men who marched away from the Padang, marched off to prison grinning and giving the thumbs-up. It was the famous bulldog spirit. You had to have it to survive.

But as they moved on she felt like an obedient school girl. You can hardly march and hold your head up when you're watching your feet, picking your way around an edge of a bomb crater one minute, then some toppled palm trees another. The road was littered with severed nuts. No doubt it was easier to cut down the whole tree than climbing it. She looked to her side. Who could tell her if there would be a stop for them to drink or to relieve themselves? No one glanced her way. It was enough trying to carry a heavy suitcase. One woman had brought a tennis racket as if she were going on holiday. She was European. The woman next to her was Eurasian. Ada tried to attract her attention, a little smile of friendly encouragement hovering on her lips, but the woman looked straight through her.

The procession was slowing now, and the women bunched together. They appeared to be skirting an object in the road. Ada heard cries of disgust and the sound of retching, and then she too saw the corpse, the flesh beginning to dissolve into a formless stinking mess. Her stomach lurched, and vomit filled her mouth. She leaned forward to spit out, and an old Chinese woman bumped into her. Ada straightened, and watched the woman as she stumbled across the broken road. She was heading towards a barbed wire enclosure set back from the thoroughfare. There was a large crowd of people behind the tall fence. All of them appeared to be Chinese. The Chinese were more hated than the British even. No one connected with the Chinese Relief

Fund would be spared, Patrick had said. Was Melanie there? Were her brothers?

Ada turned away. She must not allow herself to think the worst. It was necessary to trust that Melanie had found somewhere safe to hide. She must not worry about Amah either. It will only weaken you, she told herself.

She was conscious now that her breasts were very full, and when she heard the cries of an infant somewhere in the procession of women, the tightness was painful. Milk leaked, and her blouse became wet. Covering her chest with her free arm, she could not hide her tears.

A white haired, elderly woman, a few paces in front of her, looked back, and immediately her face grew soft with sympathy. She stretched out a thin arm ushering Ada forward, and touched her cheek gently.

"This is a nightmare, I know," she said.

"I left my daughter behind," Ada blurted. "She's with my in-laws. We thought it would be better for her to stay there. But some have brought their children. I feel terrible leaving her behind."

"Your in-laws are not being interned then?"

"They're Anglo-Indians."

"Ah. You're lucky to have people to take care of your little girl. These women probably didn't have a choice."

"I shouldn't have left her. Oh, what have I done? It's my duty to look after my baby."

"Hush," the woman said, "of course you want to protect your child. But it seems to me that a child left with loving people on the outside of a prison will have a better time of it. None of us knows what we have in store for us." Ada flinched. "Don't worry, dear, we'll manage with the good Lord's help. And if we stick together. I'm Judith, by the way." Ada gave her own name, feeling Judith's dry palm on her elbow, and noted the deathly pallor of the woman's face. "We've got to keep going," Judith said.

They passed the enclosure. Ada could see the Japanese soldiers strutting like cockerels, shouting and prodding the prisoners with their rifle butts. Some of these prisoners had their hands stamped by a soldier and were making their way towards the gates. Others, mainly young men, were being herded onto lorries. One soldier was ordering a trio of young Chinese men to stand up. He pointed his gun as if to shoot, then, laughing loudly, walked up and slapped the men's faces. Left, right, left, right. He stepped back, and another took his turn to humiliate. Satisfied, they looked about them as if expecting applause. Ada, sickened by the brutality, lost her footing and fell back in line.

Judith returned to walk beside her. "Don't attract attention. Come. We must keep walking," she whispered fiercely.

The two women were nearly at the back of the group. A lorry rumbled up beside them. It was loaded with Japanese soldiers and a few women internees. The men leaned from the truck and shouted at them as they passed, then the truck stopped. A soldier leaped down onto the road in front of Ada. He ordered her to board, grabbing her arm, his hand pressed against her breast. She tried to pull away from him, and reached for Judith, who held onto her as tightly as she could, but lost her grip. The soldier dragged his bayonet from its sheath and gouged Judith's suitcase, as if punishing her for helping Ada, then tipped the contents onto the road. Ada wrenched free from the soldier and began to pick up the clothes, thrusting them back into the case. The soldier kicked her hard. Ada keeled sideways and pointed at Judith, kneeling on the road and gasping for breath.

"She's an old woman. Let her ride on your truck. Leave me to walk. I can walk." She pointed at Judith, then at the truck. The soldier understood. Perhaps ashamed for kicking her, he gestured to Judith to get on board. She hesitated. "Go, go," Ada said. "It's better for me to walk."

"I'm sorry, dear, I'm having one of my little spells," Judith wheezed. Ada helped her to the truck. Two women leaned down and pulled her up. The tail gate slammed shut and fumes blasted Ada's face. Judith lifted her hand in gratitude.

Heavy with dread, acid fear in her mouth, Ada wondered how she would manage to complete the journey. But a few yards on, she saw several bare-chested British men in khaki shorts pushing wheel barrows filled with rubble. A crowd of locals watched in silence, bemused by the sight of Europeans doing coolie work. She gripped the slippery handle of her suitcase more tightly, swallowed hard, and straightened her back.

Nightfall brought no relief from the heat. Mosquitoes swarmed and bit. She pictured Katong, still miles ahead, the beach and the warm sea where her father had taught her to swim while Vera splashed impatiently in the shallows until it was time for her lesson. Vera. Vera dressed to kill – hat at a jaunty angle, dress new – waving to her from the deck of the departing ship. Ada imagined Vera lying indolently on a sandy Australian beach, then sauntering to the edge of the ocean and dipping in her painted toes.

Ada imagined herself walking boldly towards the water. How welcome the vast openness would be, the freedom.

Chapter 13

NOVEMBER, 1942

ADA PUT THE FLOWER IN a tin mug, and placed the mug on the concrete slab in the centre of the cell, then sat cross-legged in front of it so she could admire the soft sheen of the delicate pink petals. Once, she reflected with regret, when she had the Woods' huge garden with its extravagant green banks smothered in glorious colour, she had hardly spent any time there, had taken the beauty for granted. Even when she was helping to grow the vegetables in Serangoon hadn't she done it out of a sense of duty rather than love? And when they were in Geylang she always asked Abdul to keep on cutting and trimming. There was so much green once, so much growing life. She remembered that in the Katong camp, where they were for a fortnight before coming on to Changi, they had papaya trees. And what was difficult about digging latrines or camping in a shed overgrown with lallang, compared to being in a prison where there were no trees and only a square of tired grass?

It was only by chance that she had seen the flower on a patch of dirt in a far corner of the walled yard while she cleaned the drains. She believed it was a reward for taking on the stinking hard work. A bird must have dropped the seed one day.

She imagined the bird now, flying high over Changi village, then circling above the unruffled sea before returning to eye the plates of fried fish and sambal on the cafe tables set under the palm trees. It was hard to believe that the sea was only a short distance away from the prison.

She wished now that she was a bird flying where it chose. If she took off what might she see? Beth in the arms of the wet nurse, suckling at her breast? Ada imagined the child healthy and content. She knew she had to be grateful for that, but she rocked back and forth to ease herself from the acute discomfort of longing and stared steadfastly at the flower again, placing her hands over her ears to block out the noise of chattering and calling and stamping down the metal staircase.

The petals were already drooping. They were dying because of the noise. There was such a hullabaloo; a woman was screaming in the corridor. No peace for the wicked, as Elizabeth would say. You could not even have peace when you bathed. The guards were there, pacing, watching.

"Ada, Ada."

Ada recognised the voice and let out a sigh of exasperation. It was not fair. Lucy de Souza was Vera's friend. She had attached herself to Ada and Judith at Katong, and begged to share the cell with them in Changi, preferring the company of someone she knew rather than a Eurasian like herself, even if the Eurasian women had larger cells and running water. Not that Ada would have refused her plea, but she was an irritating presence at times, either chattering continuously, or bored and listless. What in God's name was she doing now?

Lucy was lying on the floor of the corridor nursing her arm, her dress tucked up on her thin brown legs so you could see her drawers. A woman was standing over her, scolding in a grating English voice. Others, waiting in a queue to have their fortunes told by one of the internees in the next-door cell, looked on, some shocked, some appearing satisfied that some justice had been done. Lucy saw Ada and called, "She's bitten me. I'm bleeding. Look, she's bitten me."

"You deserved it," the woman snarled.

"How did she deserve it?" Ada asked, her tone severe, although she felt intimidated. The woman was a known trouble-maker. She was coarsely spoken, the sort of English person Noel would identify as being 'nothing' in their own country, but who had come to Singapore with the belief that their white skin gave them the right to treat non-Europeans like dirt. For the first time in their life they were not at the bottom of the pile, Noel had said. You had to pity them.

"Gloating. Stuffing herself in front of us." There were cake crumbs on the floor.

And Lucy was Eurasian. Ada was aware that the Eurasians were disliked by many. Not only for having better accommodation, but more significantly because their children were allowed more food. It was rumoured that some of the Eurasians did not have a direct British parent and came into the camp because they thought it would be easier than in the outside world. Ada found this impossible to believe.

The woman's skin was badly pocked, she had a long nose and small eyes, and Ada had often thought she resembled a mongoose. Ethel – Ada had heard her being called that – poked a cowering Lucy with her foot.

"Slut! We all know what you did to get that."

Lucy moaned and called to Ada.

"Go on. Call out to your little friend. Slut," the woman shouted.

"How can you call her a slut when you behave like an animal?" Ada snapped, flushed with anger. Yes, Lucy flirted with the guards, more than flirted, who knew? But there was no excuse for biting, and ugly words. Ada braced herself, realising that now she would be the focus of abuse, but Ethel seemed too taken aback to speak. Probably no one had challenged her like this before. Ada endeavoured to appear calm, and said, in as steady a voice she could, "What good comes from fighting? We have to save our energies to work together."

"Oh, really. Listen to the little saint." The woman's eyes were menacing slits in her red face. She looked Ada up and down. "And where did you get that chichi accent? You're not English, either."

"I'm sorry to say I am, if I belong to the same race as you." The words were out, and she could not take them back. Ethel's face darkened. Someone tittered. The concrete floor wavered in trepidation; the colours of the women's dresses blurred. Ada's heart pounded, and she clenched her fists, waiting for retaliation.

Ethel stepped closer and crossed her arms, stood planted with legs apart. "Your name's Ada or something isn't it? Yeah, I've heard about you. Buttering up to the bigwigs."

Ada presumed she was talking about the doctors in the hospital. She chose to work there when the duties were being allocated in the first month of internment, and was gladly welcomed – a basic knowledge of first aid was better than nothing.

"Saint Ada," Ethel scoffed.

"A saint, am I?" Ada's anger was greater than her fear now, and she circled Ethel to grab Lucy's arm and haul her back into the cell. "Well, I don't think a saint would be thinking what I'm thinking now."

"And what's that?" Ethel snarled.

"You're a rotten bully. And you deserve a taste of your own medicine." Before Ethel could respond, a guard appeared at the top of the staircase and shouted at them.

Ada pushed Lucy in front of her into the cell as the women quickly dispersed. "For God sake, Lucy, please don't do that to me again."

"I wasn't doing anything."

"Perhaps that's the problem, Lucy. Perhaps if you did more, helped more, made friends with people, the Ethels of this world wouldn't have such a free hand with you."

"All the women are snobs. All colour bar."

"Some are. But not all. Not by any means."

She was thinking of Freddy Bloom, a pretty American woman who ran the camp newspaper. Only yesterday, Freddy had remarked quite openly to her that she could not tolerate the women who fought and argued. "They behave like children," she said, "and we have to be more grown-up than ever now. At least I can escape all the squabbling when I'm doing the paper." The news-sheet came type-written every Wednesday and was full of suggestions on how to cope, and what was going on in the prison, what entertainment was coming up, what books might be good to read. Through it, Ada had traced a pair of rubber-soled boots that would help keep her feet dry on the damp concrete. She traded her saved-up sugar ration for them.

"Look at Freddy Bloom," Ada said. She first met Freddy while Freddy had been in the hospital with an attack of dengue. During her period of recovery, Freddy had watched Ada one day bandaging a child's hand.

"My," Freddy had said in her cheery voice, "who taught you to do that? Are you a trained nurse?" This led Ada to talk about Michael, him teaching her first aid. "Well, you certainly were a better pupil than I ever was." She told Ada that she had done a Home Nursing Course in India where her first husband had been a doctor with the army before the regiment was sent to Penang. He died there at the age of twenty-seven from pleurisy. "Poor man. He was such a gentle soul. I felt so bereft." She paused, then said, "Someone told me I could try working for one of the newspapers. I was lucky. I found a job quite quickly with the Malay Tribune Group of Newspapers in Singapore." Her face brightened. "And I met Phillip, my husband. He was a doctor at the General. In the men's prison now." When Freddy had asked Ada how she ended up in Changi, Ada had told her about refusing to leave, and regretting her decision.

"You mustn't blame yourself, Ada. I refused to go. I couldn't see the sense of it. I wanted to do my bit, beside Phillip. Everybody told me to leave. The American Consul tried his best, but finally washed his hands of me. Phillip – we weren't married then – got really cross when I wouldn't go, but he gave up too, and asked me to marry him instead! We rushed off to the Registry Office between air raids, then returned to the General and got on with it. That's what you have to do, Ada. Just get on with it, don't you think?" And so they talked, and shared their sadness at being parted from husbands. Freddy did not have a child, though. On a later occasion, Ada learned that she'd had two miscarriages, and perhaps it was this loss which made her so sympathetic for Ada's separation from Beth. She had listened with tears in her eyes.

"She's not English. The Yanks are different," Lucy said.

"What about Dr. Williams? And Mrs Mulvany who runs the Red Cross corner? If not for women like them I can't imagine what a mess we'd be in. They've organised all the groups and classes too. You should join a class like me." You had to admire the camaraderie of the British women, Ada thought. They really did have that bulldog spirit. She felt proud to be English, perhaps for the first time, when they had marched into Changi from Katong singing 'There'll always be an England'. They could hear the male prisoners cheering and whistling.

"I don't want to learn shorthand or Shakespeare."

"You could go to dancing classes with Barbara Smith. You love tap dancing and ballroom. You were always going to dances with Vera."

"I really miss Vera, la. I wonder what she's doing now. She's probably going to lots of dances," Lucy said, beginning to cry.

"Oh, Lucy, I know how hard it is when we think about what we're missing. It makes it so much harder to cope." Ada put her arm around Lucy's shoulders. "I know it's awful. But we just have to keep up hope. Believe that we'll get out of here soon. And remember what Judith told us." Ada shut her eyes, trying to recall the words of the poem Judith had written out for her because she wanted to learn them off by heart. Judith, a former English teacher, was always quoting poetry, or lines from Shakespeare. She began to recite:

> "'Stone walls do not a prison make,
> Nor iron bars a cage;
> Minds innocent and quiet take
> That for a hermitage;
> If I have freedom in my love
> And in my soul am free,
> Angels alone, that soar above,
> Enjoy such liberty.'"

Ada explained, "It's a poem written by someone centuries ago. Richard Lovelace. He's writing it from prison, to a woman called Althea. She might have been his wife, or his mistress."

Ada imagined what Michael would have thought if he had heard her recite that. He would not believe how much she was learning. If she had more time she would enrol in the art class. Even run a class herself. Offer to teach sewing. Judith said she should. Everyone said she should after seeing the dolls' dresses she was sewing for the Christmas fair. If they got out before Christmas she'd give them away to the children, but would save one for Beth, of course.

Judith lay with her eyes wide open in the corner of the hospital shed. She was clearly in pain, but not in enough pain to receive the precious morphine reserved by the Japanese for the very ill. Without a fan the air lay heavily, discouraging sleep. It also carried the stench of sweating bodies.

Ada filled a basin with water and approached the bed. "Judith," she said softly. "Time for your wash."

At first Judith did not respond. Perhaps she was dreaming of her beloved Cumbria, where she used to hike over the hills with her parents and help with the milking. She spoke a lot about her childhood in England. The past was everything if you thought you might not have a future. Or perhaps even want one, Ada supposed. She sometimes believed that Judith was looking forward to death.

"Oh, Ada dear. Don't bother about me. See to someone else."

"Not on your Nellie." The word 'Nellie' was from a comedy sketch a group of women had done in a recent stage show. Ada had discovered that a little acting, a jocular voice, slightly bossy, achieved the best results in coaxing patients.

She lifted the frail body carefully and removed the nightdress. Judith was all bone, the ribs prominent, the breasts flat.

"You've never told me what my Nellie is, Ada." Judith fumbled to lift the straggles of hair from her neck. Ada breathed shallowly. The washing cooled, but without soap did not remove, the cloying smell of illness.

"It might be better if you don't know." She worked quickly, saving Judith from a prolonged loss of dignity, then gave her the rag so she could wipe between her legs. Judith dropped the rag into the basin and lay back wearily.

"Feeling a bit fresher?" Ada asked.

"Yes, thank you, dear. I could go back to the cell. Leave the bed for someone who needs it more."

"But we haven't any room. I'm enjoying the space, don't you know. It would cramp me considerably to have you back there." It would kill Judith to be back there, Ada thought. Seven feet by ten with a central concrete 'bed' eighteen inches high beneath a tiny barred window set in the wall above it. Judith had slept on the slab before her transfer to the hospital, with the two younger women on either side taking it in turns not to have their heads touching the lavatory - the 'squatter' in the corner. "I'm on the bed now," Ada said. "I get the light from the window better, so I can read more easily."

"What are you reading?"

"I've just finished *A Tale of Two Cities*. I saw it in the library." The library was a store of books someone had the good foresight to bring from the library in Raffles' Hotel. Ada recalled Michael telling her the novel was a story of a man who went to the scaffold to save his friend. She pictured Michael reciting lines from the book, his eyes shining - inspired, perhaps, to do something very brave as well. Ada wished that she could confide in Judith about Michael, tell her how she lived constantly fearing that he would come to harm. All Judith knew was that Michael was an Anglo-Indian school teacher who loved music and English literature.

"Did you enjoy it?"

"Enjoy? I could've done with something more cheerful. But Michael recommended it to me once, and I like Dickens."

"I think Sydney Carton is an intriguing character. He was a loner, but prepared to die for the woman he loved to make up for his dissolute life."

"I can understand Sydney Carton sacrificing himself. His death wasn't going to affect Lucie because she loved someone else. By going to the scaffold he was allowing her to be with her husband." Ada spoke as evenly as she could, trying to make it sound like a matter of mere interest rather than something which kept her awake at night. "But what about those who are happily married, and have families, and still choose to be heroic and risk their lives? Leave behind those who love them?"

Judith lay staring up at the ceiling. Alarmingly, she reminded Ada of an effigy on a coffin once seen in an English history book. Just as it seemed Judith was not going to answer, she replied, "I wanted Christopher – my husband – to leave Singapore, but he said that it was his duty to care for the ill under any circumstances. It made me feel small hearing that. I never challenged him again.

I realised that he simply couldn't have lived with himself if he hadn't stayed."

"He did what he believed was right," Ada said quietly, recalling Patrick's words.

"I haven't told you how Christopher died. He was working in the Alexandra when Japanese soldiers stormed in. It was a dreadful massacre. I didn't go into the hospital to help the nurses that day because I was ill. I often wish I had. And that's not because I'm brave."

Ada clasped Judith's hand. "You must miss him terribly."

"We were the best of friends. Loved doing the same things. Walking, listening to music. Poetry. I met him rather late in life when I went to London to teach. I travelled all over the world with him. He trained doctors. We never really settled anywhere for long, but we always had each other."

Ada imagined the couple talking, walking, sharing. When the war was over, she and Michael would do the same. They would spend a lot more time together. They could even join a drama group, or a music society. She had so many ideas now from being in the camp. Freddy Bloom too said that she spent a lot of time planning what she would do with Phillip when they were released. Ada told herself that she would never take anything for granted again. She would treasure every moment. And yes, she would never let Michael know that she had resented him for choosing to do his duty.

But if Michael never came back?

"You are very strong, Ada," he had said. But how strong did she have to be to get through to the end? How much courage and determination would she need? How was she going to make the small circle grow, that pinprick of glowing light, as she imagined it, nestling somewhere near her heart?

"I feel myself blessed having married Christopher, having his love. Lovelace, who wrote the lines you wanted to learn..."

"About being free?"

"Yes. He also wrote to Lucasta, supposedly a mistress. The poem says it all. He asks her to forgive him for going off to war." She began to recite:

> " 'True, a new mistress now I chase,
> The first foe in the field;
> And with a stronger faith embrace
> A sword, a horse, a shield.
>
> Yet this inconstancy is such
> As thou too shalt adore;
> I could not love thee, Dear, so much,
> Loved I not honour more.' "

Ada leaned forward, and said intently, "So is his mistress meant to think that his sense of duty as a soldier made him a better man, and as a better man his love would be better too?"

"Yes. A man with a strong sense of honour, someone loyal to his king and his country, was capable of a love that was deep and lasting." Judith closed her eyes, and her features softened. She looked contented, as if remembering her Christopher and his love for her.

Ada said nothing, but it occurred to her that Lovelace had two mistresses, and even if he did not have them at the same time, who knew if he would remain faithful? Who knew if he simply had a fine way with words and could make his wish for adventure and heroism sound unselfish? In doing what he felt was right, he was doing what he wanted to do.

She knew that she could not say this to Judith, and wished that she had not heard the poem for it made her question again Michael's motives when she was trying not to. Also, in thinking of Lovelace deceiving one mistress for another, she was reminded of the letter she received about the black woman.

Judith was asleep now, and Ada, leaving her to return to the cell, remembered how she doubted Michael's fidelity. The cell was empty, so she knelt immediately on the concrete floor, and clasped her hands. She felt angry with herself for allowing the thoughts to come, those unsettling, useless thoughts. "Dear God," she prayed, "please help me to remember those times when I miss Michael the most, and feel sorry for myself and angry with him, please help me to remember how kind and thoughtful he was, and how I respect him for doing what he believes is right. And please help me to trust that whatever transgression he might have made in the past, the dutiful man he is could not be other than a faithful husband."

It was the Emperor's birthday. At dawn the internees had been called into the yard to stand with their heads bowed for two minutes facing towards the rising sun. In the lightening pink sky, the morning star shone brightly. The beauty made Ada want to cry. When they lined up to receive their treat – a tin of pineapple for every three women, and a box of Rinso washing powder for every four – she felt oddly blessed.

Lucy sat down beside her in the shade of the wall. They could pretend to be having a picnic. In the cell (to which Judith had insisted returning) Ada had already fed Judith her share of the fruit, with Lucy hovering to see that the slice and a third was exact. Now the two young women were eating as slowly as they could. But it was very difficult; the juice was so sweet, the flesh so wonderfully tender. Ada held the final half slice in her hand and wondered when she would ever eat anything as blissfully succulent again.

People said that the food was better since the men from the P.O.W. camp had taken over the cooking. They spoke as if they were sampling the menu of a newly opened restaurant. Ada saw this as the British way of coping, a denial of adversity, in the same way they pretended that Singapore had been impregnable. This stoicism both irritated and impressed her. It took some strength of character to think well of the daily rice and water – 'bubu' – into which the men stirred bits of grass as a substitute for vegetables when there was not even a single bean in sight. Porridge twice a week, bread every second day; occasionally a few sardines, or a bit of bully beef. Although they did have fresh meat a few days ago. People said it was a dog, or a cat. But you ate any protein.

A woman was striding towards them now across the prison yard. Ada recognised with alarm that it was the mongoose woman, Ethel. She knelt down in front of Ada and dug her finger into Ada's chest.

"So you've kept that for me, have you? How kind. Thanks a lot." The voice grated, full of aggression. Before Ada understood, Ethel snatched up the remaining fragment of pineapple and shoved it in her mouth. Ada stared at her in fury. "Go on then, luv, bash me," Ethel sneered, standing up and folding her scrawny red arms.

Ada glanced at Lucy. Lucy was looking the other way, the coward. Ada pushed herself up against the wall. Ethel did not move back. They stood face to face, and then a glob of mucus hit Ada's cheek. She wiped it away, and bunched her fists, preparing to defend herself.

Triumphant, the mongoose shouted in her face, "Watch your bloody tongue when you're speaking to me in future." A guard woke up from his midday slumber by the sentry box and looked towards them. "Bitch," Ethel hissed, before heading back inside the prison. It was against the rules to gather in groups and talk.

"She was paying you back, la," Lucy whispered, getting to her feet.

"I know what she was doing, Lucy. I thought she would pay me back. I was stupid saying what I did. I was asking for trouble."

"You were protecting me, la." Lucy sniffed. "I'm not a very nice person. I know people think I'm a slut. But I want to live." She clasped Ada's arm. "I'll never forget what you did to help me. You and Judith have been good friends. I was lucky I saw you and you let me share the same cell. One day I'll do something to help you when you need it."

"Like you did just now, then?" Ada said, not looking at her.

"I'm not a very brave person, Ada."

"That makes two of us."

Lucy looked surprised.

"I'm not a very brave person either, Lucy."

"You were brave saying what you did to her."

"I said it because I was angry. I wasn't thinking. You're brave when you've got time to think about it first and still do it."

It was dawn, light enough to see. Ada could begin now. She took the baby from the box used as a cot for the very young, and placed the infant on her lap. The child had died in the night, her breathing a scorching rasp. She had been born in the prison. Ada dipped the cloth in a basin of water and wiped the baby's face gently. A fine tracery of inky blue veins showed through the transparent skin. The baby was not as dark as the mother, a very pretty Eurasian woman. Ada used to see her stand in line for food, hands resting possessively on her bulge. At least she was not alive to see her baby die.

Ada was dressing the baby in a clean nightgown, one sewn from a threadbare sheet, when she heard Dr. Smallwood behind her.

"You should get some rest after this, Ada."

Dr. Smallwood was in charge of babies and children, including dead ones. Gently, she removed the corpse from Ada's lap and took it across to one of the nurses.

Ada stood and waited for her to return. "Do you want me to do anything else?"

"No. Go and have some rest."

"And what about you? You've been up all night too. Are you going to rest?" Ada was worried about the doctor's health, not only because she was fond of the woman, but also because she was very aware how dependent they all were on the skilled. The doctors and nurses performed miracles. Trying to manage with two chamber pots, two thermometers and a dwindling supply of drugs and bandages was like having to feed thousands with a few fish and loaves. She wished that she had taken those lessons with Michael more seriously, learned more than how to bandage or dress a wound. He used to laugh at her clumsiness. He was not the most patient of teachers, probably because he had so much on his mind.

"I wish that I could be more helpful. That I was a trained nurse."

"Did you want to be a nurse? You would've been a good one. You've got the patience."

"Once upon a time I really wanted to be a teacher."

Ada remembered wanting to be like Miss de Silva, who never raised her voice and was always encouraging.

"You would've had the patience for that as well. You're doing a grand job, Ada. You're like gold dust here. Now go and get some rest."

Tiredly, Ada made her way back to her cell. Someone was playing a record on a phonograph along the corridor. It was a piano piece, sad and beautiful. Chopin? Michael loved to play Chopin, she remembered. He would lose himself in the music. Although when the troubles began he played without the customary expression of peace on his face. How she wished that he had told her more. Patrick said it was best she did not know, but how did ignorance help? The more you knew the more you could understand, and with understanding came acceptance, surely. And if he had shared more with her she could have supported him.

The music was quieter, slower, drawing the ear closer so the heart would follow – should follow, if the thought were not there that Michael had never confided in her because he feared she would not support him, but would cling and weep and drag him back. She refused to leave Singapore when there was still a chance. And before that, look how she behaved when he chased the Red Blood Brigade. He said that she was strong, but he did not believe that, she thought, not really.

Lucy was asleep. Ada lay down on the floor beside a dozing Judith on the slab and drew over the mosquito net. The music drifted down the corridor in the hot dampness of the early morning. A baby cried, and Ada's breasts carried the faint memory of early motherhood. She folded her arms across her chest and tried to connect with that time. The house would be dark and silent, and she would switch on the lamp and lift the child, hold her, nurse her, hear her eager sucking. Even on the journey through the burning streets on the way to the Selwyn Building she'd been able to give Beth comfort. But her breasts were withered and dry now.

She put her hand over her eyes, and the tears, which had been biding their time, flowed out in a torrent for the dead baby, for Beth and Michael, for everything lost, for all those days she had not realised how lucky she was.

Chapter 14

OCTOBER, 1943

SEATED ON HER MAT BENEATH the cell window, Ada dipped her finger in sugar and put it in her mouth. Her tongue circled for the sweetness, and she remembered stealing sugar cubes with Vera from the laid tables in the hotel, sucking these joyfully as far away from Amah as they could, for she would have scolded them for ruining their teeth. They also stole condensed milk – Michael's favourite. He liked it on his porridge. Or honey. Ginseng honey.

She was not sure why the internees had been called to receive the Red Cross parcel. People said it was because the Japanese were losing the war and knew they would be punished severely for failing to keep to the rules of war. There were so many rumours about the war ending, or talk of repatriation. It was a way of maintaining hope, but she preferred nowadays to stay with the present as best she could to avoid the despair that came with continuing disappointment. It was better to take advantage of every single good moment, every treat, like this sugar. She licked her finger and thought of the parcel in which it came. For every six women there was one tin of prunes, one of milk powder, two of coffee, one of salmon, one of grape jam. The coffee would be kept for a coffee morning. There was also ham, dried eggs, Bovril, Rosemell pate, eight packets of soup, ten packets of cigarettes, one packet of sugar, two bars of soap. Ada had traded her cigarettes for sugar. But the greatest joy was receiving the letters from relatives and friends written months ago and held back. Most had been nearly obliterated by heavy scorings out, but Patrick's came intact. He must have suspected that little passed the censors and had thought of a way to outwit them. Ada smoothed out the sheet of paper and read slowly, savouring the words just as she had lingered with the sugar. She had read the letter many times already, marvelling at its pedantic duplicity.

'My dear Ada,

I hope this letter finds you in the good health we find ourselves. I also hope that the British will soon give up the fighting so that we can live peaceably in the ordered society our new masters are seeking with their attempts to help all of us in Syonanto to become better citizens.

After you left, the Anglo-Indian community was summoned to the Padang and told that we must endeavour to be less materialistic and more spiritual and see ourselves as Asians rather than superior to them, as we have shamefully done. This made us reflect on the arrogance of our ways and our aping of the British as if we were Europeans. Now we know better and have the example of our new masters, who show us their superiority and good taste by their lifestyle, which surpasses the British. It is very good to see the Japanese drive smart cars and live in the beautiful Tanglin houses and play golf and tennis with such skill. If not for them the whole horse-racing industry would shut down. We are also grateful that this little island has not lost its lively atmosphere. The Japanese are a light-hearted race and enjoy life. The amusements parks are always full. In many ways we are shown what we can aspire to as Asians.

It is also good that those Chinese who have stood in opposition to change have got their just rewards. These wicked men have been set to work as coolies alongside the British soldiers who mend the roads. And the lazy women are finding occupation by serving the comfort houses. Surely, my dear, the world has rightly been turned upside down, and those who once lauded it over us such as government officials, pompous clerks and teachers, are now at the bottom, and the rickshaw pullers and clever business men who run the food markets as best they can and contribute to the Japanese fund, are at the top. You should see yesterday's top dogs wearing shorts and pushing wheelbarrows. How the mighty have fallen! The proud and haughty British have been rightly humbled by our brave new rulers.

Those people who fail to learn respect, such as bowing low before the Japanese in the street or at crossings, are given a sharp slap, in the way you might slap a child to teach it obedience - always for its own good. Yet, even with this sensible discipline everything is much more free and easy. I no longer wear a suit. I have rubber sandals which are fresher to wear, as is my open-necked shirt. How ridiculously pompous-looking I used to be with my ties and socks. Yes, we are much more natural, and fitter, because each morning our Japanese guests lead a physical education class on the tennis court which Evaline, Charmaine and I attend, and our diet is nourishing because it is plain and simple. We also benefit from the fresh air as we sleep outside our new garden quarters where Ahmad lives. Amah still has her room, and is tolerated because she looks after baby Beth, freeing us to serve our new masters, who treat us with great fairness.

We've been allowed to paint the rooms and have put down some mats to cover the floor. Without the clutter of possessions such as English books and gramophone music – all examples of the decadent colonial past we have wisely abandoned – our smaller habitation suits us very well. On the whole we are quite comfortable, and don't spend much time idling uselessly there anyway. The duties of cooking and cleaning the house adds to our sense of self-worth. Evaline and Amah are learning to cook our own meals with palm oil, which is much healthier than nut oil, I've been told. I also do the garden – we grow most of our own vegetables – and help a neighbour make paper from bamboo. This is a useful thing to know, as is learning the beautiful Japanese language - how stirring are the Japanese anthems played on all occasions.

Yes, Ada, you would find much change here, a better place for us Asians. It is not your fault that you are British, and one day, I am sure, you will join us on the outside because you have never been like your compatriots who treated Asians like dirt. You are the wife of my precious son, who has sadly gone missing while doing his ambulance duties. We have every hope of seeing him again, though, and we know how much he will be able to contribute to Syonanto. His child thrives with the food the kind Japanese give her to eat. She is a little chatterbox: very lively and curious. We have much to be thankful for.

With all good wishes and much love from us here in Serangoon.'

Ada stood up clutching the letter to her chest, feeling again an immense relief that Beth was so much better off than the children in the gaol, and that Michael was still missing, not reported dead. But it then occurred to her that Patrick had not mentioned receiving any of her letters. She tried not to sound critical, aware of the censors, but perhaps she'd not praised the Japanese enough in the clever way Patrick had done.

She searched for a carefully hidden sheet of paper, and a worn pencil, then sat to write.

'Dear Patrick,

I'm so glad to hear that you are all well, and that Beth is growing up fast to be a clever little girl. I help in the school, and every day when I sit with a little one and go over the alphabet with them, I think of teaching Beth. We've managed to find boxes and planks so the children can really get on as if they were in a proper classroom. I'm learning a lot, living in the camp. The Japanese are good masters and leave us to get on with our lives, and only interfere if we don't show the proper respect they deserve. They understand our need to worship, and we have church services. They are trying to make our lives as safe and healthy as possible. It's not their fault that the rations were very low when we first came in. The food is much better now that the men have taken over the cooking and we get eggs more frequently and sometimes sardines and green beans. Recently we were all given vaccines for typhoid and cholera. And I had quinine when I got malaria.'

The fever – she did not think she would survive – was terrible – burning hot and then freezing cold. If only there was something they could do about the bed-bugs.

'So many of the women here are talented and well-educated. Some of them teach classes in languages, some teach Shakespeare, or dance, art, music. I'm learning shorthand and trying to understand Shakespeare better. I adore the concerts, especially the ones that the men give. They are very good musicians, and we also have solo violin and piano performances. Mrs Eisinger has gramophone recitals in the tool shed. I'm growing fond of Beethoven's concertos. I've something to look forward to every week, which makes my time in the hospital easier. I love the doctors, and try to be as helpful as I can.

My best friend Judith has had to go back into hospital, but I hope she'll be out soon. She used to be a teacher, and we like to talk about books. She loves to quote lines from poems, like Michael enjoyed doing.

Recently I embroidered some handkerchiefs for a Red Cross sale and did smocking on some baby clothes. This is why I was asked to help sew some quilts for the male prisoners by Mrs Mulvaney, who runs the Red Cross. We made them out of rice and flour bags. Mrs Mulvaney got the idea from the quilt Mrs Ennis did with the Girl Guides. I was given special responsibility for making one for the camp commandant. I used satin stitch for beautiful Mt Fujiama and the magnificent Rising Sun.'

She thought it would not hurt to mention the quilts now seeing how pleased Asahi, the commandant, had been with his. He had, as they hoped, made no fuss about the other quilts going to the male prisoners. But at the time of sewing the quilts the women had needed to be careful that the guard did not catch them working. Someone had to stay outside the cell and keep watch. There were six of them, including a nursing sister, two teachers, and a former typist at Raffles' Hotel. Sewing together was a reminder of another life. It was a sort of normality. Some of them spoke of sewing circles in England. The Danish woman said she liked to embroider in the garden on long summer evenings. She stitched flowers on her square. They were determined to get messages to the men that would keep their spirits up, so there were roses and hollyhocks for the English to remind them of country gardens, shamrocks for the Irish, maple leaves for the Canadians, thistles and heather for the Scottish. Birds were to speak of freedom, flags to foster national pride, and ships and planes to offer hope of escape. One woman had wanted to embroider a mother rabbit beside a baby rabbit with a blue ribbon around its neck to let her husband know she had given birth to a boy. She had the baby with her. Ada envied her every single day.

'I've made some good friends. A New Zealand woman told me a lot about her country. It's close to Australia, but is much greener, with wonderful mountains and lakes. I'd like to go there one day, when the war is over. But first I want to be a worthy citizen of the civilised country we have now thanks to the hard work of the Japanese.'

She was especially pleased with this piece of deception and smiled with satisfaction. This letter surely would get past the censors.

'Some of the women are excellent actresses, and a lovely American woman called Freddy Bloom was allowed to put on a circus. Can you believe that! It was last November. You can imagine how surprised and delighted we were to see the tallest man, an orangutan, and the fattest woman. There was a Lion Act, which the children loved.

On Christmas Day the men gave a concert, permission kindly granted by the commandant. It was held in the courtyard. Afterwards we gave them three cheers. There was a tree, and presents for the children made by us all. The Japanese very generously showered the little ones with sweets, and the men could meet the women for a while.'

Ada's spirits flagged as she remembered watching the couples conveying love with their eyes and their carefully chosen words. She had the same sickening envy when she saw the wives pouring out their hearts to husbands allowed into the women's gaol to do the heavy manual work. Most of the guards turned a blind eye to this, but some guards were bullies, and kept the women away, striking them if they dared to venture close. There were good people and bad people in every race. Elizabeth had always said this. Oh, how she missed Elizabeth.

'As you can see, the Japanese are kind masters. They allow us to have short walks outside the prison, and I've had a swim in the sea. One lady has been allowed to lead a team to plant shrubs and papayas.'

She was wondering if she should write about the planned Fancy-Dress Ball, when brutal Japanese voices boomed down the corridor, and the metal stairs shook with the stamp of heavy-booted feet. Lucy ran into the cell, flapping her hands.

"The Nips are furious. They're slapping everyone," she managed to gasp. "They hit Mrs Fosse. They're tipping everything into the corridor, looking for something. They're coming."

Ada stuffed the letters into her blouse, and her heart pounded as she leaped to her feet and prepared to bow low in obedience. Two guards strode into the cell, and one roared at the women to get out. The other, a portly, pock-faced, middle-aged man, said nothing and glared about him. He did this in such a theatrical manner that it seemed he was only pretending, and when she saw his eyes rest on Lucy and the softness of her answering look, Ada suspected he was the one who gave Lucy the small treats which made her so unpopular. He stood politely aside to allow them to pass, while the other guard began to throw their paltry belongings about in a wild search.

✵ ✵ ✵

"I wonder what this is about," Lucy said. "One minute they're shouting at us, dragging Freddy Bloom off, and then the next we're told we can have a swim."

"I'm not sure either. Perhaps they want to confuse us so we get more anxious," Ada replied, worried about Freddy. It was rumoured that the Japanese suspected her of being a spy and sending radio messages. That was the reason for the search: they were looking for radio parts.

The guards marched the women quickly through the scattering hens and staring villagers into a disused rubber plantation, the white scars of the spindly trees a sad reminder of times past. There was a heady scent of trees and grass.

They reached the abandoned house of the overseer. The rooms had been stripped of fittings, and wires hung more thickly than the cobwebs. Excited by the thought of a swim, she changed quickly into one of the pairs of baggy bloomers that had been collected for the outing and shared amongst those – the majority – who'd not thought to pack a swimsuit when they left home before internment.

The soldiers barked in the yard for the internees to hurry. The women clattered along the verandah and down the steps, ever obedient. Ada, wondering what had become of Lucy, now caught sight of her emerging from behind an old cart, followed by one of the guards - the same middle-aged one who'd entered the cell. Was she not aware that her association with the guard would cause trouble for her, and probably anyone who associated with her?

The guards blew whistles, and the women were hurried along. Ada placed herself at the front of the group, wishing to keep her distance from Lucy, and did not look back until she heard a harsh, nasal voice behind her.

"So how are we today, Mrs Wood?"

It was Ethel, flanked by two others.

"Cosying up to the Nips are we? Like your little coloured friend. Going to offer to sew Asahi a pair of pyjamas? I expect you'll get the chance to do a fitting in private. They say he's got a big cock."

They had come to the beach. The guards blew their whistles and ordered the women into the water, a flat, still pond with a single, ruffled edge of white. Ada ran forward, wanting to escape the bullies, and threw herself into the warm, silky sea, then began to swim towards the pagar.

But her strokes were laboured; she was feeble from lack of food, and soon had to stop and tread water. When she looked towards the beach, she saw that only one other woman was swimming out to sea. The rest were splashing and frolicking about as if they were on a happy family outing, while the guards sat on the sand and smoked like indulgent parents claiming time for themselves. She could not see Ethel or her cronies, so she lay on her back, spread-eagled, and, staring up at the magnificent sky, tried her best to concentrate on its expansive beauty, to keep her mind clear of upsetting thoughts, to forget the prison and Ethel.

But where was Lucy now? Treading water, Ada scanned the crowd and caught sight of Ethel. She was making her way along the shore-line followed by her henchmen and looking out at the bathers as if searching for someone. Now, as she headed into the sea, appearing sure of her direction, Ada noticed a lone figure standing waist deep in the water. She was thin and angular, her straggly black hair caught up in a knot. It was Lucy. Lucy, who would not swim with the others as everyone shunned her. She was on her own, and helpless. Ada struck out towards her, kicking as hard as she could.

When she reached Lucy, the bullies had surrounded her, and Ethel was pressing down on Lucy's head. Ada pushed between the smirking sidekicks and tried to wrench Ethel away. Rough hands grabbed Ada's shoulders, and coarse nails dug into her flesh. A knee shoved hard into her groin, and she yelped loudly with pain. Whistles blew, and the guards began shouting, ordering all the bathers to get out of the sea.

Before she could obey, two guards dragged her from the water and threw her onto the coarse sand. Aware of other bodies falling beside her, Ada felt a boot in her side, and drew up her legs, expecting more blows, then wondered why they did not come as she heard the thumping and beating, the cries and moans of women. She looked up and saw a crowd of internees staring with horror at soldiers flogging Ethel and her friends.

And then there was Lucy pushing forward, allowed to push forward. She reached down, caught Ada's arm, and hauled her up. Next, they were staggering along the beach, Lucy supporting her, urging her not to look back, to walk. Ada forced her legs to move despite the ache in her side, and only glanced over her shoulder when they came to the plantation house. A thick-set middle-aged Japanese was standing in the shadows of the scarred, secretive trees. He was watching them. Lucy waved to him.

Chapter 15

MAY, 1944

MICHAEL WAS LEANING OVER TOO far. He would fall in. The river was deep. He would drown. She called for him to be careful. But he could not hear her there on the bridge; her voice was lost in the din of the cascading water. Down it came, lustrous as satin, endlessly falling into the bottomless pool beneath. She felt helpless, and exhausted by all the travelling they had done through the Highlands. Thankfully, he took a step back and picked up a fishing rod, but still did not look at her. Frowning intensely, he flung the line into the water. She remembered that he always had an ability to block out any distraction and focus completely on what he was doing.

And what was that he had caught? A pair of knickers? Surely not. A fish was what they wanted. They needed fish. So why was he smiling triumphantly at her as if he thought she would be pleased? He could not expect her to want the knickers. They were soaking wet, and they stank. She turned away in disgust. But the smell carried up to her, it was so powerful. She shook her head to rid herself of it, and woke, conscious immediately of the gnawing ache in her belly.

The stench in the prison was worse than it had ever been, nearly as bad as in the hospital, now the water supply was cut off most of the time. She had one last memory of the waterfall, and a longing for a torrent of clear water to swirl along the foetid corridor, before she dragged herself up and pushed her feet into her sandals. The straps cut into her swollen flesh. She dared not let herself think it was beriberi. Some of the women already suffered, their bodies bloated with fluid that threatened to press its weight on their hearts. Ethel was one of these. Yesterday, Ada had seen her in the hospital looking very ill, and had wondered, somewhat hopefully, if she were being punished for her trouble-making. But the question then arose: if you believed God would do such a thing and punish the bad, you had to ask yourself why He would punish the good - punish Freddy Bloom and Dr Williams. They had been taken in by the Japanese Military Police, the Kempeitai, and had spent months in the Smith Street lock-up. Ada remembered them returning to the camp, Cicely Williams emaciated, Freddy bloated with beriberi, both of them covered in sores and bites. And yet they carried on – Freddy had recently started up a domestic science course; Dr Williams was working as hard as ever. Neither of them spoke of their ordeal – perhaps because the Japanese had forbidden them to, or because what they had undergone would be too distressing to recount.

It was their example of fortitude that Ada was following as she struggled into her dress. Yesterday she had put it in the sun in a vain attempt to cauterise the dirt. It was stiff with sweat. Now she tugged a comb through her dry, tangled hair. It had felt like a capitulation when Lucy cut it short for her. She refused to look at herself in Lucy's mirror these days. She did not want to see her face, either. Her skin was grey, her eyes sunken and dull, the tight skin on her bones pimpled with bites.

Lucy was curled up asleep like a baby in the womb, legs stick-thin. She often did not bother with breakfast. Deciding not to wake her, Ada made her way slowly to the dining hall. There was a pool of vomit outside the door. But this was nothing to the lingering smell of boiled rice. She thought to turn away and go straight to the hospital, but knew she had to force down the gruel with its trace of sweetness, and drink some coffee, watery as it was. It would fill her, keep her going until tiffin when she would have boiled rice, and, if they were lucky, a few beans, and, if they were very lucky, a scrap of fish. She would eat the fish first. Yesterday at tiffin someone had snatched a sliver of fish from another's plate. It was distressing to see the women grabbing at each other's hair, one cramming the flakes into her mouth, her eyes flaring with desperation, the other baring her teeth like a wild dog. You had to hold onto your dignity. That was all you had.

There were a few women still in the room. She noticed Mary Thomas, one of her fellow workers in the school, but she chose to sit on her own. The ordeal of eating was best done alone. She sat and stared at the gruel on the tin plate. There were weevils and scraps of dirt in the thin mess of bloated grains. The women who cleaned the rice probably did not care anymore, as they were simply too weak and ill, or losing their eyesight. Dr Williams said this would happen if you did not get enough protein.

Ada scooped up a teaspoon of gruel and placed it in her mouth, stored the food in her cheek, then took another scant spoonful, stored that, and crammed in another. Face pouched, she braced herself, forced her mind to picture a succulent prawn, and then swallowed, gagged, gagged again, put her hand across her mouth as the food rose in her throat, grabbed the mug, sipped, swallowed, held her hand like a fence, a strong fence that found comradeship with the muscles in her taut belly, and the food went down. She looked up, heart beating fast, eyes watering, and noticed at the corner of her vision someone flapping their arm - an irritating flapping. Reluctantly, she turned her head, and saw Mary Thomas beckoning to her. Mary had a forceful nature; she persuaded the Japanese to give some books and pencils to the school. She looked haggard, her skin tinged with yellow. She had been ill with dysentery.

"Ada, Ada," Mary said urgently, coming up to her. Mary leaned close, her breath was sour. "I want to show you something."

She tugged Ada's arm, and they went outside into the blazing yard then along the back of the tool shed. Mary pointed to a hole in the concrete beside the rotting boards.

"I've eaten one. I swallowed it whole."

Two tiny pink shapes were curled up against each another. Baby mice. "Go on, Ada, take one. Don't think about it. Swallow it down." Ada recalled how, when she was too late for school to eat breakfast, Amah would whip a raw egg with a dash of Lee and Perrins sauce for her to swallow. You got used to it. You held your breath and tossed it down.

"Go on. It's protein, Ada."

"I can't."

"You can. Watch me." Mary bent down and snatched up a mouse by its tail, flicked its head against the boards of the shed, shoved the creature into her mouth, and gulped.

"Go on."

Ada took a step back.

"Close your eyes and open your mouth. Think of something delicious. Go on. I'll pop it in."

Ada opened her mouth and kept her jaw rigid. She tried to imagine the piquant taste of the sauce as soft flesh brushed her lips.

"Swallow hard now," Mary ordered.

Ada swallowed, gagged, then leaned forward retching.

Mary grabbed her shoulder and pulled her back. "It's protein. Don't waste it."

Nauseous, chest heaving, Ada buried her face in her hands. Mary shook her arm, trying to distract her.

"What's your favourite dish, Ada?"

It was a popular past-time in the camp, talking about food. The English women spoke with intense longing of stuffed chicken, beef with all the trimmings, legs of lamb, stews with dumplings, jam tarts, treacle sponges and chocolate cake. Milk puddings too, the comforting food of innocent childhood.

Ada closed her eyes and, breathing out slowly, tried to picture a disc of pancake batter thrown like a shawl over a hot griddle. Her gut lurched, but she kept her gaze on the crisping pancake. On went a spoonful of spicy meat and a scattering of vegetables.

"Satay," Mary suggested encouragingly.

Ada groaned, thinking how she would die for that again. Meat, she wanted meat. "Beef rendang," she replied, and remembered the last time she had that. It was on honeymoon in the Cameron Highlands. "I can't choose a favourite. My mother-in-law has the recipe for the most delicious devil curry." Her mouth filled with saliva as she remembered the dishes carried in by the servants at Wood banquets: dhal, and at least three vegetable curries. "I would give anything for fresh pineapple. With Chinese sauce."

Mary had her own list as well. They sat with their backs against the shed and batted the names to and fro, smiling as the memories flooded in, until they grew conscious of the deep ache in their guts. How had it been possible to have taken so much for granted?

"It's time to collect up the children," Mary said, standing up wearily. Ada stood too. She felt exhausted, but knew they must carry on. The children were too weak and ill-nourished to concentrate on lessons these days, but they liked to be read to, they wanted to be cuddled, they needed the attention that their ill and listless mothers could not always give them.

When Ada returned to the cell, she found Lucy still lying on the central slab. They no longer took it in turns to sleep on this. Lucy needed it more. It was not that she was more malnourished or in poorer health, but her spirits were worryingly low.

Lucy opened her eyes. "What are you doing, Ada?"

"I'm going off to the school." She folded her mosquito net.

"Will you have time to pray with me first?"

Lucy prayed several times a day, kneeling on the hard floor. She'd been attending the daily church group and knew the prayers off by heart. She sang hymns in a breathy voice – tunelessly but rich with feeling. The latest in her repertoire was 'Jesu Joy of Man's Desiring'.

"I can't, Lucy. Mary wants me to help her."

Lucy shut her eyes again. "I miss him so much I want to die." She was speaking of her lover who'd been posted to Burma.

Sometimes Ada wondered if it were genuine love that Lucy felt, if it were the man himself that she missed, and not the extra food he had given her. But who could say that loving someone because they fed you was better than loving someone because they made you laugh, or that you respected them? Who could say what words of kindness were shared in those times when Lucy gave her body to him? There had been an exchange. Body for food. Yet out of that exchange perhaps true love had grown. Who had the right to judge?

"You mustn't talk like that, Lucy. Everyone's saying that we're going to be repatriated soon. I heard someone say that Germany has surrendered. We mustn't give up now." She patted Lucy's arm consolingly. "Come and help me collect up the children. If you help me, I'll pray with you later."

✹ ✹ ✹

"Give her half an aspirin, will you, Ada, and sponge her down, but go carefully on the water. It's off again," Sister Jeffries said.

Judith was on fire. The aspirin would not be enough. Ada filled a basin with water, stored in a kerosene tin, and carried it to the cot. Judith remained inert, barely conscious, but as Ada wiped the cloth over her face and neck and down her arms, she turned and said, quite clearly, "What would I give for a bit of snow, a snowflake, just one, to fall on my face."

"Take this, Judith." Ada offered the fragment of pill in her cupped hand.

"No. Keep it for someone who needs it more than me."

"You're burning up, Judith. Come on."

"No." She tightened her lips, and as Ada stood there helplessly, said, "I've been dreaming of Christopher. We were walking together in a garden. It was autumn. Beautiful autumn. The trees were gold and red, and it was so lovely and cool. I was wearing a coat! And then it turned to winter. And that was even better. We were on a sledge and the snow was coming up and spraying us. How silly. When I was in England in the cold, I would daydream of living somewhere hot. Like Singapore! And now I only want to be back where it's never too hot. England has the most perfect weather, I think. It's just right for people like me. I'm ready to go home. I want to be with my Christopher."

Ada could not speak, and her eyes filled with tears.

"Please, Ada, don't cry. I don't fear death, you know." Judith's hot dry hand touched Ada's. "Keep up your reading. It will help to keep you sane, my dear."

"And free," Ada whispered. "Like the angels alone that soar above, eh?"

"Indeed. And if you stay free in your mind, no one can hurt you."

"Ada," Sister Jeffries called. Ada turned to see a young Japanese guard standing to attention clutching a rifle.

"You're to go with this soldier, Ada. I don't know what for." She smiled reassuringly, but her voice was strained.

"What about Judith? I don't want to leave her," Ada said, coming closer.

Sister Jeffries shook her head, and the guard stepped forward. "You've got to go, Ada," she whispered.

"Where am I going?" Ada asked the guard. He grabbed her arm and pushed her in front of him when she turned to say goodbye to Judith, then used his rifle butt to propel her forward into the hot yard.

"Where am I going?"

He did not answer and nudged her hard in the direction of the sentry box. Her legs buckled as they approached the door in the wall. She was not prepared for this. What was happening?

"Where am I going?" she said to the guard as he pulled back the door. She stared into his face and could read nothing.

Fear made her head swim, so she thought at first it was a mirage - the sleek Packard standing there with its back door held open by a tall Sikh. He was looking towards her. For one ecstatic moment she believed that Patrick had won her freedom, that he had managed to convince the officers in the house that she was an Asian at heart. They had listened to Patrick because he learned the error of his ways and had become a trustworthy and obedient servant.

But an abrupt shove from the youth instantly dispelled the hope. "You leave camp now!" he shouted, as if he despised her, as if she had done something badly wrong.

The car smelled richly of polished leather. Beside the driver was a Japanese man in a light suit. He did not turn his head to look at her. He said nothing. His hair was cut neatly, his collar pressed. Perhaps she could ask him where she was going? But she did not speak a word of Japanese, and she was frightened.

The car began to move, and the young guard stepped back into the prison. Her heart pounded, and she had an overwhelming desire to throw open the door and run after him and beg to remain – to remain with the filth and cramped cells because she dreaded the unknown far more than she hated the stench, the disease, the terrible food.

She tried to steady herself as the car sped on. When she looked out of the window, the strangeness of being in the outside world lent itself to the nightmare she was living in, so she felt the same protective detachment that she experienced on the way to the shelter in the Selwyn Building when the city was burning. There were no fires now, but it still seemed unreal - the derelict buildings, the swarming workers, the long queues, longer at the market stalls than she had ever seen.

When they reached the city the limousine moved slowly. Not a single car or rickshaw was in sight, but the road was clogged with trishaws. People glanced at the car then turned their heads away, as if frightened to look. Ada sat back, her detachment now giving way to fear. What was going to happen to her? She had never felt more alone. Even on the first day of internment when she walked to Katong with no idea what was in store for her, Judith had been there. Judith, whom she might never see again. Mary, Sister Jefferies, the doctors, Freddy Bloom, Lucy, Mrs Eisinger, those in the shorthand typing class before the teacher wasted away from countless bouts of malaria, all those women, would she ever see any of them again?

The car drew to the side of the road and stopped. A group of sharp-featured Javanese boys were sitting on the pavement. They looked thin and desolate. She stared beyond them, at the building they were parked beside. It was the Smith Street lock-up.

Chapter 16

THE GUARD, A ROUND-FACED JAPANESE woman, demanded Ada remove her knickers. Ada felt ashamed. They were dirty, and her body was unwashed. Embarrassment stained her cheeks. She was not ready for whatever it was that lay ahead. The woman, stony-faced, snipped the elastic before handing back the pants. Ada's legs trembled as she stepped into them and secured the top, folding it like a sari pleat.

With a rifle butt pressed hard on her back, she entered the corridor. Was this where Freddy Bloom and Dr. Williams had walked? Would the Japanese do to her what they did to them, so terrible that they never spoke of it? Would she have the will-power of these women? Ada pressed her hands against chest. Her heart was beating frantically.

The narrow corridor was lined with cells fronted with thick wooden bars placed close together; shoes and sandals were neatly arranged outside, and within there were the dark shapes of people seated in rows - all men, it seemed. Hearing male voices screaming above and beneath her, she could hardly breathe with the sudden and violent thought that she'd been brought here because Michael was a prisoner.

She was pushed through the low door of a cell lit only by the light from a small barred window. There were two rows of men - about eight in all, she estimated at first glance. Most of them appeared to be Eurasian or Chinese, but she noticed an elderly European and a thin, bearded Indian in the front row. The prisoners were seated cross-legged on a platform and facing the bars. Behind them, in a corner, there was a lavatory with a tap above it. She could look at the men directly, for they glanced at her quickly and then away. They were mute, faces wooden, and they had their hands on their laps like obedient children frightened of their teacher.

"Sit," the guard barked. The elderly European and the Indian made a place for her in the front row. Still no one looked at her, and no one spoke when the guard left. She wondered if the cell was bugged, or if not speaking was simply a rule that must not be broken for fear of being flogged. Others surely had broken the rules. She noticed that the men in the opposite cell also sat motionless, facing the corridor, and it struck her that she was the only woman. Filled with a sense of being utterly alone, she felt abjectly weak.

Hours seemed to pass. The guards tramped back and forth, stopping from time to time to shout an order, or receive a moaning body from other guards and throw it into a cell. There was a metallic smell, which she knew from her work in the hospital to be that of stale blood.

The men kept looking straight ahead, and in the terrifying silence, broken only by the agonised cries of men in pain, the same questions kept revolving in her mind. Is Michael here? What do they want from me? What will happen to me?

Her mouth was bitter; she could taste dread. It filled her gut and churned her bowels. She pressed her legs together and clenched her buttocks, trying to hold in the filth that struggled to escape. At last she whispered, as soon as a guard had passed, "I want to use the lavatory." The Indian nodded towards the smeared bowl in the corner, and looked kindly at her, then bowed his head and shut his eyes, giving her privacy. She saw the others do the same as she hastily pulled down her knickers. The men are blind to me, she told herself, they do not care about the foul smell. I cannot help it. I want to die. She turned on the tap and washed herself. The humiliation robbed more of her strength, and when she took her place again she swayed backwards.

"Sit up, sit up," a voice shouted, and a sullen face stared through the bars. She began to sob, snot poured from her nose, and she clamped her hand over her mouth. The Indian grasped her arm firmly but did not glance at her. Too much pity was bad for you. She must cope. There was no choice. You're one of us, the message seemed to be. Do like us, and you will survive.

Another hour, perhaps two, passed, then doors banged along the corridor. A guard appeared with a trolley and pushed two steaming bins into the cell. Immediately, a young Chinese man at the end of the row stood up and dipped a can into one bin, then inclined his head towards Ada. She rose to take the hot can of tea, winced as it scalded her fingers, and noticed that the other bin contained boiled rice. She was not hungry, but she knew that she must eat, and when it was her turn to scoop up the rice with her can, she managed, to her surprise, to swallow more easily than when in Changi. Perhaps this was because her mind was grateful for the distraction. It was a respite from sitting and thinking and dreading. It was nearly ordinary.

Once the bins had been taken away, the European man stood and walked around the cell. He swung his arms and bent his knees. It was all slow, hard work, because he was an old man, nearly bald, and very frail compared to the thickset Chinese with his greasy black hair, or the Indian with the kind eyes. The old man sat, and the Indian commanded the floor. He looked directly at Ada and inclined his head fractionally as if acknowledging her as his audience, which he was about to entertain. She offered a tiny smile of gratitude as she watched him rotate his body, bend, touch his toes, then sit in a lotus position and flex his ankles. His long, lean body reminded her of Michael.

After they had all taken their turn to exercise, the guard returned and drew the blackout over the window. When he switched on the naked electric light that would remain burning all night, Ada lay down on the platform closest to the wall and the fat cockroaches, and was grateful rather than embarrassed when she felt the press of Indian-Michael's body next to hers, and his faint whisper, "It'll be all right. Try and sleep". It was more soothing than a lullaby, and she sensed a quiet strength in his steady breathing, which helped her to lie still.

The European man began to mutter. Was he calling his wife? The word sounded like 'Mary'. Elizabeth used to pray to Her, Ada remembered, because she believed that women listened to women and understood. "Mary, Mary, the mother of Christ," Ada prayed. "Please help me to live through this. Please watch over my child and husband. Please may we all live to see one another again. Please let Michael not suffer wherever he may be."

Tiny feet ran over her legs. It was probably a mouse. She did not move, not even lift her head to see where it had gone. Instead, she began to think of Freddy Bloom and Dr. Williams. Frail as they were, they continued with their duties. Women with wills that could not be crushed. Freddy had said that she was determined to live and be with her husband Phillip again. You could not give up. Ada pressed her hand against her heart and tried to visualise it there, the small circle. "I must not die. I must not die. I will live and be with Michael and Beth."

She was losing sense of time – days passed, then weeks, with nothing to mark their way except the dragging out and dumping in of battered men any time of day or night, so terrifyingly unpredictable that the routine of the rice meals and the time for exercise was a welcome relief.

Ada watched the Chinese youth trying to do his press ups. Each day it was becoming more difficult for him. His stomach was distended. Her stomach was swollen, too, as were her legs, and she could not fasten her dress. She feared the advance of beriberi. If she became really ill, what would the Japanese do? Would she be allowed to die, like the old man? He could not do his exercises now. He lay all day with his eyes shut. He did not eat. When the guards had brought him back to the cell, his pants were soiled. The Indian had taken them off and washed them under the tap.

When the old man died, perhaps it would be the Indian's turn to go upstairs? And then she would lose her friend, whose occasional touch, whose body next to her when they slept, and whose unvoiced will to survive, helped her to keep sane. What would she do without him? There would only be the words then - songs, stories, the lines of plays learned from Judith. Always, Ada wished for more words, the store-house of Judith's memory. Sometimes she tried to imagine – even if the pictures filled her with a sense of unbearable loss – Michael listening to her and sharing his own love of language. They were in the bedroom after his return from school, or they were walking on the beach in the cool of a moonlit night.

She fingered the side-gape of her dress. She needed another frock. With the practice of having done it many times, she turned quickly to the pattern book in her mind. Today she would choose something simple, in a floral material because it would hide the dirt. And she would make a child version for Beth, with a smocked bodice and flowers embroidered on the pockets - satin stitches for the open buds, as she'd taught the women in Changi. She would be open with the Japanese when they came for her, would tell them that because she was such a good sewer she'd been given the honourable task to do the quilt for the commandant. Yes, it was a most honourable task. She would behave very modestly, shyly, like a simple woman, and they would not thrash her until she bled.

She forced away the image of being flogged, and replaced it with another, which she used to find difficult to create but which now came easily to her – she and Beth, no longer a baby but a young child who resembled her father in her colouring and fine features. They were holding hands and entering the shade of the large tree that overhung a corner of the tennis court in Serangoon. Bright birds flitted in the shadows of the woods; it was early morning, not too hot. They sat on the grass, Beth in her new dress, and Ada opened a picture book: *Sleeping Beauty*.

But for some reason Beth was fidgeting today, anxious. She did not believe in handsome princes coming to the rescue. She was tired of fairy stories. Ada understood. She felt the same restlessness, a deep sense of foreboding. She clasped her hands tightly on her lap, and the words she wished she could tell Beth tumbled fast through her mind. "When I was a little girl I loved to go to the sea, Beth. My father would take us. Vera couldn't swim as well as me, but she was a much better dancer. It's a pity you didn't know your grandmother. She used to have the most beautiful long hair. Like mine used to be and will be again one day. Anyway, what was I saying? I loved to swim. And eat ice-cream, and go to the fun parks. The Great World, the New World. You couldn't make up your mind what to eat. Lacquered duck, barbequed chicken wings, pork rib soup, stuffed dumplings, fried rice. And it was such fun dancing. When we're with Daddy again he and I will go to dances a lot more. I've improved from having the lessons in Changi. And we'll go to the pictures. You can come too. We both loved Charlie Chaplin."

The walls of the cell drew in, and her heart beat faster, her breath shortened as she thought of Michael. "Where is he? What have I done to deserve this cruelty?"

★　★　★

The next morning, they came for her. She was breathless when they shoved her through a door into a smoked-filled room. There was a barred window above a long table, behind which three men in civilian clothes sat smoking.

She bowed, and then obeyed the order to sit on a wooden chair underneath a sluggish fan. A bald-headed, bespectacled man stood up. He looked like Asahi, the prison commandant, an educated man, but his voice was harsh.

"Ada Wood. Husband, Michael Patrick Wood?"

Her tongue cleaved to her palate, and her body shook. She clasped her jittering legs to try and still them, but could do nothing to stop the wild beating in her chest. She nodded. He shouted at her to answer.

"Yes," she croaked.

"You married how long now?"

How long? How long? Sweat poured. Her dress stuck to her body.

"How long?" he barked again.

She could not think clearly. What year was it now? What month?

"We married in 1941. March."

"When last you see your husband?"

"Just before the end."

"What end?" He jerked his head at her. His face was severe, ugly.

"When the British lost."

"Ah!"

"Where your husband teach?"

So they knew he was a teacher. What else did they know? What did they want from her?

"Raffles Institution."

"Husband taught English and music?"

"Yes." She swallowed the vomit that rose in her throat.

"Husband know many languages?" He stared, waiting impassively.

"Yes."

"What he know?"

"Malay and Tamil mostly. Some Cantonese and Hindi." She shook her head, confused. "And English, of course."

"Japanese. He know Japanese?"

"He was learning." Her mind raced. Was that the wrong thing to say? Michael would sit at his desk for hours. She used to nag him to finish.

"He spy on Japanese. He spy. You know this, hah?"

She shook her head vehemently. It was a lie, a trick. She could not speak. The words, 'it is wise not to know' travelled through her mind. She pictured Patrick warning her, and her eyes filled with tears of longing to be with him again, to know safety, to be free of this terror.

"Husband work for British? Who he work for? Give names."

She wiped her wet cheeks with a shaking hand. "I don't know," she whispered.

"You lie. You know husband was spy. Clever man. He use radio. He running dog of British Imperialism."

"I was not told. I was not told anything."

The officer pointed to the floor. Her dress tore as she knelt.

"Why you stay in Singapore?"

She looked up at him and saw a gleam in his eyes. He wanted to catch her out.

"I was afraid. I was frightened to go on the ship in case it was bombed. I was frightened for my baby." She would not say that she did not want to leave Michael because then they would ask her why. They would be angry to hear that she loved him. They did not like to know of such things because they were hard, pitiless men.

"Stupid woman. Husband caught and punished."

She clasped her head, she gasped for air, and her body shook with fear. "Is he dead? Please, don't tell me he's dead."

"Tomorrow you come and we say. Now go." He barked an order. She was tugged to her feet and hauled onto the landing. She moaned and wept as she was dragged down the stairs. The concrete scraped her legs, and she cried out with pain.

A stinking hand covered her mouth, and she fought to breathe. She thought to bite the hand. She had done that when the soldier had tried to rape her, and she did it again, but she could hardly see...

And then there was nothing.

Nothing.

Until a man approached. His chest was naked and he had a thick beard. He was smiling kindly at her, but she drew up her legs and crossed her arms, cowering from him. He knelt on the floor beside her, and wiped her face with his shirt, whispered her name, and lifted a tin of water to her lips.

"Drink. Don't give up," he said. She realised that she was back in the cell. A guard shouted, and she heard the Chinese youth answer, "Dying." The guard moved away. She began to whimper. She did not care if she died, even though she knew that a child was waiting for her.

She slept in fitful bursts, drugged with misery, and two guards came for her when the electric light still burned. She felt as limp as a rag doll, she was so weak, nearly defeated, almost dead, and again she wondered if she cared. Confused and lost, she looked at the Indian. He was mouthing words. Hate, Hate.

Her mouth moved, breathing out with the H, lingering on the T, and for a brief instant she tried to imagine a small glowing circle somewhere near her heart as they forced her to climb the stairs, prodding her with their rifle butts.

Seated on a stool in the smoke-filled room, she kept her gaze straight ahead, and did not see the man until he spoke.

"Ada Wood. You stay in Singapore. Why you stay?"

The voice was different. She was sure that she had heard it before. When she looked at the man as he stepped closer to her, the face did not seem completely strange. She glanced down at his hand that clasped a sheaf of papers, and saw a silver scar. He was not wearing his silver tie to match, but she knew that this was the photographer, Mr Tanaka, who'd taken Vera's passport photo. Ada could remember his polite bow, the pity on his face. Perhaps that civility remained?

She dared to speak. She could feel every word that issued from her mouth like a weak flare from the dying embers in her chest.

"I was a loyal wife. You told me I was when I came to your studio with my sister. She belonged to a group, the 'Oriental Jewels', trained by a Hungarian woman, Madame Varga. You took photos of the group. Vera, my sister, came to you for her passport photo because she was leaving Singapore for Australia. You asked me if I was going to leave as well. I was pregnant." She looked directly into his face. How had he become a member of the Kempeitai? He'd lived in Singapore for a long time. Who had persuaded him to do this evil work?

"We discovered that your son was a pupil in Raffles Institution where my husband taught."

He coloured. Of course, he remembered Michael, the man whom his son respected. He was ashamed that he had allowed Michael to suffer. He said that Michael was a patient, good man.

"My husband didn't tell me anything. He didn't want me to worry, I expect."

The voice that answered was gentler, but what was said cut more viciously than a knife.

"You will not see your husband again. He died September twelf."

"He's dead?" She stared blankly ahead.

"Yes."

She clenched her teeth but could not stop the surge of grief that came from her stomach and flooded upwards, a monstrous wave that forced its way through her heart and rose in her throat. A high-pitched wail filled the room, and she was shaking her head and shouting, no, no, no, as they pushed her down the stairs and back into the cell where the Indian waited, clutching his shirt.

Chapter 17

September, 1945

LUCY EXAMINED HERSELF CRITICALLY IN her compact mirror and applied another coat of lipstick while Ada looked anxiously towards the entrance of the ward. Any moment now they would appear – Evaline, Patrick, Amah, perhaps Charmaine too – and with them, a little girl. They'd look down the row of beds, then, unable to recognise her amongst all the ill women, would turn around to walk out. So she would wave vigorously, and they would come forward with huge smiles. Her heart fluttered thinking of how it would be. She'd lift Beth onto the bed and hug her with all her might.

She touched her cheek and tried to reassure herself that the yellow of her skin was fading and that she did not look so gaunt. It had been a bad case of dysentery - a terrible blow, as it had come right at the end when she thought that the worst was over, that she'd had her share of misfortune and, although grieving bitterly for Michael, she was as healthy as anyone near to starvation could be.

She had been taken from Sime camp to the General Hospital as soon as the Allies had Singapore under their control, but even with the mepocrine, vitamin and iron tablets, which the posh English doctor had assured her would work miracles, she was still not herself. She was very weak, and her heartbeat felt erratic at times. And what would make her teeth less grey, or replace her rotten molars? She feared that her breath stank. As for her hair, it would never regain its lustrous thickness.

"I'm worried I'll scare Beth," she said. "I look dreadful."

"She's your daughter, Ada. She's been longing to see her mummy for years, la." Lucy looked directly into her face and smiled. "The face cream I got you has worked wonders." It had been in one of the Red Cross parcels. Ada had been helped to the door of the hut to watch them landing with an unearthly billow of silk above them. It was on the same day that news had come of the atomic bombs in Japan. The enormous devastation in contrast to the gifts falling from the sky had seemed like the difference between Heaven and Hell, the difference between reward and punishment.

"You're as beautiful as you ever were, Ada."

"You've always had a lot of imagination, Lucy." Ada pressed Lucy's hand, grateful for the reassurance, even though she believed it to be untrue. "I don't know what I would've done without you."

It was Lucy who had called her name as she drifted away, wanting to die. She'd heard the voice but knew what was awaiting her – the annihilating pain of fully-conscious grief – so had drawn further into herself. The voice would not let her go. "We're leaving Changi soon, Ada. We're going to the camp in Sime Road. You'll see grass, and we can grow vegetables, la. You'll be all right." Ada had kept her eyes shut. "You'll soon see your daughter, Ada. You want to see your little girl, don't you?" She heard a strange whimpering, and a hand had clasped her neck; a spoon touched her lips. The whimpering continued until her mouth filled with a fishy liquid. She swallowed, and it was then, she supposed, that life had begun its struggle to reclaim her. Dr. Williams had crushed a vitamin pill into the watery broth. The camp commandant had given the doctor tablets to combat the beriberi. Perhaps he'd done this through compassion, or perhaps, Ada wanted to believe, he had been instructed by her second interrogator, the Japanese photographer, who had felt guilty for what had happened to his son's respected and loved teacher, and felt pity for his widow. It was surely the photographer who had her sent back to Changi. If not for him, and the Indian man who'd nursed her after the interrogation and had, she believed, willed her to live, she would have given up the ghost. She would never forget the Indian man who had so reminded her of Michael.

"I don't know what I could've done without *you,* Ada. It was you who tried to teach me how to behave so I could survive. And when you weren't there I knew that I had to become strong like you were, and I learned to work hard. We're good friends, la. I'm going to miss you. But we can write to each other." Lucy was leaving Singapore for Ipoh to stay with an aunt - the one who'd brought her up after her mother's death. "I still can't believe we're free at last," she continued. "I thought it was all a dream when I saw the planes flying over the Padang and heard the bands. Everyone was hugging each other. I lost my voice cheering. You should've heard the commotion when the Union Jack went up. They said Mountbatten was very handsome."

Ada wondered if her own joy would have been equal, if for a few moments she could have escaped the shadow of Michael's death. When the church bells had rung out the day the British planes flew over low, and the skeletal P.O.Ws came in from the men's camp with V-marked cakes, she'd watched the women with a miserable envy as they'd laughed and wept before venturing to join the men like delirious teenagers on their first tryst.

"You look sad, Ada. It is hard for you, I know."

"I'm all right. Just tired."

She had slept badly, disturbed by a lurid dream, the one she had most frequently. It always started with a body being dragged by its feet up a steep staircase. The hair trailed over the dirty steps, the skull thumped against the concrete. She took out a dainty handkerchief and began to dab at the blood left by the head, but when the screaming began she stopped and wrung her hands together. Next, she was on the floor, and a Japanese man in a spruce uniform came towards her, smiling broadly as he removed his jacket. She cowered from him, sobbing. He knelt beside her and, try as she might, she could not push him away. She had woken with her nightgown soaked.

She looked anxiously towards the door again.

"Do you want me to stay?" Lucy asked. Ada shook her head. Lucy leaned forward and kissed her. "I'll come in again before I leave for Ipoh. Don't worry, Ada. Your little girl will take to you as soon as she sees you. Blood is thicker than water, la. It's natural."

Wasn't it natural that Beth would not smile at a stranger, Ada told herself, trying not to stare at the child holding Amah's hand, to marvel at her leggy height, the thin wrists, snappable like twigs. She was very sunburnt, and her thick, straight hair with uneven ends looked as if it had been cut around a pudding bowl. Ada was surprised that Evaline had not trimmed the child's hair neatly and had allowed her to get so dark.

Ada tried another smile, not showing her teeth, and Beth ducked behind Amah. How foolish to have imagined an instant hug, a wide-armed welcome. The child was frightened of her ugly mother. Amah, who rarely allowed her worry to show, had tears in her eyes.

Amah was clucking. "Be good girl. Go kiss mummy. You like see your mummy. Go kiss." She pushed the child in front of her.

"Hello, Beth. I know you don't remember me, but I'm your mummy, and I'll be home soon to look after you." Ada spoke softly, and hoped her expression was one of appealing kindness. Beth stared at her, seriously, critically. Ada felt a leaden weight in her gut. It made her despair to think that it would take time and patience to win Beth's trust, that she would need more forbearance when she'd been patient for so long. And who knew if it were ever possible for a mother to gain a child's love after a prolonged absence?

"She like speak Malay," Amah offered.

"Selamat. Selamat, Beth." Ada injected the greeting with as much bright energy as she could muster. "Selamat." Still Beth remained silent, frowning a little.

Amah said, "Beth shy now, but you wait. She learn English better. Quick, quick. She very clever, and talk, talk all time."

Ada was wondering how Beth would behave in a familiar place when Amah came forward and clutched Ada's hand firmly, reassuringly. Ada realised that she was allowing her worry to show and forced a smile. Amah exclaimed, "Very rough. Hand very rough. You work hard for Japs?"

"For ourselves. We tried to keep things clean. And when we got to Sime Road I did a lot of gardening." Once she was fit enough, Lucy, with Dr. Williams's encouragement, had made her work in the vegetable garden. They said that contact with nature was the best way for curing the spirit, and indeed Lucy was proof of the claim. She was no longer, to Ada's surprise, the moping, self-absorbed Lucy of Changi days, but a cooperative hard worker.

"It was wonderful to have open space after Changi. Do you help in the garden, Beth?" Ada asked in Malay. No answer came, so she addressed Amah. Perhaps ignoring Beth was the best for now? "We grew sweet potatoes, lemon grass and chillis. To liven up the rice and tapioca. The sandflies were a terrible nuisance, though." And all the extra internees, she recalled. She felt ashamed of her resentment because she was sorry for the new arrivals - bewildered women of the small Jewish community in Singapore who had for some reason escaped internment until then - but the huts had become filthy with overcrowding, not to mention the one they used as a hospital, which began to run out of bedpans and anything you might call linen. And the food ration had been cut in half. She would never forget the sight of women sitting motionless all day with their eyes shut.

"Bad time. Very bad time. Japs very bad. You very sad."

Ada looked away, not wanting to answer. Apart from Lucy, who was sworn to secrecy, she told no one in the camp about what she'd suffered in the Smith Street lock-up. When she returned to Changi, Freddy Bloom and Dr. Williams had been the first to greet her. They hugged her, they expressed their joy and relief at seeing her again, but asked no questions. Ada remembered they had not spoken of their ordeal in Smith Street, and felt they understood that although the terror of those months came to you in the uncontrolled times of sleep, you tried to keep it at bay in your waking life. Any expression of compassion made the task of banishment more difficult.

"It could've been far worse. I could've been on one of the ships that was torpedoed, and had to spend the war in Borneo or Sumatra, like some of the women I've spoken to in here. The stories they tell me of what they went through make me realise that I was lucky to be in Changi."

After Smith Street, Changi had seemed like a safe, loving home. A couple of days after she had learned that Michael was dead, they came for her again. This time she had been taken along corridors and down stairs stained with blood, into the blinding light. During the journey in the car, she had no eyes for the teeming streets, but she'd wept with relief to see the prison.

"Not all the Japanese were cruel. Some of them cried at the end and said they'd miss us." When they'd known it was all over for them, they left the gates open to allow locals from the nearby kampongs to bring in eggs and pork and chicken. They distributed withheld letters and Red Cross parcels. A young soldier had brought her chocolate in his ring-wormed hands. Then there was the one who had given her his rubber boots before he left to go into his own internment camp and await the official handing over to the Allies. Some of the women had wanted to leave as well, and who could blame them, but they were warned to remain where they were. Japanese soldiers, shamed, and refusing to admit defeat, had still occupied the island in large, angry numbers.

"There's good and bad in all races, Amah." Ada would make sure Beth understood that, and that she would grow up to have her father's intelligence, his open-mindedness, his sense of fairness. He had hated discrimination of any sort. In fact, he had a lot of respect for the Japanese. And wasn't it better to think that it was the war, the wish to serve their emperor and win, that had driven them to do bad things, than to allow hatred to eat away at her?

"I wrote to Patrick to tell him about the classes and concerts we used to have in Changi. I don't suppose you know if Patrick got my letter?" She was conscious now that Amah had not mentioned him or offered an explanation for his absence. "Patrick couldn't come with you? Or Evaline? Are they ill?" Ada asked anxiously.

Amah remained impassive. Before Ada could repeat her question, Amah blurted out, "Abdul. He more bad than Japs. He come back to house one day, and he like...*big* man. He beat me. I still have cut."

Ada frowned and shook her head in sympathy. She remembered the old feud. It was an act of revenge.

"I'm very sorry to hear that, Amah. You must've been very frightened. I hope he didn't hurt anyone else. Did Beth see him beating you?"

"No, no. He hurt old woman. He coward. He run away when Patrick come." She looked at Ada with her head tilted to one side.

Ada detected that she was hiding something, and asked more insistently, her worry increasing. "Patrick and Evaline. How are they, Amah?" Had they not come because they were deep in mourning and did not leave the house? It occurred to Ada that Amah had not offered sympathy. Did she think it was not her place to do so? Or did she not want to do this in front of Beth?

Or perhaps the Woods had not learned yet of Michael's death. Which meant, she realised, that there remained the dreadful prospect of having to tell them.

Amah shrugged. "Patrick old man. Very tired. He send you love. And give you this." She placed an envelope on the bed. Ada sensed an awkwardness in Amah's manner. What was she holding back?

Amah rummaged in her bag. "You like chicken? I have mango too." She placed a parcel wrapped in newspaper on Ada's lap. "I cook you good food when you home again. Make you strong." She took Beth's hand. "We go now. You rest." Eyes wide-open with amazement, Beth was staring at a sleeping woman in the next bed. The woman was one of the internees who'd spent the war in Indonesia. Her nose was missing, eaten away by rats while she'd been unconscious.

"Yes, take her home, Amah. This is no place for a child," Ada said, noting that apart from her blue eyes Beth was the picture of Michael.

"You kiss mummy now," Amah said to Beth. The child looked curiously at Ada but made no move towards her.

"Please give my love to everyone, Amah," Ada said quickly. "And tell them I can't wait to see them again. I should be out of here very soon, God willing."

Amah patted Ada's cheek, her expression sorrowful. "All over now. You get better quick-quick. Come home soon." She turned and hurried away, towing Beth as if desperate to escape.

Ada watched to see Beth disappear through the doorway. Of course, she did not look back. Ada folded her arms across her chest and tried to contain her sorrow. She'd not touched her daughter at all.

Tears in her eyes, she opened Patrick's letter.

'My dear Ada,
    I apologise for not accompanying Amah to see you, but I've been very poorly and am confined to my bed.

Charmaine sends her apologies and love. She has been married for a few months now, and has gone with her husband, John Whitworth, to Kuala Lumpur, where he has been sent for a while to sort out matters to do with the postal system. The two met through friends.

It saddened me greatly to learn from your friend Lucy that you are so ill. Both your body and mind are suffering. I know that you were taken by the Kempeitai. They told me when I also was interrogated after they'd captured Michael.'

Ada looked up from the page. So they knew. There was no bad news to break. At least she'd been spared that.

'I only hope that you're getting the right treatment now. Many drugs and equipment have been stolen from the hospitals. The country is in a sorry mess, and we've had a hard time of it. Everything is bought on the black market. Thank goodness I buried our valuables and title deeds and did not leave them in a bank safe, as the Japanese raided the British banks. The Japs printed only rubbish money, worth hardly a cent, and we had to hand over our British currency. It was daylight robbery! I had to sell most of the jewellery for us to survive, though not your rings, of course. With my overseas investments, and with the money from property that I have here, which I can sell when it is wise to do so, we will manage quite well, unlike many people I know.

I have to say the Japs soon lost all the respect some had been prepared to give them. But at least the officers who took over the house made sure it was cared for. They repaired the front verandah steps. One of them was a very cultivated man. He played Schubert very well,

and Brahms. We were invited sometimes to a little recital
- after we'd cooked and served them at table of course!

And now, Ada, brace yourself for sad news which
I wish that I could keep from you because you have
suffered so much already. It grieves me to write that
Evaline died a year ago. I didn't want to tell you while
you were still in hospital, but thought it would be worse
for you to come back here and find her gone.'

Gone? Gone? Evaline striding down the hallway, coarse hair
tightly pinned back, chest thrust out, bossy, in control. No.
Evaline haggard, Beth in her arms, standing on the verandah,
calling goodbye. Ada began to cry more freely and had to keep
wiping her eyes in order to read on.

'The hard work wore her down, even with Amah
to help her. Charmaine was working long hours in a
government department managing rice distribution.
She got the job through one of the girls who did her
shorthand writing course. In the evenings, she had to
go to Nippon-go classes at St. Joseph's. One of the
officers in the house would test her! It's not surprising
that Evaline developed heart trouble. I think it could
also have been the palm oil we had to cook our food
in while the good vegetable oil was reserved for the
Japs. At least we got fresh vegetables and occasional
fish and chicken. Believe it or not, people accused us
of being collaborators. It was a way of venting their
anger, I suppose, and it's stopped since they learned
about Michael.

It makes me very upset still to think that we couldn't
get the care Evaline needed. I miss her with all my
heart, but I comfort myself with the thought that she
didn't live to hear about her son and go through the

suffering that I know you went through, even more than I experienced, when he was captured. But I do know that she would have shared my great pride in him. My forebears gave their working lives to the British. Michael went one step further and gave them his life.'

An unwanted image of Patrick appeared. Ada could see him at one end of the dining table, a chunk of pineapple half-coloured with the black of Chinese sauce suspended on his fork, relating his beloved tales of Anglo-Indian bravery and great deeds. Was it there that it started, Michael feeling he had to be a hero? She gripped the sheet more tightly; her hand was shaking.

'Now let me tell you about Beth. She is a healthy lively child, and you can see how much she resembles both you and her father. Amah has taken great care of her, and it's not at all surprising that the child sees Amah as a mother. We've spoken a lot about you, her real mother, but in the end it's what the child experiences that creates the bonds. I'm telling you this, Ada, in case Beth does not take to you immediately and prefers Amah. It will take time for you both to get to know each other properly. Beth's English is poor, I'm sorry to say, though Evaline and I tried to encourage her to learn in the privacy of the servants' quarters. Amah spoke to her in Malay, which is what the Japs required us to do, though they really wanted us to speak Japanese. We pretended that we were very stupid. It's a great relief to have burned the Nippon-go books. Evaline would have loved the bonfire, as she would have loved to be mistress of her home again. Yes, our home, to which I welcome you back as soon as it is possible for you to join us. I will do my utmost to buy the right food and medicine for you. I cannot tell you how much Charmaine and I are praying for your recovery.

God bless you.'

✻　✻　✻

Ada, though weak, was well enough to leave hospital ten days later. When she returned to Serangoon, Patrick, hearing the car turn into the driveway, came out onto the verandah to greet her. Seeing him at the top of the steps, Ada was reminded of when she had first visited the house and how impressed she'd been. It was only four years ago; it had taken less than four years for a family to be wrecked by loss.

A beaming Ahmad appeared from around the side of the house.

"Ahmad, I'm so pleased to see you," Ada cried.

Ahmad bowed, and said in Malay, "It is very good that you have come back at last. It is a day to remember always."

"You look well, Ahmad."

"Thanks to God, I am still going strong. It is good to be working for Mr Wood again." He smiled and bowed, then hurried away with her case - the same one she'd packed for internment.

She climbed the steps. Patrick raised his arms in welcome, and she hugged him, feeling his thin bony frame. When she stepped back, she noticed with a shock how much he'd aged. His skin was dull and wrinkled, dry as parchment. His Adam's apple protruded more than ever.

"How are you, my dear?" he asked.

She dared not look into his eyes in case they revealed a horror at her appearance.

"I feel all right. I get tired quickly."

"It'll take a while for you to regain your health." He cleared his throat, as though embarrassed. Was it the way she looked, or was he thinking that physical ruin was nothing to what they must bear in their hearts?

~ 203 ~

"Come. We'll have some refreshment. Not a feast, I'm afraid. And Amah will bring in Beth after her bath."

Ada followed him into the darkened room, the shutters drawn against the heat, and against the outside world too, perhaps. There was a strong smell of newsprint; the floor was covered in papers.

"I'm reading everything I can lay my hands on," Patrick said. "I was starved of good journalism. We didn't get anything but the Jap papers. 'The Synonan *Shimbum.*'" The emphasis was made with scorn. "It's probably the reason I get headaches." Ada imagined Patrick shutting himself in the room, away from the world, his skin growing papery through lack of sunlight. "My memory is not what it used to be, either. Here, you'd better have this before I forget. It's got a New Zealand stamp."

"I knew a New Zealand woman in Changi," Ada said, recalling the woman in the quilting group who had described the beauty of the country to her. "But she would hardly be settled back in New Zealand yet, and I wouldn't expect her to be writing to me anyway." Ada took the letter and recognised the spidery writing. "It's from my sister. I thought she was in Australia, though."

"I know you wanted me to write to her and tell her what had happened to you, but I didn't have her address. If she'd written to say where she was, nothing reached us," Patrick said, his gaze now on the doorway. Ada turned and saw Beth. Shy at being noticed, she scampered to Patrick and clung to his leg.

"Go and give your mummy a kiss," Patrick urged. Beth glanced over her shoulder at Ada, then pressed her face against Patrick.

"There's no need to be shy of your mummy, Beth."

Amah appeared. Beth let go of Patrick and ran to her. Amah looked apologetically at Ada. "She tired. Bad mood."

Ada tried not to show her disappointment. "I'll see you in the morning, Beth," she said in Malay. "Good night." She hesitated, then stepped forward to kiss the child on her forehead, before moving swiftly into the next room. She sensed that the more attention she gave Beth, the more the child would resist her. It was going to be a wearisome game of tactics.

A servant, a bashful Indian boy, not much older than a child, brought in a bowl of dhal, rice, and a curry of sweet potato and spinach. Ada was anxious to read the letter, and Patrick told her to go ahead while he served himself.

She ripped open the letter written on one sheet of flimsy paper. The date was 20th July, 1945.

'Dear Ada,

I'm writing this now as everyone says the Japs will not hold out much longer. I've written several letters to you - to the Wood's home, but I expect you didn't receive them.

I hope with all my heart that whatever has been going on in Singapore, you were not imprisoned by the Japanese as you are married to someone who is not British, and that you and Michael and Beth are as well as can be expected. I think of you a lot, and pray for you all, including Michael's family, girls from the Sea View, Lucy, the Sinathambys - everyone I left behind.

As you can see by the stamp, I'm not in Australia anymore. I'm married now. I met Jim, a New Zealander, when I was living in Melbourne and working in a munitions factory because the pay was much better than shop work. He'd been working on a dairy farm in New Zealand because the doctors considered him unfit to return to active service after recovering in Wellington hospital from hepatitis. He'd come across to Australia on a short break. He had an idea to buy land there once the war was over. But finally he decided he'd be better off back home. We'd been seeing quite a lot of each other, and corresponded when he returned. Then he asked me to marry him! So here I am in Godzown – God's Own

Country, they call it here. It's a beaut country, Ada, and I hope you and Michael will think seriously about coming to join us. It'll be a better place to bring up a family than in poor Singapore.

I miss you, and I hope that I'll hear from you very soon. I enclose a photograph of us on our wedding day in Wellington. It's the capital city, but we're hoping to move further north where the weather is better.'

Vera was standing on the steps of a large, stone building with one arm looped through that of a lanky, fair-haired man who seemed a little astonished - perhaps at his good fortune of capturing a beauty for a wife. Vera was smiling radiantly, and looked very smart in a flared skirt and a fitting jacket with a large corsage pinned on the shoulder.

Ada looked up.

"Sorry, Patrick. It was rude of me. I just needed to know what Vera was up to." She realised that her tone was overly light – that she was making the long separation of sisters sound like a mere pause in daily life. "She says that she's written several times. Nothing came here?"

"Not for us. We didn't receive any mail at all until after the surrender. That letter only arrived a week ago."

"Shall I read you what she's written?"

Patrick cocked his head, waiting for news. Ada read the letter to him and showed him the photo. He nodded, and said immediately, "You should go to New Zealand. As soon as you can. I'll pay your fares, and maintain you and Beth. It will be the best thing you can do to go, Ada. This is not the country it was before the war and might never be again."

She looked helplessly at him. She was not ready for more change. And spirits did not cross water. Elizabeth always said that.

"The British can't get rid of the black market and control prices. If they don't get everyone working hard and begin to expand trade soon, the country will go to the dogs." Patrick's voice was breathy, and he wiped his brow. The fans were not working, and the air was unbearably sultry. Ada could feel the sweat collecting in her armpits and between her breasts.

Patrick smacked his hand on the table top.

"Merdaka, merdaka, that's all they talk about. Strike for this, strike for that." He let out a loud sigh. "In a way I don't blame the Chinese who are behind it all. Most of them have had a very hard life."

Ada remembered the tenement that Amah had taken her to, the foetid smell, the dire poverty.

Patrick continued, "You should've seen them when the Japs turned up to sign the papers with Mountbatten. If they hadn't been stopped, they would've torn the Japs to pieces." He shook his head. "But what do the communists know about getting a country ravaged by war back on its feet? They're exploiting the misery of the people." He dabbed at his brow. "The truth is the British have lost face. I too haven't the respect for them I had. Look at the way they condemn Pagler. You know, the president of the Eurasian Welfare Association. And then forgive Lai Teck as if Eurasian collaboration was more treacherous than the Chinese. It's a sad state of affairs. You wouldn't believe the corruption. This is not a country to bring up a child. New Zealand is far away from such troubles. Go, Ada, go. Take Beth and get a better life. You deserve it, Ada, after everything you've been through."

"You've suffered as well, Patrick. Don't you want a better life too? Would you leave Singapore with me?"

"I'm an old man. A young country has no room for old men."

"Who will care for you when I go?"

"Charmaine will live here with John. He's a serious, dependable man. He'll see I'm all right. And Amah will be here. Until she decides to become an aunty and live with her fellow amahs."

"Charmaine is happily married, then?"

"Yes." The answer was brief, as if he wished to save a widowed Ada pain by not dwelling on Charmaine's married happiness.

"I'm pleased, very pleased for her. She always wanted to be married." Ada noticed the compassion on Patrick's face, and looked away into the garden. The hump of pipe still took up most of the space, but she could see that Ahmad had begun to move the camouflage of earth and plants. She remembered her incarceration in the sweltering heat, the hiss and crumple of bombs falling, and how she bitterly regretted her stubborn refusal to leave Singapore. She used the excuse that the sea was treacherous, and it was preferable to die on dry land. So what was her excuse now?

"Don't be afraid, Ada. You can always return to Singapore if New Zealand doesn't suit you. But you must give it time. And you will not be on your own. You'll have your sister."

"I can't use up your money. Do I have the money from my mother you invested for me?"

"Better to leave that invested. There is no need for you to touch that. Keep it aside for Beth."

"Oh, Patrick…"

He put up his hand to silence her.

"What is money when I know that the wife of my son, and his child, my grandchild, are living in a safe and peaceful country?"

She sighed. "You are very kind, Patrick. In the camp I thought often about your kindness, and how you had my interests in mind." She stroked her brow. "Give me a few days, Patrick. I'm very tired. But I hear what you're saying."

"I know, Ada, that the thought of uprooting yourself and travelling to a far corner of the earth is very frightening. You'll need to summon all your courage."

Courage. Determination. You've got it in you, Michael had said. The small circle. Make it grow.

"I will do my utmost for Beth, Patrick."

PART TWO

New Zealand

Chapter 1

April 1947

The taxi driver drove them up the steep tree-lined driveway from the main road, cursing when a rock hit the axle. "All right for a ute," he said.

"We don't have a ute, or a car. We bike. We're fit." Vera issued it like a challenge, and he dumped their suitcases unceremoniously at the gate and took the money without a smile.

In the moonlight Ada could make out the outline of a box-shaped house with what resembled a stiff feather at the pointed crest of the roof. The feather, and the large sash windows on either side of the front steps, gave the house an alert, expectant air. A pillared verandah ran the width of the building. Ada, climbing the battered wooden steps to the front door, was reminded of the old Geylang boarding house, and felt a surge of homesickness.

Vera stamped her feet and rattled the door handle impatiently. "Can't understand why he locks up."

"Keep your hair on." There was the grinding of a key, and the door was pulled back to reveal a tall man wearing an apron. He had the distracted air of someone interrupted in a major task.

"It's freezing out there," Vera said, and walked briskly past him down an ill-lit wide corridor before disappearing through a door at the end. Ada, left standing with Beth butting her thighs, offered a faint smile of conciliation. The man barely glanced at Ada but nodded at Beth.

"Go on, get yourself warm. You don't want your aunt hogging it all."

Wondering if she should introduce herself, Ada took Beth's hand and followed Vera into a small square room. The 'it' was presumably the fire – a modest version of the one she remembered from the Cameron Highlands. Vera was standing squarely in front of it with her hands outstretched.

"It's lovely and warm in here," Ada said, wishing she could be closer to the fire, and was reminded of Jane Eyre excluded from the hearth on a cold November day.

"Finding it a bit chilly, eh? Thought you might." He picked up a poker and shoved it viciously into the coals losing their shape in one molten mass. "It'll get colder, but you'll get used to it."

"You don't get used to it," Vera said, "but you learn to dress warmly. Good thing you thought to bring coats." She rubbed her hands together. "If you haven't guessed, this is Jim, Ada. Jim, this is Ada, and little Beth."

Ada and Jim nodded at each other, Ada with a smile. "A good thing," she said, agreeing with Vera. She had managed to make two coats from a voluminous green one bought from a stout Welsh nurse who had come to Singapore with no idea of tropical heat. Patrick, despite constantly praising the benefits of New Zealand, saying it was the England of the South Seas, had warned that the temperate climate did not necessarily mean it would always be warm.

"I was surprised how much colder Wellington was than Sydney. Quite windy," Ada said. She tried not to make it sound like a criticism.

The flying boat had landed in a large bay, a wide expanse of smoky blue where sea and sky were blended with mist. The bay was banked with hills smothered in pines, and bushy shrubs specked with yellow, amongst which were dotted red and green-roofed houses. She recalled noting how quiet it was in the terminal building. There were a few cries of welcome and a rush to embrace, but the emotion was soon hidden away in intimate groupings. Not a hawker in sight, not a single outburst of raucous laughter or loud chatter, not a sign of tears. This was a moderate country, temperate, with everyone behaving civilly, always. No bombs, no killings, no looting.

"Well, you won't have to worry about the wind here," Jim said. "It's why I told Vera we would come up north more, find a bit of land, grow things you couldn't begin to think of in Old Windy. I'll show you around tomorrow."

"Ada might be tired," Vera said discouragingly.

Jim winked at Beth, but avoided Ada's eye, and pinched the shiny triangular top of his long Roman nose. Sensing his shyness, and at a loss for what to say, Ada looked around the small, square room. Beneath a window, and set against the wall opposite the fireplace, there was a table covered in a brown oil-cloth and laid for a meal. In one corner, a black glass-fronted cabinet housed a row of fine sherry glasses. Above the cabinet was a two-dimensional celluloid frieze of a kitchen – an English kitchen, Ada thought, a Judith kitchen with a fire and a coal range. On the mantelpiece were bits and pieces of Elizabeth's – a nest of ivory balls and small jade figures. It was East meets West; a curious combination, like that of Vera and Jim. Beside the balls was a lean kangaroo carved out of smooth chocolate-coloured wood.

Noticing her curiosity, Jim took it down and held it for Beth to see.

"Got that for one orange from an abo. Y'know, a black fella in the desert." He frowned, as if he despised it for being a bargain, then turned abruptly and strode into the small adjacent kitchen before Ada could ask him when he had visited Australia.

"The wash-house is out the back, through the kitchen, if you want to use the loo. And you can hang your coats in there," Vera said.

Ada, holding Beth's hand, edged past Jim who was stirring something on the stove. She thought to offer help, but when he barely moved to give them space, his attention given over to his task, she sensed that he would not appreciate being interrupted. On their return to the dining room, he was placing steaming bowls of soup on the table, his features set with concentration.

"Come on. Sit yourselves down. You too, Vera. Don't let it get cold," he said. The soup was stocked with potatoes, carrots and meat. Golden pools of meat stock shimmered on the surface. Beth sat with her hands in her lap. "Go on. Dig in," Jim said, looking at her. "It'll warm you up."

"She's tired," Ada apologised, and smiled at Beth. It was no use getting annoyed with the child. You had to make a game of it or she would use the non-eating trick as a weapon – a very effective weapon against a mother who knew starvation and could never waste a morsel of food. On the voyage, Beth had made a fuss at meal times, complaining loudly in Malay about the food, and asking tearfully for Amah.

This was what the two sisters, middle-aged Dutch Burghers, had described to Ada. They used to bring drinks to the cabin where she had lain bedridden with seasickness for most of the trip. They were emigrating from Singapore to Australia. Both were teachers, accustomed to children, and took over the care of Beth, who, in their opinion, was only being difficult because of all the changes. Grateful as she was, Ada had not offered the reasons for these changes when the women had hovered, inquisitive, except to say she was interned for three years, and that Beth was now missing her amah who had cared for her and to whom the child had been very attached.

Although Beth had been told that they would soon return to Singapore, and that Amah would be waiting for them in Serangoon with Patrick, the parting of Amah and Beth – the child sobbing and clinging to Amah - had been one of the saddest moments that Ada had ever witnessed. Patrick, visibly moved, had looked out onto the Roads where the British and American warships and passenger liners were anchored. "This reminds me of the Liberation. We can all look forward now to a better world. We must look forward," he announced firmly, as if leading troops into battle. Amah had wiped her eyes roughly with the back of her hand, and fetched a parting gift for Beth from her tunic pocket. It was a small bead purse. Then she turned to Ada. Her gaze was flat. Ada understood that Amah did not want to add to the pain of separation, but when Ada held her close, she pressed her cheek against Ada's chest, and her body shook with grief.

Before the sisters had disembarked, they gave Beth a gold crucifix and kissed Ada in a reserved way. Ada sensed that she had disappointed them with her reticence.

Jim eyed the food with pride before beginning to eat hungrily. A few mouthfuls in he turned and said to Beth, "It won't bite, y'know."

Ada, noting that Beth brightened at this, picked up a spoon and began to feed her. The child was ravenous, in fact, having eaten only a ham sandwich when they stopped at the draughty station cafe on the slow journey from Wellington. Ada had drunk the stewed tea as if it were a life-giver. She felt drained by the passage through a deep gorge. The train had seemed frail and unsteady on its perilous height. Beneath them, a fast river had leaped wilfully over dark jagged rocks.

To Ada's relief, the soup soon disappeared.

"Bob's your uncle!" Jim said cheerily. "Not bad tucker, eh. What else do you like?" Beth stared silently at him. "Cat got your tongue?" he asked.

"Leave her alone," Vera said, raising her head. She'd been eating methodically, appearing preoccupied.

Beth looked quizzically at Ada, who winked at her. The wink meant, 'hold on, it'll be all right soon'. It had become the way she could manage Beth's impatience, make the glimmer of grateful relief appear in the child's large eyes, when sometimes it had been impossible not to be drawn back to the past. Although she would try hard to remain attentive to Beth, sometimes she simply could not do it, and the wink was a sort of code between them.

Jim began to clear away the plates, stacking them noisily.

"I couldn't tell you two were sisters. And this one," he gestured with his head at Beth, "isn't like either of you."

Ada said quickly, "She's like her father." Suddenly, tiredness and sorrow pressed a muffler hard against her face and she could not feign politeness anymore; she could hardly breathe.

"Come on," Vera said, looking at her, "I'll show you your room."

Rooms lay on either side of the hallway: Jim and Vera's bedroom at the front opposite the seldom-used sitting room - or 'lounge' as Vera called it - with a worn, grey three-piece settee; a spare room in the middle next to the bathroom; and Ada's at the back, opposite the dining room and nearest the kitchen. Vera opened the door.

"It can be freezing in the mornings, especially in the winter if we get a hard frost. The sun usually comes out later, though. It can get quite hot then. But use the heater to get dressed. I do. Remember to switch it off or Jim will go mad." The room smelled of paint. The walls were a light and chilly blue.

"We got this ready for you. It was a real sight. Jim made the wardrobe. It's built-in." She stroked the varnished wood of a cupboard, which filled in a space beside a small fireplace. "Jim's good with his hands. I'll give him that. He would've done a lot more, got the other bedroom ready for Beth, but with the property to take care of his time's cut out for him."

"I'm used to sleeping with Beth," Ada said. She preferred it. When she woke from a nightmare, she could fasten her eyes on the sleeping child and regain some calm.

They stopped at the chilly bathroom. The walls were planked, the paint worn.

"The people we bought this from let the place go to the dogs. Which is why we could afford it." Vera gestured at the bath, a yellow-stained, clawed-footed monster. "Wouldn't sit in that if you paid me. I make do with a throw-over. But you and Beth can have a bath, if you want to."

"No thanks," Ada said. She was not at all inclined to have a bath. The Woods had installed modern showers, but did not bother with bath tubs, not wishing to follow, as they believed it to be, the English custom of 'sitting in your own dirt'.

"I'll give Beth a sponge down tonight."

"All right then. Look, I'm going to get changed for bed. I can hardly keep my eyes open. You settle down too, if you want. Jim will wash up."

Beth was standing in the middle of the dining room and looking up at Jim when Ada returned. Jim was asking the child what she liked to eat.

"Marmie," Beth said.

"Strewth. Why would you want to eat your mother?" Jim ran a hand through his light, springy hair, which stood high above his forehead and gave his long oblong face a surprised, boyish air.

Ada took the bemused Beth by the hand. "It's a Chinese noodle dish," she said. Amah used to cook it most of the time for Beth. But she did not say this. To mention Amah would be most unwise.

"Your soup was delicious, Jim. You'll have to teach me how to cook it."

"So you can't cook either. The servants did everything, eh?"

"No, I can cook," Ada replied in an even tone. "But not soup. I can learn, though. I want to be as helpful as I can. I'm very grateful to you and Vera for letting us live with you. Make sure to tell me how much our board is. I don't want to be a burden."

Jim shrugged, and stared into the fire. Ada could not work out if he were embarrassed by her gratitude, or by the mention of money. She blushed, sharing his discomfort. Patrick had paid their passage and was prepared to maintain her - that is, supplement Michael's meagre teacher's pension - and although she did not want to continue taking from Patrick, either, he was at least Beth's grandfather. She hated this dependency. As soon as possible, she wanted to make her own way.

Jim ran his hand through his hair again. "I'll be up early. Hope I don't wake you. I've got to get on. I'll lose most of Sunday because of the Anzac service."

"Anzac?" Ada asked.

"Service for returned soldiers at the cenotaph. Aussies and Kiwis," Vera said, as she came in. She was wearing a flowing dressing gown, a glossy burgundy - out of place, Ada thought, in the humble room.

"Are you coming with me?" Jim asked Vera brusquely.

"Why don't you take Ada this time?" Vera replied calmly, standing with her back to the fire, arms stretched behind her to the warmth. "She's got more right to be there than I have."

Vera was referring to the war, Ada guessed, and the fact that she survived like the returned soldiers.

"What about Beth?" she asked.

"Oh, I'll look after Beth," said Vera, smiling kindly at Ada.

Ada said nothing, which was taken as an agreement, but she did not want to go, no matter the solidarity she might feel with the soldiers. She did not want to break down and cry in public.

Chapter 2

Aᴅᴀ ᴡᴏᴋᴇ ᴡɪᴛʜ ᴀ ɢᴜᴛᴛᴜʀᴀʟ cry, and clutched the sheet tightly, as though it were a life-line that could haul her out of nightmare. At first, she thought the rough blanket on her shoulders to be Amah's dry hands, but when there was no soft, insistent mutter – "You no worry now. Forget. Forget" – she knew the struggle to escape the abyss must be done alone. She licked her dry lips, wishing for a glass of water and the reassuring gleam of Amah's eyes and gold tooth. In the dusk of a hot room they had been a beacon of safety when she would suddenly awaken, fearful and confused. It had been the same nightmare - the high walls shutting her in so that she could hardly breathe. In panic she stumbled after a body being dragged like a rag-doll up the steps before her.

She pushed herself up on her pillow and saw in the grey morning light that intruded around the edge of the blind the glimmer of the dressing table mirror, then a soft gleam of the wardrobe door. She heard the sound of a tap running.

A return to sleep was impossible. The room was cold. She glanced at the clock Vera had lent her. It was nearly time to get up, anyway. With a sense of guilt, thinking of Jim, she reached from the sanctuary of her bed to flick the switch of the electric heater. Lying on her side, she watched with fascination the birth of artificial warmth - two coils of wire, stretched across the midriff of the silver visor, singing into red life - before she reluctantly rose, careful not to wake Beth. She slipped on her thin kimono, and stepped cautiously into the wide, draughty hallway. Praying that Jim would not appear, she headed for the wash-house.

She was relieved to see that Jim was outside. She could see him through the dining room window pumping the tyres of a bike. She noted with surprise the carefully-laid table – rolls of butter, a milk jug with a bead-fringed muslin cover, and marmalade in a china dish sprigged with blossom. She would not have associated his blunt manner of speech and gaucheness with this display of careful domesticity.

She was dressed and sitting on the fireside chair when she heard him fling open the back door.

"Good on ya. You got yourself up on time. Nice to have a woman around who knows what a clock is." He spoke gruffly, but Ada could tell it was high praise.

He went back into the kitchen, then returned with a teapot in a purple knitted cosy, and a rack of toast. As he poured the tea, she noticed his hands. They were immaculate - no dirt beneath the nails, as one might expect of a man who laboured hard, and the cuticles were pushed back. But then again Vera had said that he worked in a department store as head of women's fabrics, where his hands would be in full view. He was wearing a waistcoat, well-creased black trousers, and a white shirt, the sleeves clenched by two metal-elasticated arm bands. He was clean shaven, and she noticed the ice-blue of his eyes.

"I can make you some more hot toast," he offered, lowering his gaze as though to hide his shyness. It felt awkward to Ada as well, to be sitting there with him in the silence of the morning. It was like being a married couple.

He said abruptly, still not looking at her, "Do you want to ride Vera's bike? I can pump the tyres."

"I don't know how to ride a bike, I'm afraid."

He sniffed, and she felt herself to be a nuisance as Jim explained that it was too early for the bus to run, and too far to walk. The town, which she knew to be spread out below on a flat plain, was four miles away.

The sky was lightening to a pastel clarity in the dew-filled morning when they walked down the driveway, Jim pushing his bike until they reached the road. Then, with Ada seated on the carrier, clinging on to Jim's waist as he instructed, they coasted down the hill. The brim of Jim's hat, which he wore low on his head, presumably to prevent it falling off, forced Ada to lean back as far as she could without altering the balance. Once past the village store, a row of houses, and the school, which Vera had pointed out from the taxi the previous day, they came to a vast space on either side, an openness that only gave way to an orchard, the trees garbed in pale russet and yellow, standing in obedient rows.

The town began with a string of square bungalows set well back on either side of the road. Next was a church, a cinema, then a row of shops, all closed. Ada was reminded of a Wild West town you might see at the pictures. She could nearly imagine a cowboy leading a horse up to a lamp post. The buildings were all two-storied, with tin roofs coming out from the top of the first level to overhang the pavement, the space beneath resembling that of a five-foot way but devoid of clutter. It was all so clean and quiet.

They neared a clock tower with a cenotaph in front of it. Jim slowed, waited for her to get off, then parked the bike in the gutter, and bent to flick off his bicycle clips.

"All right?" he asked, standing up. Without waiting for an answer he strode off to join a line of men, leaving her to find a place with a group of women, all wearing hats. She felt under-dressed, out of place, and unprepared. She wished again that Vera had not put her up to accompany Jim, and hoped Beth would not miss her, even though the child appeared to have taken to Vera, and had chatted quite happily to her on the train.

Three flags, those of Britain, Australia and New Zealand, were propped against the stone of the war memorial. Men were coming from all directions towards it. They were dressed in black, some with wide-brimmed felt hats like Jim's. They walked in the self-conscious, measured way of funeral attendants. A minister was standing on the steps of the cenotaph in front of two rows of men. He held a Bible in his hand. A faint ray of sunlight shone on his white hair, appearing to anoint him and set him apart from ordinary people. Ada remembered the Bishop of Singapore, how he had given evidence at the trial of the Kempeitai; a special man, a brave man whom she blessed with all her heart.

A bugle played. The men bowed their heads, and the women copied them. The minister's voice carried in the still air. The woman next to Ada began to weep. To prevent herself from crying too, because she knew how hard it would be to stop, Ada looked to her left at the department store on the corner. Behind the wide display windows she could see a model wearing an ankle-length dress, and she was reminded of what Vera had said in the hotel where they had spent the first night after arriving in Wellington.

"The women here get togged up for the pictures. They actually wear long frocks, Ada. Like those women. The ones staring at us." Vera had flicked her head at the bevelled mirrors, and Ada noticed the reflection of a group of women seated around a table between fluted columns. They all wore satin dresses and clutched fluffy stoles, and had long faces, as if the whole social event was rather an ordeal. Vera had not lowered her voice. "They don't have balls here, you see. Going to the pictures is a real occasion. I'll probably never go to a ball again."

The hotel was above an empty street. An occasional tram beat out a metallic rhythm. "It's so dull here," Vera had said.

"Everything shuts at 5.30, and nothing opens at the weekends, can you believe. You're going to have to get used to that."

"Good," Ada had replied. "It's peace and quiet I've come for." What did it matter if there were no balls? She was just thankful to be alive.

The woman standing next to Ada was blowing her nose. "They shall grow not old, as we that are left grow old", the minister intoned. Ada's jaw ached with the effort of trying not to cry. To distract herself, she scanned the windows for evidence of dress material. Next week, she intended to see if there were any cheap off-cuts with which to sew Beth a new frock. One with a wide sash. Red. The child could wear red. Something bright.

"Age shall not weary them, nor the years condemn."

The dress would have buttons down the front. And pockets. She'd edge them with lace. It was the attention to detail that counted. Patience.

Now there was a stir in the waiting crowd, and women craned to see their men start to lay wreaths. The minister was still speaking. "At the going down of the sun, and in the morning, we will remember them." Several people were sobbing, and as a bugle played again Ada could no longer hold back her tears.

Thankfully, Jim stayed to talk with a few men after the service, so Ada had time to gain some composure before he joined her, though she suspected her eyes were red. Anyway, he did not look at her, and was caught up in his own thoughts, so she was able to ask him, quite conversationally, "Is that where you work, Jim?" The sun was shining on the shop-windows of the department store.

"Yep. It's quite new. Built after the big earthquake. It flattened the whole place. We get lots of earthquakes here. You have to stand in the door-frame in case the chimney comes through the roof." Ada wondered if this was the pay-off for living in a country blessed with peace. Jim snapped on his trouser clips, took hold of the handlebars of the bike and wheeled it in a semi-circle to face the way back.

"I'm not one for this sort of get-up on the whole," he said. "But you've got to pay your respects. We're the lucky ones." Ada thought he was referring to her. Three bulky men came up alongside, one with a pronounced limp. Jim called out, "G'day, how yer goin', mate." They enquired in the same matter-of-fact tone, question but no reply, and Jim walked on.

"Bill back there," he said in a confidential tone to Ada, "nearly lost his leg. We were on one of the islands. The Solomon Islands. It's got a funny name. You wouldn't know it. We were ordered to clear out the Japs. Got a fair number of them, but more of them got away. In the middle of the night, would you believe? Lost some of my mates. I got hepatitis soon after that and was sent back here. Sometimes I think it wouldn't hurt if they said something about what was won, rather than just going on about what was lost. I mean we beat the Jerries and the Japs, didn't we? You should've heard us when we got wind of the end. Roared our socks off."

Ada tried to imagine such jubilation. It had been very different in Sime when the end came. It was more a seeping out of news than a profound declaration. There had been rumours of a Japanese defeat as early as July, after the Americans started bombing Singapore. The bombs had fallen in batches. The women would stand and count as they came down in fours, then ten, nineteen, back to four.

She did not want to share this with Jim, to think any more about the war, drained as she felt after the service with the mournful bugle, the dour men in their felt hats. She hoped that he would not mention Hiroshima and Nagasaki. He would expect her to agree that the Japanese deserved everything they got. She remembered Patrick saying that for all the cruelty committed by their military, the Japanese people – the women, the children, the old – should not have suffered such devastation.

Jim swung his leg over the bike and waited for her to get on. Cautiously, she positioned herself on the carrier, and self-consciously, aware of the men close behind watching her, held on to Jim. If it was the last thing she did, she would learn to ride a bike.

They left the town behind and came again to open country. The colours of the orchard trees had deepened to gold and orange in the bright sun, and Ada was reminded of Judith, her desire to see an English autumn before she died. Ada remembered the terrible loss she had felt when she returned to Changi after Smith Street and was told that Judith had died.

It was still painful to think that she would never see Judith again, so when they reached the village she tried to put memories aside by concentrating on the spruce lawns, and regimented rose-bushes along the driveways of the bungalows. It was like an illustration in a child's story book. The picket fences were painted, the lawns carefully mown - including the strips of grass in front of the fences next to the pavement.

"It's so neat and orderly," she said, loud enough for Jim to hear. In Singapore you would never find that, she thought, people taking care of property not their own. But then there was so much to do keeping back the greedy jungle.

"Yeah, but it's let down by this place along here." Jim slowed as they came up to an old colonial building. It was like Jim and Vera's, but whereas Jim had painted the tin roof a shiny red and the wide weatherboards a glistening white (in the Spring, as soon as they heard Ada was coming, Vera said, impressing on Ada in a roundabout way that her arrival was important), this house had a rusting roof and scabby walls, and two verandah posts were sagging. As for the lawn, it seemed never to have been cut. The grass, entangling tyres and bits and pieces of discarded furniture, grew like lianas in through the windows of a car with missing doors. The seats had been ripped out and put on the verandah.

"There's a whole tribe of Maoris living there. Mum, Dad, grandparents, cousins, the whole bang lot of them," Jim said morosely. "None of them lifting a hand to tidy up. They just sing and play their guitars."

"Like the Malays. The whole family sticks together," she said, ignoring the criticism. It was comforting to think the Maoris were like the Malays - easy-going, like the ones in the kampong across from the boarding house.

"Your house isn't worth a brass razoo if you've got Maoris next door," Jim said.

Vera had pointed out a Maori settlement from the train. The children had rushed to the fence to wave, their black hair flapping across their faces. They were barefooted and wore clothes that were too big for them. They had broad smiles.

The road began to rise. Jim's breathing quickened, but he kept pedalling steadily. The low hills were gathering colour after the summer drought, turning from khaki to moss green. Their undulating curve was interrupted only by dark clumps of pines and stands of eucalyptus. In the distance, Ada could see the silver glint of a river edged with yellow-leafed poplars.

Sheep grazing by the wire fence raised their heads for a moment to watch the bike pass; one, with an offended side-glance, heaved itself up in its heavy coat onto a tussock rise.

A red truck overtook them, and the driver tooted. Jim pushed harder. She could hear him panting.

"I don't mind walking, Jim."

He did not reply, and she wondered if she had insulted his manliness in some way. She remained silent, and the world around was silent with her, until a blackbird on a telegraph wire directly above began to warble loudly. It seemed to be trying to cheer her up, and she smiled at the joyful sound.

Thick tree-trunk lamp-posts lined the roadside. They appeared to Ada, with their outstretched arms, like crucified giants. Sturdy and upright, the posts continued right up to Jim's property, where a low flimsy cloud hung over the top of the high ground behind the house and thinly shrouded the windbreak of pines. The haze made it all seem mysterious, like the setting of a story - her story, and Beth's. It made her anxious to think what the plot would turn out to be.

"You can hop off now," Jim said. As soon as he put his foot down, she dismounted, suddenly feeling impatient. The ground was uneven, and her ankle jarred. It hurt, but she was not going to complain. She did not even bend to rub it, and continued to walk up the hill.

Chapter 3

May 1947

It was going to be a beautiful day. The lawn was white with frost, but the sky was blue. By eleven it would be warm enough to be in the garden.

"Get a move on, will you," Jim muttered, standing behind Vera, who was putting on her make-up in front of the mirror above the mantelpiece. In the mornings, she always did her make-up in the living room as the rest of the house was like an ice-box.

Ada, too, wished Vera would hurry. She wanted them gone so peace could return. The mornings always had this jagged edge. Jim paced and fussed while Vera sipped her tea and ate her leathery toast in squeamish bites. She hated the frost. If it lay tarnished under a grey sky, the day promising to be witheringly cold and sullen, Ada would feel nearly sick, sensing Jim's mounting tension when Vera continued to lie in bed until the last moment.

"Here," Jim said, comb in hand. Vera smoothed her eyebrows, pressed her scarlet lips together once more, then turned to him and took the comb. He bent his head, and she drew a line down his parting. The teeth scraped his scalp with little tenderness. Jim stood up, flexed his shoulders, and adjusted his trouser braces. "If you could bring in the milk bottles," he said to Ada.

She would do more than that. It had not been voiced, but there was an understanding that she would take over a lot of the housework. It was little wonder, Ada thought, that Vera, released from being Jim's much desired helpmeet, had remarked more than once how pleased she was to have her there. Who'd helped Jim on Saturday morning to feed the clothes into the monstrous wringer, and lug the tin bath to the line while Vera lay in bed? "Seen a wash as white as that?" Jim had asked. What point would there have been in replying that it looked grey compared to the beaten clothes the dhobis strung before their longhouses, the plaster walls polished with rock crystal so they shone like marble? Vera had appeared around noon to sit in the sun, her hair washed and in curlers.

Yet Ada was aware she was being uncharitable in believing that Vera had only wanted her to come in order to do the housework. "You will have good schools and good food and lots of space so Beth can grow up healthy", she had written. "You can get permission to come if Jim and I promise to be your sponsors and give you a home. Because Michael's father will be able to show he can maintain you, there should be no problem with the immigration people. And of course you won't have to do a dictation test. You're English."

Jim strode out to get his coat, telling Vera to get a move on again, and bidding Beth, who was still eating her cereal at the dining table, to be a good girl. Ada, wanting to be out of the room while Vera fussed with her handbag as if delaying on purpose, placed the guard in front of the fire and hurried down the icy hallway to fetch the milk bottles, thinking of the chores she had to do by the day's end. Jim was very particular. Everything had its allotted place in the neatly arranged cupboards. So Vera would know what everything cost and be more thrifty, Ada guessed, he'd call out the prices for Vera's instruction as he unpacked, then smooth out the bags with the side of his hand to remove the creases before putting them in a drawer to wrap his empty beer bottles. Ada suspected that he did not want the bin men to know that he drank - too much, in her opinion. He had a reputation in the town to maintain. It was a small place; people gossiped.

With relief, she heard the bikes crunch down the shingle driveway. When she returned to the dining room Beth was sitting cross-legged in front of the fire and combing the hair of her doll, a new one given to her by Patrick just before they left. It had black hair, and its skinny limbs were pale brown rather than white – a Eurasian. Beth was already dressed. Ada wanted her to get into the practice of washing and dressing as soon as she woke up, in preparation for a school routine. She looked sturdy and warm in the thick jersey which Vera had recently bought for her, promising to knit one when she had the time. The bought ones, she said, did not give you the wear. Jim had laughed hearing that, and said wonders would never cease.

The peace was immense. Ada felt the tension slip from her shoulders. Dust motes pranced in a spiral of sunlight, and she noticed a fine coating on the cabinet. As much as she wanted to sit down with a cup of coffee, she imagined Jim slicking his fingers over the furniture that evening. She said to Beth, "I've got a bit of housework to do, darling. So why don't you get on with your drawing, and practise your letters." Beth ignored her. "You haven't done any lessons for a long time, Beth. What a lucky girl you are, starting school." Beth had visited the school once, before it broke up for the May holidays. When Ada had asked her if she was looking forward to going to school, she nodded as if that was expected of her, but did not look very excited at the prospect. "Come on, Beth. Here's your book. You can draw a picture first if you like, with your new colouring pencils, and then we'll make up a sentence to go with what you've drawn and do a bit of reading."

Ada was concerned that Beth, having missed the first term of school, would be behind the other children, and prayed every night that she would settle well. Patrick had told the child to keep up her lessons so that one day, when Singapore was a better place, she could return and be top dog. Anyone could be top dog these days, now that the British had gone down in the world. He also said that Michael had learned to read before he went to school. "Your father was a very clever man, Beth. He had so many gifts. Music, languages. They came as easily to him as drinking water. If he had lived, he would've been an excellent headmaster. You'll be like him, Beth," Patrick had said encouragingly, but his face had been sad. Ada knew what he was thinking. It was such a waste.

But before Beth could be taught to read, Ada had needed to persuade her to speak in English first. It had been difficult. Beth had seen no reason to speak in anything other than Malay. She had been in Amah's company constantly, following Amah around as she did her chores, or Ahmad in the garden, especially after Evaline died and was not there to ensure that she stayed out of the sun.

The idea of how to encourage Beth to speak in English had come to Ada the day she heard the child talking to her doll. The doll had been given to Beth by the Japanese officer, the pianist, who had a girl of his own the same age, according to Patrick. Ada had drawn closer and said quietly in Malay to the doll, "If you're good I'll sew you a new dress. You can tell me what you'd like. You can have any colour. But you'll need to ask your Mummy to listen to you and tell me in English, because I don't speak Malay very well." Beth had been solemnly alert. "She's saying something? What's she saying, Beth? Tell me in English." Beth, Ada had realised since her return to Serangoon, understood more English than she wanted people to know. "What *warna,* colour does Susie want?" Ada had said, picking up the doll. "Red, green, black?" she asked, pointing to the red of a cushion, the green of Beth's dress, the black of the doll's woolly hair. Beth had shaken her head and had pointed to Ada's blouse. "Oh, she doesn't want black, green or red. She wants white. Ask her what *warna,* colour she wants for her new shoes."

Beth's eyes had widened with pleasurable wonder. "Merah."

"Say it in English, Beth. Red. We don't want to get this wrong. And later, we'll have tea and you can tell me what Susie would like to eat. Come let's see what we can find for Susie's dress." She held Beth's hand, and together, like a couple on their tentative first date, they started to explore the dusty labyrinth of the house. It had been the start of numerous tea parties and expeditions into the garden and then the street – Ada naming and pointing – followed by quiet story times with picture books salvaged from the horde of Charmaine's childhood possessions. Ada had treasured every second, delighting in holding the child on her lap, and Beth had begun to see her as a friendly and interesting companion, someone who could compete with Amah, if not win complete trust, because there were times when Ada could not help retreating into her own miserable world.

Gradually, Beth had been tempted to play at schools - drawing on her slate, for instance, learning her alphabet. It was all done in a leisurely, playful way. But when it had been definite that they were going to New Zealand, Ada had become more earnest, and immediately Beth had started to resist her. The more the child was coaxed to learn English words, the more she was determined to speak in Malay, and would finally run away, leaving Ada to stare helplessly into the garden. Seeing Ahmad making good headway with the beds, she envied the uncomplicated work of managing obedient plants.

Ada took the colouring pencils from the side-board drawer and placed them on the table.

"Here we are, Beth."

Beth continued to comb the doll's hair.

"All right. I've got to make the beds and do a bit of dusting. I'll be back in a minute, and then we can do something together."

She switched on the radio then hurried to the front bedroom, leaving the door ajar so she could hear the music. A band was playing a dance tune. It sounded like a Victor Sylvester number, and she was instantly reminded of the dancing classes in Changi. One of the internees had brought the record with her to the camp, and they played it again and again. The classes were held in the dining hall, which used to smell of burnt rice. Hopeless dancers, most of them, but you laughed at every small thing. She and Mary would partner each other, trip over each other's feet, giggle a lot.

It struck her how important that companionship had been, all of them trying to keep their spirits up, all of them coping with hardship together. She wished that she had not been ill in hospital at the end, and that she had managed to exchange addresses with some of the other women, like Mary. She wondered how Freddy Bloom and Dr. Williams were faring in England. Did they keep in touch with each other, and share their memories? It must help sometimes to do that. Who in this safe, peaceful country would ever understand what it meant to have suffered and lived so close to death? Vera, for instance, knew that Ada had been interned, that the cell was minute, that the food was terrible, and that she got beriberi, but she had not told Vera about the beatings she saw, the women and children who'd died, the disease, the starvation, and certainly nothing about Smith Street. And as for Michael, Vera believed what had been told to Beth - that Michael had been killed doing ambulance duties. Vera had been very sympathetic, though she had not continued to ask anything more - which was hurtful, Ada admitted to herself, but then reasoned that Vera probably did not want to upset her by asking questions. It was also possible that Vera felt guilty for her own good fortune. Besides, she had not been told the truth; had not been told how hard it was trying to come to terms with how Michael had died.

In Serangoon, Ada had tried her best to live in the present, and during the day it was possible by keeping busy with housework, and of course with Beth. She used to try and avoid the library, but if she had happened to walk into it, usually in a pain-shielding semi-daze, the memory of Michael playing was no longer the comfort that it had been in Changi when she still hoped for his survival. Instead it caused a sickening bolt to the heart which had her crying helplessly. Yet even this shock was nothing to the times she glanced at the clock checking for the hour Michael would return, and then had to cope with cruel reality. It had been at night, though, when no longer anchored by routines, that it was impossible not to think of Michael and how he might have suffered.

Now, as she plumped the pillows and smoothed down the quilt, she realised that she had never been on her own so much of the day. It was hard to believe that in Serangoon she had to retreat to her bedroom if she wanted to think or to study. And before that, in the boarding house, Elizabeth and Mrs Sinathamby had been there, not to mention the constant comings and goings of the boarders.

When she returned to the dining room, blessedly warm from the murmuring fire, Beth was seated at the table, busy with her colouring pencils. Beth held up her drawing.

"What a lovely picture, Beth."

It was a circle with a line at an angle at the top, and two lines extending from the bottom. Beth had begun colouring it in with brown.

"It's Mr. Rooster," Beth said. "Can we feed him soon?"

"Of course we can. When the sun's up properly, and we've done a bit of reading." Ada came to stand by Beth, and stroked the child's hair, glossy in the sunlight coming through the window. "It's going to be a beautiful day."

Ada placed the tea tray on the table Jim had made from logs, and shaded her eyes, searching for Beth. The brightness was dazzling. The sun had transformed frost into glassy points of light. Glittering beads of water clung to the fence wires that divided the garden from the three paddocks that stretched out to a bush-covered hill. To the right, beyond a walnut tree, was a small orchard, into which Beth was disappearing.

"Come and have your drink and biscuit, Beth," Ada called. Beth paid no heed. She was tracking the trouping of the rooster with his brood. They had come to a patch of edible weed at the edge of the orchard. He stood back in a proud, gentlemanly way and let the females eat first, then, with a couple of the most faithful in his harem, began high-stepping across the lawn. He seemed to show in his aloofness how any self-respecting hen should do it: pick your way fastidiously as if wearing high heels, and haughtily toss your head. Beth rushed after them, laughing, and Ada smiled at the child's happiness.

In the orchard there was a smell of decaying fruit lying in piles of fallen leaves. Jim had stored most of the apples. Ada had been a little disturbed by this storing. It was like the Woods preparing for the worst. Yet it was hard to believe that anything bad could ever happen here. The sky was a heavenly blue; the light very clear, not a scrap of humidity.

A mass of birds suddenly shot upwards from out of the bush. There several colonies in there, all different. They sounded like quarrelsome tribes with the noise they made at roosting time. Ada paused to look down the valley, and heard the long, pure call of a bell-bird.

"Look, look, Mummy," Beth cried. "Aren't they funny? Jim wants me to stop them getting into the vegetable patch."

The vigilance was not necessary. Jim had caged the silver beet and the cabbages against greedy beaks. Ada appreciated that he was trying to make Beth feel useful, help her to belong. It was kind of him, she thought, and regretted her impatience with him those times he would come in from working on the property and wanted her to go out and see what he had been up to, expecting her to stop whatever she was doing immediately. On the very first morning, she recalled, when he strode into the house and whisked her away, it was as if he'd been waiting all his life to show off his land, once a derelict chicken farm. He'd gestured in a lordly way at the small flock of grazing sheep. The hill behind also belonged to him. With all the space, roundabout ten acres, he had known right away it was the place he had been looking for.

"Too right, I did. You could breathe out here, I thought. You could get stuck in. Honest hard physical work. Only trouble, I was short of a few bob. But a mate of mine said he would give me a loan and wrote out a cheque right there. A good mate, eh." Jim had frowned and scratched his chest. "He's promising to give me a hand with the dipping, and I'll hire a shearer. There's only so much you can do on your own when you've got a full-time job as well." Ada had gathered from Vera that it was not unusual for people to have jobs and also manage a small holding with a few animals. It was part of the Kiwi character to want to stay connected to the land. And for Jim, Vera believed, it was also the fulfilment of his father's dreams when he left the old country after the First World War with the hope of owning land and becoming his own master, but ended up doing what he had always done - running a draper's store, a trade which Jim had followed him into and was keen to abandon. Ada had thought of Noel, and how he aimed to make his own way in Singapore.

Jim was intent on getting the place up to scratch. Everywhere you looked there was an immense amount of work to be tackled - fences to mend, beds to weed, vegetables to be planted, logs to cut, and all of it done with not a soul to help. There were no servants in this country. Ada had remembered how hard Ahmad used to work in Serangoon, and how he tried to get the garden back to how it had been before the war. Too late for poor Evaline, though. "It's going to be wonderful, Jim. It's a beautiful place. A paradise," she said. Ada respected the man for his determination, even if his possessive, somewhat childish pride was overbearing at times. How different he was from Michael who kept things to himself. But she'd not liked that either, had she?

Beth was standing with her head cocked on one side, her eyes on the hens. "Mummy, is Jim going to kill anymore chooks?"

Ada had no answer for this, but she hoped that he would not slaughter them in front of Beth again. He did it so quickly that there was no time to turn the child's head away. Beth had burst into tears when she saw the headless feathery bundle desperately keeling around in a rapidly waning circle. Jim had stood with the bloody axe in his hand.

"You can't be a sook like the blighters in town," he told her. His grin had been sheepish, though, as if he had sensed she was angry with him. "You shouldn't hide it from them. Does them good to know where their food's coming from. Respect it more."

She had wanted to say that if anyone should know about the value of food it would be her. And yes, children should know that food did not appear magically on a shelf, yet why need they witness brutality? But she had kept quiet, aware of her place, resenting it.

Chapter 4

VERA DUMPED THE SHOPPING BAG on the kitchen bench.

"Haven't got any lap chong, I'm afraid. He tells me he can't get any. I had to bribe him for the soy sauce." She had referred to the lack of these ingredients before, and Ada had visualised the stacked shelves of the shops in pre-war Chinatown – bottles of sauces, noodles, Chinese sausages hanging in coils from the ceiling, wreaths of dried mushrooms sharing space with oiled umbrellas.

Vera kicked off her shoes and reached for the cup of tea Ada had poured her.

"I hope you're feeling at home, Ada. Not regretting coming at all."

"I'm really pleased to be here. And very grateful to you and Jim for letting us stay. I never had any doubt it would be the best place for Beth to grow up," Ada said, slicing a carrot into fine slivers. There was no need to tell Vera that there had been a moment when she had wavered in her decision to leave Singapore.

It had been on the afternoon she visited the cemetery. She walked between the shattered headstones and the blind child angels stranded on their backs, to lay flowers first on her parents' grave, and then on Evaline's tombstone, which now bore the newly carved tribute to a son who lost his life in service to his country. Nearby, a group of boys were feasting on durian. The disgusting smell of the fruit had reminded her of Noel, who was the only member of the family who'd eaten it. To tease him, Elizabeth would feign utter repulsion as he feasted. Picturing her parents laughing together, Ada reflected on how happy their marriage had been, and remembered Elizabeth's grief when it ended. Elizabeth said that she wanted to die, too; that she could not live without Noel. When relatives urged her to return to England, she refused, claiming that spirits did not cross water, and all she had now was Noel's spirit. Recalling these words, Ada had thought how unbearable it would be for her not to have Michael – at least in spirit – and that she would return home and tell Patrick that she changed her mind.

She would not tell Vera this. To think that she had given in to her fear, even for a moment, that day in the cemetery, had put her own needs above Beth's welfare, filled her with shame.

"God, I miss the food in Singapore," Vera said, watching Ada peel an onion.

"It's different there now, Vera. The rice ration is not much more than what people were getting under the Japanese. You have to queue for everything. People are starving. I've seen them eat out of dustbins. It really is bad. There's T.B. everywhere. Water off a lot of the time. And electricity. Medicines are still scarce. It's a long way from getting back to what it used to be like. It might never get back. Who can tell what the communists are going to do? They're ruthless. There are bomb attacks everywhere. Singapore is a dangerous place. It's very frightening." She shook her head. "You have to count your blessings that you live in this country, Vera."

"Don't say that in front of Jim. He'll go on and on about it being a paradise here."

Ada made no comment. Perhaps abashed for sounding ungrateful, Vera added quietly, "The war must've been terrible for you."

Was this an invitation to tell more? To tell her about the Kempeitai? To tell her the tragic tales Patrick had obsessively wanted to relate? How his friend Dr. Wong had his nails pulled out and his ear drums pierced; how scores of Eurasians had been forced to dig their own graves in the Ulam Tiram massacre.

No, she could not tell Vera this, not now, perhaps never, because what good would it do? Vera would be horrified and try to comfort her, but what could she say that would take away the pain? And she might even add to it by not really understanding. "It would've been worse without friends," Ada said as evenly as she could.

"Oh, I'm sure. Friends are so important. I don't know what I'd do without the girls at work and having a laugh together. They can be a bit boring sometimes, though, especially when they talk about the best way to iron shirts or bake scones."

Ada could not imagine the women on the haberdashery counter where Vera worked – on the opposite side of the department store from Jim – gladly doing household chores. Lined up like cut-out dolls in front of the glass cases of ribbons and buttons, they all appeared so sophisticated – hair set, makeup perfect – and far removed from domestic toil. And she most definitely could not match their fragrant grooming with their sly and gleeful stories, passed on to her by Vera, about certain men being 'out for a poke', and which of their female friends had been 'thrown-over and nearly topped themselves' or who had been 'caught and had to bring it down'. Ada noted the discrepancy between their claim that it was necessary to get away from all pursuing males – 'all the wallies chasing them' – and their stocking up of trousseaus with blankets, sheets and saucepans paid for by weekly instalments.

Whenever Vera related the stories of the wronged and discarded women, sometimes with a pitying contempt, Ada vowed that she would never give anyone the chance to gossip about her. Not that she'd done anything to be ashamed of, but no one would ever know what had happened to her in Smith Street.

"I'm not sure how I would've coped without Lucy," she said, tearing meat from the chicken carcass. Vera knew that Lucy had survived the war, and was living with her aunt now.

"After I heard Michael had died I didn't want to eat. Lucy had to feed me. She made me eat. She told me I had to survive for Beth's sake. And when we were moved to Sime, she got me gardening with her." Ada pictured herself lying on a mat watching the rain fall in a steady trickle through the thatched roof of the hut. She had not wanted to move, or to talk. Someone had given her something to darn. She stitched, then ruthlessly unpicked and stitched again, mindlessly seeking distraction from her grief. For hours she would do that, like a mad woman.

"It must've been terrible for you. Oh, Ada. Thank God you had Lucy there. Thank God you had a friend." Vera was clearly upset. "I wonder why Lucy hasn't answered any of your letters?"

Ada had written several times but had received nothing in return. "Perhaps she prefers to leave the past behind. I don't blame her." It was a friendship of circumstance; she and Lucy had little in common, really.

"I had other friends as well. Women I owe a lot to." She was thinking of Mary, of Judith, of the doctors and nurses, of Freddy Bloom. "Of course, not everyone was kind and helpful." Ethel, for instance. And she did not have the close friendship with any of them, which she'd had with Melanie. "You remember Melanie, don't you?" She heard about Melanie a few months after returning to Serangoon from hospital. Melanie whom she trusted; her dear, dear friend, the only one ever invited to the house when Frugneit was there; Melanie who lent her books and read Shakespeare with her. "The Japs put her in a comfort house. She was shot when she tried to escape." Would it ever be possible to forget the anguished wailing of Melanie's mother as she spoke of her sons and daughter, all taken from her? Ada remembered her own noisy sobbing, and how Mrs Chow had reached out a comforting hand. It was thin, the knuckles swollen like memory knots in string.

"Oh, my God. How dreadful," Vera said, hand over mouth. "Oh, my God."

"Yes. That's war for you," Ada replied, her eyes smarting with tears. "I hope Jim likes the meal," she said, changing the subject, and concentrated on dicing the meat.

Vera answered quickly, sounding as keen to talk about something else. "He'll be so blotto he won't know what he's eating. He's meeting Bill for a jug. Or two."

Ada's heart sank. Jim was so talkative when he had been drinking. "Is Bill the one who lent him the money?" she managed to say.

"Yeah, Bill's his best mate." Vera shrugged. "He loves having a laugh with Bill. Although when he's at home all he wants to do is work, work, work."

"We need to work to get on, Vera. To have a better life."

"But can't you have some fun on the way? He never wants to go to the pictures with me, let alone a dance." Vera picked at a cuticle with her nail. "Do you remember Madame Varga? And how I wanted to be a dancer?"

"I do. You were a beautiful dancer," Ada said, remembering Vera showing off her steps for Elizabeth in the front room of the boarding house, her cheeks flushed with pleasure and exertion. It was true that Vera had escaped the suffering of the war, but the war had ended her dreams. "It doesn't do any good to look back, Vera. We have to keep looking forward."

"I never thought my life would be like this." Vera folded her arms and sighed. "I remember Mummy saying that if you made your bed you had to lie in it."

Ada wondered why it was that Jim and Vera could not meet halfway, could not find something that they both enjoyed doing.

But perhaps that was impossible if they were too different in character and simply did not want the same things out of life.

Vera was studying her nails again. It saddened Ada to see her looking so despondent, and it occurred to her that if Jim and Vera had a child it might help Vera to come down to earth, and help Jim to take it easy more.

"Do you want to start a family one day, Vera?" she said, washing grease off her hands.

"I always thought I would. But I'm not so sure now. I don't think Jim is very keen."

"Jim's so patient and good with Beth. She follows him around like his shadow." Last Sunday afternoon, Ada had watched her, through a bonfire's oily curtain of heat, standing on the brown molar of a tree trunk and chattering to Jim as he forked in the rubbish. "He seems to me like a man who would love having children."

"He hasn't said. Probably thinks I wouldn't be a very good mother."

"So you really don't know what he thinks."

"Well, you know he thinks I'm useless. Especially compared to you."

There was nothing in Vera's tone or expression which indicated that she was jealous. Jim's praise did make Ada feel uncomfortable, as when he would compare her with his mother whom he claimed had been a very practical hard-working woman, but she believed it was his way of irritating Vera for her seeming indifference to his criticism. Ada had seen the longing on his face when he watched Vera sometimes. When they went to fetch their bikes from the shed, his hand would hover at Vera's waist as she picked her way in her flighty heels over the uneven ground.

Vera suddenly said in a bright tone, "And how's my beautiful niece? Now, here's someone who'll know how to live." Beth, who'd already had her supper – a new favourite, macaroni cheese – was standing in the doorway wearing one of Vera's old dance dresses, which Vera said was terribly dated and which she would never wear again. Ada had shortened and taken it in to fit the child. The gown was conspicuously glamorous. The net and taffeta flounces swept the floor as Beth did a little turn in the coquettish way Vera had instructed her, and swung her leather bag of cheap paste jewels which Vera used to wear in her dance shows. The child was more attached to the shiny beads and sparkling chains and bracelets than she was to her doll. Ada did not see this as a good sign. But when Vera jumped up and switched on the radio, dialled to find a station with suitable music that blared out into the small living room, and grabbed the hands of laughing Beth, Ada was aware that she envied Vera. It was not anything to do with a fear that Beth would love her vivacious aunt more than her mother, as once the child had preferred Amah. It was the sense of having lost the ability to be perfectly light-hearted, as in the days when Noel was still alive, or when she worked at the Municipal and had gone to tea-dances with the girls before Frugneit showed his true colours. It was a long time since she had been able to live entirely in the present, and without worries.

"Come on, Ada. Come and dance with us. This is a three-person foxtrot." Vera grabbed Ada's hand, tugging her forward. Ada bumped into the cabinet and began to giggle. Vera kicked back a chair. "Come on, girls, keep up with the music." Her eyes shone, and there was something defiant in her manner. Ada could see she was in one of her reckless moods, but the music was so loud, so persuasive, that all you wanted was to give in to the danger of it all, despite the risk of Jim coming back and finding them cavorting. She dipped, she swayed, she bumped into the cabinet again.

They were all laughing when Jim walked in with the cold night air around him, his hat at a jaunty angle, and his cheeks red either from the bike up the hill or from the beer. His coat was half-buttoned, and his eyes very bright. Ada stopped, tense, and with her experience of Frugneit and his drunken homecomings, hurried to switch off the radio.

"Oh, Jim we didn't expect you back so soon," she said. She glanced at her watch. "Goodness, it's time to get Beth ready for bed."

"It doesn't take long to down a jug," Jim said. "Bill had to get away. His old lady's under the weather, so I brought home a couple of bottles." He pulled off his coat and went back through the kitchen to hang it up in the wash-house.

"I'll get Beth ready for bed," Vera offered.

Ada frowned and shook her head. "Don't worry, Vera. I can do it. You finish off the meal." It was her greatest desire not to be in the same room as Jim. "I've cut up everything. You just need to heat the oil. Make sure it's very hot before you put in the onions. Fry them for a minute, then put in the carrots." She could see Vera was not listening. Vera began to tickle Beth, who ran laughing into the hallway. Vera followed, growling like a deranged lion.

Jim called out, "I see you're using up the chook."

Resenting Vera, but realising that it would be pointless to follow her and insist she do the meal when she would probably not do it properly anyway, Ada hurried into the kitchen, sloshed oil into the frying pan, and turned up the heat to full.

"Good on ya. We're the same you and I, Ada. We know about hard times," Jim said.

"It'll only take a minute or two. I expect you're hungry. It's a Chinese dish. Very tasty."

"Chinese, eh. Went to a Chinese in Wellington once. I'll try anything." He snapped off the top of a beer bottle, poured and drank thirstily. Ada put aside a small plate of ingredients to fry up later for herself, then tossed thin onion slices into the pan.

Jim bent over a plate of cooked omelette she had made earlier to lace over the fried rice at the end. "Smells good. A lot of people don't have fresh eggs even now. Still baking without them. And butter. People overseas think because it's a farming country we have baths in milk. But they forget we sent our food over to the Poms in the war." He emptied his glass, then immediately refilled it.

"You can eat in a minute. I'll get Vera. And read to Beth. I can have mine later." She added the carrots.

"Your sister should be watching you do this. She can't cook to save her life. She's got the recipe book that I gave her, too."

Ada knew this to be the Whitcomb's Peace Recipe book. It showed how resourceful New Zealand women were. No one starved, they did not eat mice or worms, but they made do with little - pig's feet with leeks, calf-head soup, cereal coffee made with bran and treacle.

"Y'know, every bit of this meal, apart from the rice there," Jim said, gesturing with his head to the cooked rice in a bowl on the bench top, "comes off this land. It does me a world of good being able to say that."

After suggestions for mock egg sauce, mock this and mock that, there were also listed the ingredients for being a good wife - patience, understanding, laughter, kindness, and above all a wish to serve with meekness. You had to make a house 'so sweet that no one wants to roam'. They groaned when Vera read that out. "And open your legs for them", Vera had added in a rough voice. Ada guessed the expression came from the haberdashery ladies, and was reminded of Elizabeth's advice on wifely duties, the 'giving into them'. No doubt Elizabeth had good intentions, preparing her daughter for the wedding night, but all she had done was to instil anxiety - which Michael detected. Ada had recalled how patient and gentle he had been with her in the Cameron Highland hotel, and had pictured his face, the trace of doubt, when she told him of her pleasure. Remembering all of this with Vera's crude remarks, she'd glanced out the window to see Beth in conversation with one of the hens, and had vowed never to use Elizabeth's expression with her when the time came.

"I hope you'll like this. It's a popular dish in Singapore."

"I'll eat anything you put in front of me, Ada."

She scraped the chicken off the chopping board, then reached for the soy sauce. "Don't give me that muck. A pinch of salt will do me," Jim said, then added, perhaps recognising he might have sounded rude, "you're a good woman. I like hard-working sheilas."

Trying to ignore this clumsy gallantry, Ada concentrated on finishing the meal, then quickly filled two plates and carried them to the table. Jim sat down to the meal immediately. She left him taking in big spoonfuls, and hurried into the bedroom where Vera was reading to Beth in bed.

"I've dished up yours, Vera. I haven't made Jim his pot of tea."

"He can get his own. There's no need to run after him."

"Go on, Vera. I can read to her now. Your food's getting cold." Ada reached for the book. Vera got up reluctantly, and Ada took her place. "Now where did you get up to?" she said to Beth, ignoring a lingering Vera.

"I want another story. I don't like *Sleeping Beauty*. I don't like the witch."

Vera had left the bedroom door open, and obviously the dining room one as well, because Jim could be heard complaining to Vera from across the hallway.

"All right. How about *Cinderella*?" Ada asked. Beth nodded emphatically, and Ada turned to the appropriate page and began to read, soon finding that she had to raise her voice.

Jim sounded as if he were addressing a large gathering. "It's the way you were brought up. I should've known better."

"If you've told me that once, you've told me a million times," Vera cut in.

"Search me, then, that you still keep pissing it up the wall."

"What's pissing, Mummy?"

"Sssh. I don't know. It doesn't matter."

"Jim's angry. Why's he angry? Is he angry with Vera? Has she been naughty?"

"You can talk about pissing when you come back pissed to the eyeballs," Vera said.

Ada read more loudly, but Beth was not listening.

"Wait, Beth. I'll shut the door so we can concentrate."

She would shut both doors. She stepped carefully across the hallway, and just as she raised her hand to close the dining room door, Jim turned and saw her. He was standing in front of Vera, who was seated at the table. He had one fist resting on his hip, the other holding a glass of beer. It was his customary stance when singing the virtues of Godzown, or boasting of all the impatient women waiting for his assistance and clever advice on how to make the most of the scant stock of dress fabrics.

Jim swayed back slightly. "No, don't shut the door. Come in, Ada. You and I know what the war was about. Not like her ladyship here. Just because she's living in a country where there's security from the cradle to the grave it doesn't mean she can spend money like lady muck. And why shouldn't I have a drink or two with my mate? I work hard, I work damn hard. And I'm not flakers. Strewth, you should see them, those who can't hold their booze, chundering as soon as they get out the door, not even out…"

"Shut up. You're disgusting," Vera snapped.

Ada dearly wished to leave the two of them and return to Beth, but thought that if Jim had his audience for a moment he might calm down.

"Your sister just doesn't cotton on that you have to get off your acre if you want to get somewhere. Strewth, I need a good woman to work with me. Like my Mum did with Dad. It wasn't their fault the Depression came." Ada predicted that he was about to embark on his favourite story, the one concerning his parents. A father who had been forced on the dole when he lost his draper's business because no one had the money for dress materials. But there was no pay without work, so he moved the family to a smaller house and did forestry work, when he had to live in a tent with a dirt floor and wash in a horse trough. Jim's mother, left behind with the kids, had to learn to make clothes out of sugar sacks, and keep the home spick and span because someone would come and check to see if you were one of the deserving poor. It had occurred to Ada that was how Jim had learned the importance of doing things properly. She did not know what had caused Jim's tirade, and was repulsed by his drunken behaviour, but she felt some sympathy for this tall, fair man with bafflement in his eyes. If you wanted to succeed, you had to work really hard. She could understand Jim's frustration with Vera.

Beth was clinging to Ada's arm, then she slipped past her into the room.

"Come on, Beth. It's time you were asleep." Ada drew back, flapping her hand to coax the child out.

Jim turned to Vera. "It can't be family blood that has you sitting on your backside. Look at your sister."

Ada grabbed Beth's hand, glimpsing Vera's face – the red showing on the pale skin, her big eyes opened wide in fury – before she shut the door.

"Why are they angry, Mummy?" Beth, frowning, looked up at her mother. "I don't want them to be angry."

"Jim's had too much to drink, and Vera's tired, darling." She tucked Beth in and knelt to hug her tightly. "Don't worry. It's all over now. Try and go to sleep."

"There's too much noise."

The door across the hall slammed, and Vera ran down the hallway to the bedroom. Ada held her breath waiting to hear Jim's heavy footsteps in pursuit. Nothing followed. Her heart was beating fast as it used to do when Elizabeth fled from Frugneit. He would hammer at Elizabeth's locked door. What was Jim going to do?

"Can I have another story, Mummy? I can't get to sleep."

"Ssh. I'm going to lie down as well. Turn over and I'll cuddle you. It's very late. Far too late to be up for someone going to start school soon."

"I don't want to go to school."

"Don't you want to have other children to play with? You're very lucky. You'll learn all sorts of interesting things."

"What things?"

"Ssh. Go to sleep. Shut your eyes."

"Are you sorry you can't go to school, Mummy?"

"Very sorry."

"Will Jim kill another chook soon, Mummy? I don't want him to. I like chooks. They're my friends."

Ada steered onto the path of chicken talk, their silly habits, and Beth began to quieten. She loved her cuddles, and she was tired. Ada hoped that she would accept the quarrel as something people did when they were drunk or exhausted. It was all part of a new reality, like the paddock, the birds, the chooks. And soon Beth would start school, and hopefully make friends. Ada knew she had to hold on to the thought that Beth would be all right, and try and put aside her disappointment that life with Vera and Jim was not what she expected.

As soon as Beth began to breathe steadily, Ada sat on the edge of the bed. She preferred to miss her supper than to be with Jim. Soon she could hear radio music playing quietly, the sound of running water in the kitchen, the clink of china. Jim would never leave the dirty dishes until morning, and relieved as she was that he seemed to have calmed down, she wished that he would go to bed. She needed the lavatory, and would have to go through the kitchen to get to the wash-house. She crossed her arms and stared morosely into the darkness. Jim was too particular. Life could not only be about work. There had to be a balance. All work and no play makes Jack a dull boy, Elizabeth used to say.

There was a gentle tapping on the door. She looked up, alarmed, then went cautiously to open it. Jim was standing there. He looked serious, repentant.

"Do you want anything to eat, Ada? I've left the pan for you to fry up your meal."

"Thank you, Jim. I might later." When you've gone to bed, she thought.

"Good on ya." He hesitated. "I'll leave you to it, then."

She smiled faintly and closed the door. It was the drink which made him argue, she told herself. Drink changed people's personalities. She did not dislike him. He was not vicious like Frugneit. What a shock it had been to live with him after Noel, who only drank on special occasions, and then only in moderation. Michael also, she recalled, hardly ever touched liquor. He had never lost his temper with her. He was a good man. She had been wrong to suspect him of betraying her, although it had been a shock to get that letter about the black woman. She remembered how desperate she had felt, how she had needed someone to talk to, and pictured the crowded restaurant in Market Street with Mrs Sinathamby seated across the table from her.

Dear Mrs Sinathamby. Ada had visited her before leaving Singapore. Her grey hair was unravelled from its bun, her sari clean but crumpled, and she'd stared mournfully at the ruins of the boarding house on the other side of the waste ground. It had been directly hit. "Everything gone," she'd moaned, wiping her eyes with the back of her hand. "My husband, your husband, so many of my good good friends. Elizabeth did a clever thing, leaving this world behind when she did. I will miss you, Ada. Oh boy, I will miss you and the child. But you must go and get a better life."

Ada pressed her hands to her flushed cheeks. How she missed Singapore. How she missed them all. Mrs Sinathamby, Patrick, Charmaine. She sighed. But you had to live in the present. Take each day as it came. Freddy used to say that. Freddy now back in England with her Phillip, Ada supposed. And as she imagined a tall, thin man – like the doctor who had treated her in the hospital at the end of the war – with his arm around Freddy, Ada felt acutely bereft, and very alone.

Chapter 5

June 1947

Jim stood up, flexed his shoulders and adjusted the braces beneath his suit jacket.

"Now is the kid ready?" he asked. "Are you ready, Beth?"

Beth shook her head. Ushering Beth from the chair, Ada could feel the stolid antagonism in the child.

"Jim and Vera are late, Beth. Let's get your coat on."

"I don't want to go to school. I feel sick."

"Where?" Jim demanded, standing over Beth as Ada placed her hand on Beth's brow. "Let's see your tongue." Beth opened her mouth reluctantly. "Can't see anything wrong," Jim said.

"I feel sick in my tummy," Beth countered.

"You've missed quite a lot of school recently, Beth," Ada said. "You really are well enough now."

"I don't want to go with Jim and Vera. I want you to take me, Mummy." It had become the practice for the child to be delivered on the back of Vera's bike to avoid the scene at the school gate of Beth clinging to Ada and begging her not to be late in the afternoon. Not that the pleading was necessary. Ada was always one of the first mothers to arrive, and would stand impatiently awaiting the appearance of a senior boy with a large brass bell. After he'd shaken it for the last time and put in his hand to choke the clapper, Beth would run out from the small wooden building that housed the infants, her face alight with joyful relief, which always cut Ada to the heart.

"I'm coming up at play-time, darling, to see how you're getting on, and to have a little talk with your teacher," Ada said. She could not put it off any longer, but the thought of a possible confrontation with the fierce looking Miss Mathews made her feel apprehensive.

Vera, who'd come in from the bedroom and was standing in the doorway, nodded in judicious approval, then stepped forward quickly, took Beth's hand firmly before she could protest further, and stalked out after Jim.

Ada felt the need to hurry down the hallway and stand at the window of the front room to watch them coasting down the driveway on their bikes, Jim's trousers clipped at the ankles, Vera's coat arranged carefully so as to be protected by the skirt guards. Little Beth was holding tightly on to her waist, face up against Vera's back to keep out the cold air. The child was a picture of misery. As soon as they disappeared around the shadowed bend, Ada cleared the breakfast dishes, then hurried to make the beds. She was unusually heedless of the cold, her thoughts focused on what she would say to the teacher and how she would say it.

She was still rehearsing her lines when she set off for the school, heading down under the heavy pine trees where the long grass was stiff with frost. The sky was a faultless blue.

In the village, the houses on the dark side of the street brooded behind unmarked lawns that spread towards the fences. Ada chose to walk on the sunny side of the road, past the Maoris' house, where the sun flashed off the dirty windows and called out welcome. Of the inhabitants there was no sign. And then passing the store she came to the village school - two wooden buildings, both painted cream with red tin roofs.

The playground was empty as she approached, but soon out ran the boy with the bell to announce morning play-time, and the children filed out to collect their bottles of milk from the senior pupils standing guard over the milk crates. Ada saw Beth take her bottle and sit on the bench fastened to the side of the classroom wall. She liked her milk, she liked drinking it through a straw. When she'd finished and returned the empty bottle to the milk monitors, Ada saw her going back inside the classroom while the other children paired off or made groups to play with marbles, or a ball. One group of girls had a long skipping rope. They all seemed perfectly happy. Ada waited for a moment to see if Beth would come outside again, but when she did not reappear Ada pushed open the gate and made her way, with as much assurance as she could muster, through the riotous playground to the infants' building.

The room was warm, and a wood stove burned in a corner. There were paintings on the wall of stick people with big heads, and arms stretched out sideways in rapturous welcome. Ada heard a woman's voice in the corner screened off by a low bookcase. It sounded like Miss Mathews. A child spoke, and Ada knew it was Beth. She waited, and a head appeared above the case, then turned quizzically towards the doorway, perhaps because the sun was blocked out. Ada moved aside and light streamed in. The teacher shielded her eyes, momentarily blinded.

"Miss Mathews? Good morning."

"Ah, Mrs Wood, I recognise your voice." She rose stiffly, and Beth sprang up with delight, ran towards Ada, and clung tightly to her waist. Ada hugged her briefly before untangling herself.

"If it's all right with Miss Mathews, I'd like to talk to her now, darling."

"Off you go, Beth. It's a sunny day. Thank you for your help," said Miss Mathews, flicking her hand at Beth, who immediately obeyed. Ada knew that she was afraid of the teacher's sharp tongue, which showed itself with some of the naughty boys and created respect in them all. Miss Mathews, a plump middle-aged woman, moved heavily towards Ada. She had a pronounced limp.

"I understand you're worried about Beth?" she said, looking about the room, perhaps for a full-sized chair other than her own. Seeing none, she faced Ada again. Ada tried not to look anxious, and straightened her back, then, aware that the teacher was shorter than herself, relaxed her posture a little. Miss Mathews continued, her voice breathy.

"You wanted to see me about how well Beth's settling, I understand. Well, I must say she's a very good little girl. You have nothing to worry about as regards her behaviour. She's very well-behaved. She's clever, too. None of the other children has started to read yet. Who taught her?"

"We, her grandfather and I. We were worried that she might be behind the other children when she came here. Her English wasn't good at all. The Japanese took over the house during the war and everyone had to speak Japanese or Malay, and Beth was with our Amah a lot. She'd had her own way for years, and was very active. It was quite difficult."

Miss Mathews looked mystified. Ada, daunted by the thought of having to explain further, was relieved to hear, "Well, you did a good job, Mrs Wood. She's very fluent. She can express herself better than a lot of the other children."

"She was always with adults, I suppose."

From where she stood Ada could see into the playground. Her eyes scanned the quadrangle for sight of Beth. At the far end, boys hurled themselves at the icy patches on the concrete, out of sight of the teacher parading the yard. A couple of children were chasing each other in quickly flagging bursts. And there was Beth, wearing her new woollen dress sewn up on the machine lent by one of Vera's friends. The child was standing in a sunny corner by the drinking fountain, her thick, wavy hair parted down the middle and tamed with white ribbons that sat on the top of her head like floppy rabbit ears. She was watching some girls with a skipping rope.

"If we'd known Beth's capabilities at the start we might've put her up a class," the teacher said. "But it certainly wouldn't be a good idea to move her now. It's more important that she gets to know the other children."

Ada spoke quietly. "That's really why I came. Beth says she doesn't have any friends." Ada hesitated, her heart beating a little faster, then added, "She doesn't like coming to school." Did Miss Mathews hear that as a criticism of herself?

Miss Mathews frowned. "I don't like to see her out in the cold by herself when her aunt drops her off in the mornings, but I do send her out when the other children arrive, otherwise they would think I'm favouring her. She was inside this morning because you were coming."

"I'm not saying it's your fault at all, Miss Mathews. As I said, Beth's used to being only with adults."

Miss Mathews did not seem to hear this. "She's always very neat and tidy. You sew her dresses?" Ada nodded, and the teacher, glancing at Ada's sober woollen coat, said, "She stands out." Was this a reference to Beth's colour? Ada flushed. Miss Mathews continued, "She's very conscientious. Always applies herself seriously. Which makes my life easier, of course. But a child who acts in such a way is quite exceptional, especially one as well-dressed as your daughter. And children are wary of difference."

Ada looked out the window again at the group with the skipping rope. She thought their clothes were ill-fitting and drab. She felt sorry for the girls. But perhaps the mothers could not sew and knew nothing about fashion? Vera sometimes brought home trimmings from the haberdashery counter such as buttons and rick rack, and American magazines featuring pictures of Shirley Temple, which gave Ada ideas. Jim brought home unsaleable ends of material bales. It did not take much to make a pretty frock, pin-tuck the bodice, put a bit of lace around the cuffs.

But was it also being suggested that Beth should not work so hard, not take her lessons seriously? To tell her to do that, Ada thought, would be against everything she believed; everything Michael had believed.

Ada looked at the dolls stacked on a shelf, a tea set, little pots and pans. Beth had told her the girls fought to play with them whenever they could. No wonder Beth stood out. She was at school to learn, not to play. In Singapore, you had to pass your end-of-year exams before you went up a class. And if they had uniforms, as they did in Singapore – navy blue, box-pleated – there would be no bother about a child having pretty dresses.

Miss Mathews was speaking. "I'm sure she will settle in time. She's such an attractive little girl. Spanish-looking." The woman's brown eyes sparked with curiosity.

What did she mean by 'settle in time', Ada wondered. Did Miss Mathews understand what it was like to be uprooted from your country and have to begin again? Did she have any idea what it felt to be lonely? Ada, upset and annoyed, noticed the older woman's thinning hair, the dark freckles on her scalp, the mole like a fat raisin on her forehead.

"Her father was an Anglo-Indian," Ada said, standing more erect. She was tempted to go on, say Michael had been a teacher – which would indicate that she might have some idea about education – but the bell monitor come out to signal the end of play-time.

Ada thought Miss Mathews looked pityingly at her, having registered the past tense. Or was it because she'd learned Beth was of mixed blood? Ada smiled wanly, thinking of what she might say to make the teacher understand how important it was that Beth should want to come to school and learn, but already Miss Mathews was moving away.

"I'm sorry, but we have to end now, Mrs Wood." She said this without looking at Ada and began to search through the clutter on her desk.

Ada hesitated, wondering at the way she was being dismissed. Feeling slighted, she murmured thanks, then turned abruptly towards the door. Body taut with frustration, she walked quickly towards the gate, hoping Beth would not see her and insist on accompanying her home, although she wished at that moment to take Beth with her, far away, back to Singapore.

Chapter 6

AFTER HER UNSATISFACTORY INTERVIEW WITH Miss Mathews, Ada wondered how she could help Beth through her own efforts. Beth wanted friends, though not just any friend it seemed, such as the little girl who wore spectacles, or the plump one. When Ada took reconnaissance walks past the school at break-times during the following week, she saw them seated on their own outside the classroom. Beth, also on her own, was standing a few yards away watching a group playing with a long skipping rope. It was obvious that Beth was desperate to join the skippers. Ada observed a pretty blond-haired child, the apparent ring-leader, pointing out which two should hold the ends, and who should run in first to join her as she jumped up and down, her ponytail swinging with easy authority. Ada also noticed that none of the skippers was a Maori girl. The Maori children played in a group apart from the others.

At the end of the week, she suggested to Beth that she play with them. "I don't want to play with them. They don't wear shoes. And they have dirty feet."

"It's because they're poor, Beth. You can't not like people just because they're poor."

"They don't like me. They run away."

Ada wondered if Beth were as strange to them as she was to the white children, the Pakehas. Perhaps, Ada thought, the

Pendels had been viewed with suspicion by the locals in Singapore as well, at the beginning, and it was Noel's determination for them to integrate with the Asians and Eurasians which made it possible for them to have close friends who were not white.

"We could invite some of them to tea one day after school, Beth, so you could all get to know one another more."

Beth shook her head emphatically. "No. I don't want them to come here to tea."

"Who else would you like to come to tea, then?"

Beth frowned, then looked hopefully up at Ada. "Linda Watts."

"Which one's Linda?"

"She's in charge of the skipping rope. It belongs to her big sister."

Ada guessed Linda was the girl with the ponytail. Ada had seen her being fetched from school by a slim, attractive woman who seemed to gather other mothers around her - someone accustomed, like her daughter, to being in control, Ada suspected.

Ada spoke to Jim and Vera that evening of what she had discussed with Beth. Jim said she was a fool to want Beth to play with the Maori children.

"You'll be sending her right to the bottom of the pile."

Vera added, "You can't expect too much from her. She's only a kid." Ada could not argue with that. "Try and make friends with Linda's mother," Vera advised. "Or some other mother with a daughter. I expect they'll be truly glad to have a chat after being stuck indoors all day." She sounded full of sympathy for these women. "You've got to push yourself forward. Go up to them and introduce yourself."

As yet, Ada had not sensed that anyone would welcome a chat. The women, all white (most of the Maori children were bussed in from a settlement a few miles out of the town) kept in tight groups and were familiar with one another. When anyone happened to glance her way, all she ever received for her smile was a faint one in return; no one came forward and spoke. She wondered if they suspected she was a single mother who might be needy and become dependent on them. It did occur to her that they might be wary of someone having a child of mixed race, but she dismissed this thought quickly. It was too unpleasant.

A few days later, having decided that she must now act on Vera's advice and 'push herself forward', starting with Mrs Watts, she prepared herself with a little more care than usual before setting off to fetch Beth from school. Dabbing on some lipstick, she felt a fluttering in her stomach. Calm down, Ada, she told herself, you're only going to talk to another mother, not the Kempeitai.

Before she locked the door, she checked her stockings for ladders and straightened the line of the seams. When she went outside, she glanced into the shadows of the orchard. Jim had warned her of burglaries in the district. He'd recently become the proud owner of a rotund, secondhand fridge, and believed crook blighters would start nosing about. "Anyone who took a mind to it could get away with murder up here," he'd said. "It's an isolated spot. Let him try though. I'll have him off to his maker in no time."

Recalling this at a moment when she felt anxious made her think of Jim with annoyance. He had this tendency to dramatise things, and to try and prove he was manly. On the previous Sunday, he had come back from a weekend deer shooting with a mate. Beth had gone running out as soon as she heard the truck, then back again squealing, "come and see, Mummy. Jim's killed a deer." The beast lay there with its bound legs extending stiffly from its body. Ada noted that Beth did not appear upset, as she had been when Jim had beheaded the chicken, perhaps because seeing a corpse was not like witnessing an actual slaughter. Beth had nudged the animal tentatively with her foot.

"Don't do that, Beth," Ada had said. In the half-light the carcass was like a shadow in a nightmare.

"She can't hurt it now. It went down at the first hit. Got it in one," Jim had said with obvious satisfaction. Ada, angry, had dragged Beth into the house. All right, you killed for food, but you did not need to relish the violence.

Remembrance of her anger helped to feel less nervous as she drew closer to the school. She positioned herself in a conspicuous place on the quadrangle and watched a group of women, including Linda's mother, gather in their usual place. They all looked much the same to Ada, with their set hair and twinsets.

Mrs Watts was, as usual, the centre of attention. She was relating something, and the other women, who'd been intent on greeting and meeting one another in a gossipy huddle, had the satisfied expressions of people being fed dollops of juicy information. In her numerous imaginings of this scene, Ada had fantasised that the woman would look up, and, intrigued by her friendly direct gaze, hasten over, start to talk warmly, ask about Beth, invite them to tea even. But when Mrs Watts did stop talking and glanced at Ada, perhaps aware that she was being watched, the glance did not settle; Ada was of no interest to her. And the bell was ringing.

Ada edged closer to the group as Beth ran out. Sighting Ada, she hurtled towards her. Ada hugged her, then instead of walking off immediately, waited until Linda, with the long blond tresses and the unfortunately dowdy frock showing untidily beneath her coat, decorously approached her mother like a little princess, and took her hand. The two turned and Ada was in their path.

"Mrs Watts?"

The woman smiled faintly and raised her brows.

"I'm Beth's mother. Mrs Wood." She wondered about the etiquette of a handshake, but it seemed too forward and formal, like arranging a business transaction. Mrs. Watts looked puzzled. "Beth's in the same class as your daughter." The children were eyeing each other solemnly. She continued in a rush, "Beth would like Linda to come and play after school one day."

Mrs. Watts looked more than doubtful. Linda said, "Can I, Mummy? I want to see the sick hen."

Last Sunday, Jim had brought it into the house wrapped up in an old vest. He'd said it needed the warmth of the fire, but he was also trying to cheer up Beth. Ada had smelled the sour musk of the hen house when he'd walked through the kitchen. "It's got a cold," Jim had said.

Beth had knelt to the hen and stroked it gently with the tip of her finger. Jim had filled a spoon with liquid from a cup. "If you hold this, Beth, I'll open up its beak so you can pour the stuff in." Beth stayed watching the hen until supper-time when Jim took it out to the wash-house. Next day, she went to school more readily than usual, and had apparently spoken to someone, perhaps Miss Matthews, about sick Clucky - which seemed to have drawn the attention of the prized Linda.

"How sick is it?" Mrs Watts glanced at Ada with a suspicious curiosity.

"Jim says it's going to live," Beth said.

Mrs Watts looked down at Beth. "And who is Jim?"

"Jim's her uncle," Ada answered quickly. "You might not have seen him when he and my sister drop Beth off in the mornings. We're living with them. Until we find a place of our own." Saying this gave Ada a momentary sense of power, and she offered a date for Linda to come with the air of someone who did not expect to be refused.

"Well, all right then," Mrs Watts said grudgingly. "Where have you come from?"

"Singapore."

"Singapore. That's where the Japs were." Mrs Watts leaned back slightly and looked at Ada for a few moments with eyes of cold blue. The woman's stare bore nothing of compassion for a woman whom she might have suspected had experienced hardship. Indeed, Ada considered it to be unfriendly, somewhat accusing, and her initial feelings of embarrassment and nervousness gave way to anger. She watched silently, lips compressed, as Mrs Watts took Linda's hand and walked away.

Ada decided that she would not allow the encounter to bother her, and two afternoons later, as had been arranged, she fetched the two girls from school with the brisk efficiency of someone who had been doing this all her life, who was not a stranger to the district, who had the right to mix with others and have her child do the same. The mothers stared, but she ignored them.

It was a grey afternoon. The frost had come without sun, a black frost which signalled rain, and dark clouds were mounting over the ranges. Beth took Linda's hand, and the three walked slowly up the hill in silence. Ada felt anxious about the cake she'd bought from the shop, the one Vera would go to no matter what Jim said about learning to bake. The cake, a sponge with coconut icing, looked a little dry, and though it was stored in the fridge would be even drier today. Ada suspected that Mrs Watts was one of those New Zealand women Vera talked about who baked scones and whipped up a light sponge or a moist Madeira without thinking about it, whereas she, like Vera, had never baked a cake. Elizabeth had no interest in baking or in instructing Amah to do so. She preferred the Indian sweetmeats bought from the Indian hawker to any English confectionary, and expected the boarders to prefer the former too, or fresh fruit, or milk puddings.

Ada need not have worried, for Linda gulped a glass of milk and refused the cake. She wanted only to see the hen in its box in the wash-house. But once she had watched it for a few moments, she screwed up her nose and said, "It's smelly in here."

It was the sort of remark her mother would make, Ada thought, sighing inwardly.

"Let's take Linda and show her your doll, Beth, and your new tea-set."

She led the girls through the kitchen into the bedroom, where she placed the tray, with the tiny porcelain cups and tea-pot that Vera and Jim had bought Beth, on the floor. "Here we are. You can pretend to have a party," Ada said cheerily, putting Beth's doll in front of the tray. Linda stood sucking her thumb as she stared dismally at the tea-set, and Ada watched Beth as anxiously, expectantly, sadly, as Beth watched her guest. "I know," she said at last. "Why don't I read you both a story?"

It was *Snow White*, a recent favourite of Beth's. Linda listened at first, but soon began to fidget. "I want to go home now," she said.

"Your mother's coming soon." Ada smiled encouragingly, and Linda began to snivel. "Look, I know. Why don't you recite some rhymes, Beth? Go on, darling." Beth was reluctant but began after Ada's prompting. Linda watched her, round-eyed. It was as if she had never heard verse, or never heard a child of Beth's age reciting anything off by heart, word perfect.

Mrs. Watts arrived earlier than expected, nervous and flustered as if something wild and horrid might emerge from the surrounding bush. Jim's house was a rambling, shabby structure in an untamed landscape; Ada knew that the Watts lived in one of the neat bungalows. Linda was sitting mutely and, if not smiling, thankfully did not rush to her mother with the relief of someone who'd undergone an ordeal.

"Will Linda want to come again and play, Mummy?" Beth asked immediately after they'd left. She sounded doubtful and worried, subdued by her guest's lack of enthusiasm.

"She was a bit quiet. But perhaps she was getting used to being in a different place. I'm sure it will be different next time." Ada wished she could believe this, she really did, not that she considered Linda to be all that special. But Beth wanted to be Linda's friend; she wanted to play with the skipping rope.

★ ★ ★

Although Ada did not expect that Beth would at last have a friend in Linda Watts, she was upset for Beth when the child said at home-time the following day, "Linda said she didn't like coming to my house. She told everyone that you spoke funny."

Ada flushed, loathing the idea of people commenting on her. Of course, anyone could tell she was not a New Zealander, but why be so rude?

"And she said her mother said I wasn't your real child because I wasn't a white person like you, because I've got a brown skin." Beth looked up at Ada. "Have I got a brown skin, Mummy?"

"You're one of the lucky ones who go a lovely brown in the sun easily. Not like me, who goes red and freckly". Ada pointed to the faint smattering of dots across her nose, leaning forward for Beth to examine them, wanting to distract her.

"She said I was a half-caste. What's a half-caste, Mummy? Linda went eeurgh, like that," Beth said, pulling an ugly face.

Ada had suspected, from the way people stared at them when they were in town, and the curious glances of the mothers in the playground, that people were trying to fathom the connection between a fair-skinned, light-haired woman and a dark child. But now the suspicion had been confirmed, and she felt that it smeared her somehow, it smeared Beth. Ada tried to manage her feelings of anger and hurt by imagining herself striding across the playground and taking smug Mrs Watts by the shoulders and shaking her. "It's a mix of two races," she said as calmly as she could, placing Beth on her lap. "I'm English, and Daddy, whom you look like, was an Anglo-Indian. Which means he was a bit Indian and..."

"An Indian?"

"Yes, a bit Indian." Beth looked puzzled. "An Indian is someone from a country called India. I'll show it to you on a map one day. We'll go to the library in town."

"They call me a Maori, too."

Ada sighed. "It doesn't matter what they call you, darling. What matters is that you're beautiful and clever and a good girl."

"I don't want to be a Maori or a half-caste."

"Why, Beth? What's wrong with being a half-caste, as you say, or a Maori? The Maoris are friendly people nowadays." Jim had told them about the fierce warriors, the cannibals, and Ada had insisted that was a long time ago.

"I want to be like you, Mummy."

"Well, you have my blue eyes. But you're very lucky because you have your Daddy's handsome features and lovely colouring." She rose, took Beth's hand, and led her into the bedroom, where she removed two photographs from under the paper that lined her underwear drawer. "You see how handsome he was. And he was a very clever man," she said, reminding herself that she ought to have the photos framed.

Beth had seen the photos before, but she took one photo from Ada and studied it carefully. She remembered to hold the snapshot on the edge. It was one of the two of Michael that Patrick had found amongst Evaline's belongings and had given Ada. The album of wedding photos and framed photos of the family which Evaline had cherished had been destroyed along with much else when the Japanese took over the Serangoon house. All of Michael's belongings - his clothes and shoes, his schoolboy memorabilia, his satchel, his conductor's baton, which Patrick had kept with him in the servants' quarters - were discovered by the ransacking military police and removed after Michael's capture.

In the photo, Michael was seated on the front verandah in a high-backed rattan chair, a peacock chair, and he looked quite the peacock himself with his upright posture, his immaculate white suit, stiff collar and bowtie, his hair slicked back very straight and smooth. He would comb it with great concentration, before dabbing eau de cologne on his clean handkerchief. It was a morning ritual. He took care of his appearance; he liked to look his best.

"Here, look at this one, Beth." She preferred this photo; it showed Michael's playful side. He was wearing a boater at a jaunty angle and leaning on a croquet mallet - like Fred Astaire with a walking cane in one of his dance routines. One leg was crossed over the other, the foot angled so the toe of his shoe was pointing on the ground. He was pretending to be a dandy.

"Daddy loved to play games. He was a very good tennis player. He had a great sense of fun sometimes. He could be quite a tease."

"What's a tease?"

Should she tell Beth about his pranks on Charmaine, and chasing his mother around the garden with a dead snake, or the stories his friends had of him? Or would that confuse the child? Children saw things in black and white. You spent a lot of time teaching them what was right or wrong. They got that from the fairy stories, as well. Good triumphing over bad. Snow White and the wicked stepmother. Gretel and the witch. You had to live a while to learn that people were more complex.

"Someone who likes to play tricks and make people laugh. But he worked very hard. He was an excellent teacher. And he could play the piano beautifully."

"Was he brown?" Beth asked. Not waiting for a reply, she insisted, "He's a man, I don't want to look like him, I want to look like you."

It made Ada feel sad to think that the child had no memories of Michael, had never listened to him play, and never heard him recite poetry. He'd have been such a good example to her with his education, much more able than herself to help Beth with her studies when she grew older.

"I've never showed you this before, Beth."

She returned to the dressing table, and from the bottom drawer withdrew a small leather box.

"Look at this."

It was the medal she had received on Michael's behalf for duties performed in the Field Security Section. She learned that he had been working in Malaya under a new identity as an itinerant music teacher, and had transmitted information about Japanese activities by assembling a radio – the parts left with his different students when he went to their homes to give them individual lessons, then collected together when he needed to pass on messages to the British.

"Your Daddy was a very brave man. And that's why he got this medal, because people were very grateful to him."

"Why?"

"Well I've told you he died in the war when he was driving an ambulance - the big car for taking sick or hurt people to hospital. It was a very dangerous job. You can be very proud of him. I know he would be proud of you. He always wanted you to do well at school so you could grow up and do good in this world."

Beth took the medal from Ada, and, as she studied it curiously, Ada thought with anger of the insults, and the child's hurt and confusion. How dare they treat her like dirt! Ignorance: it came from ignorance. The people here were so far away from the rest of the world. Probably few of them had travelled to the East.

"You can tell the class tomorrow at morning talk time about Singapore, Beth. All the different sorts of people who live there, the different foods. How you spoke Malay all the time with Amah."

"When can I see Amah again?" Beth said.

"One day soon."

The following afternoon, Beth approached with a sad face, hardly glancing at Ada and dragging her feet.

"What's the matter, darling?"

Beth said nothing, and, head drooping, took Ada's hand. They began to trudge up the hill without speaking. At last, Ada asked, "Did you give your talk?"

No answer.

"Did they like your talk?"

No answer.

Ada did not probe further, but as soon as they reached the house Beth said tearfully, "I'm not going to tell them anything again. I'm never going to tell them about Daddy playing the piano, or Amah. Or anything. Bruce Evans stood on my shoes and dirtied them."

Ada glanced down and noticed the smudges. "Don't worry about your shoes. Jim will easily get them spick and span with a bit of spit and polish and elbow grease," she said jocularly, using Jim's words for strong effort.

"He called me a Moriori. And David Prescott gave me a Chinese burn." She grabbed Ada's wrist with two hands and twisted, glaring up at Ada, blaming her. "Everyone called me a skite." The child began to sob loudly.

"Did you tell your teacher?"

"No. They hit you if you tell on them."

Ada placed Beth on her knee and stroked her hair. "They're just ignorant. Take no notice of them, darling. They're not worth anything."

When Beth grew quiet, Ada made them both a cup of sweet milky tea and stole some of Vera's chocolate biscuits, which were stored in a tin for the unlikely occasion of someone dropping in. As mother and daughter sipped and nibbled in silence, Ada's mind whirled with plans. She would go up to the school the next day and tell the teacher that something had to be done. And if nothing was done, she would take the law into her own hands. She would find out who those wretched boys were, and speak to their parents. And most certainly she was not going to allow the matter to rest with regard to the Watts woman.

☆ ☆ ☆

Ada waited at the school gate to waylay Linda's mother at home time. She'd decided that she would not approach the parents of the boys. After what Jim had said, she was guiltily aware of her own part in the matter.

At first, when he heard of the bullying, he had reddened with anger and vowed to beat the living daylights out of the bullies. Vera, her large eyes wide open and bright like headlights on full beam, claimed that the bullies needed a taste of their own medicine. The two had glanced spiritedly at each other. Ada had never seen them in such full agreement. But after they'd calmed down a bit, Jim said, "Kiwis don't like anyone getting above themselves. That's probably what they thought she was doing talking about the amah."

"She was just telling them a bit about herself. I wanted them to see…" Ada began.

"Yeah, but they thought she was showing off." Jim had stroked his chin and looked thoughtful. "If I was you I'd let the kid off a bit."

"What do you mean?"

"She picks up on your anxieties, Ada," Vera had cautioned.

"Too right," Jim said. "You push her too much to do well at her lessons." Ada knew that the pair had been discussing her and she felt hurt and angry, but she realised that the morning talk had done more damage than good.

Ada sighted Mrs Watts approaching the school gate. She was on her own so Ada stepped forward.

"Mrs Watts."

Ada spoke in a low calm voice; she was determined not to lose her temper. "Mrs Watts, can I speak to you for a little while?" The woman looked offended, but gave a slight shrug and followed Ada through the school gate and a few paces to the side by the perimeter fence. "Mrs Watts," Ada said, launching herself immediately into her much deliberated speech for fear her resolve to speak her mind would desert her, "I'm sorry to have to bring this up, but I'm afraid I'm very worried about Beth. She really doesn't want to come to school at all. I had to drag her here this morning." She refused to leave with Vera and Jim, and Ada had taken her down after the bell. "She loved having Linda to play, and was very anxious that Linda have a good time. As I was. However, it seems that Linda didn't enjoy herself at all, and in fact next day said something unpleasant about us, which apparently came from you."

"I don't know what you're talking about, I must say." Mrs Watts wrinkled her nose as if disgusted by a nasty smell, and looked at Ada with such scorn that it took all of Ada's will not to slap her.

"In fact it's more than unpleasant. It's unforgivable that you said Beth wasn't my child. How do you think that made Beth feel? We've just had a war, where many have suffered. Don't you think it's time we showed that humans must try and be kind to others? I'm sure you would be as angry and upset as I am if Linda felt alone and disliked for being different."

The children were streaming out of the classrooms.

"Why don't you go back to where you came from?" said Mrs Watts, and she thrust out an arm as if to strike Ada. "If you don't like it here, go home." She half-turned and shouted this over her shoulder.

Ada, shocked and beside herself with anger, could not speak as she walked Beth home. Her hands felt clammy and her body remained tense while she brewed a cup of tea and warmed some milk for Beth. She was not even aware that Beth had left the table and gone to the bedroom until she went in there herself to fetch a handkerchief to blow her nose because she had begun, pitifully, to cry. It was all too much, she thought, crossing the hallway. Patrick might think this was a country of possibilities, a land of milk and honey, but he did not know about the prejudice of people here, people who knew nothing of the world. Well, he was going to be shocked. He would tell them to come home immediately.

Ada rummaged in the drawer, then, glancing miserably at herself in the mirror, noticed Beth standing behind her. The child's face was very pale. Ada swung round in alarm. Beth's large eyes were dark circles in a white mask.

Ada, horrified, cried out, "Beth, what have you been doing?" There was no need to ask. She could smell the talc. Beth had coated her face with a thick layer of powder. "Oh, Beth. Come here, darling." She put out her arms.

Beth stood where she was.

"I don't like brown skin. I don't want to look like Daddy. I want to look like you."

"You don't want to look like me. Insipid like me. You're so lucky with your colouring. In Singapore the really beautiful girls..."

"I want to see Amah. I don't like it here. I want to see Amah." Beth shook her head, and the tears were rolling down her cheeks.

"Darling, darling," Ada said, and took a handkerchief from the drawer, knelt in front of the child and gently began wiping off the powder. "Amah's thinking of you all the time. Remember the day she took us to her temple? She threw paper money into a big oven to bring good luck for us." The doors of the temple had been heavily studded with nails and emblazoned with thrashing spike-tailed dragons. In the courtyard, beside a rotund Buddha, a group of old men in shorts and singlets had sat in the sunlight spinning down through the red rafters.

"When is the good luck going to come, Mummy?"

"Soon, very soon, darling. It'll be all right." She forced a smile. But they would need more than luck or prayers. An image came to her of a man in dirty khakis standing in a crowded noisy room. "I have duties," he had said. "You are strong, Ada." She sat down on the end of the bed, placed Beth on her lap, and facing the mirror stroked Beth's hair. Give me the pain, she wanted to cry out. I can take it. Not this child. This beautiful, innocent child.

Chapter 7

THE SCRIPT WAS SHAKY. ADA immediately pictured Patrick limping around the house, a frail old man, and, remorseful for having worried him, read with guilt.

'Dear Ada,

It saddened me greatly to read that Beth is facing such unkindness from the children. Of course, this is how they learn to be from their parents. Children are taught to be prejudiced, and you really cannot blame them for what they pick up from their elders. The only thing that you can do is to teach Beth to ignore the taunts because stupid people are making them, people who will come to nothing. They know very little about the world and hate everything that is unfamiliar to them. Their prejudice is something they hold on to because they are frightened of people from other places, and they hate what they fear.

There is only one way for Beth to overcome the ignorant, and that is to do better than them. You tell me she is doing well at her school work. Don't let this suffer. Ask her to send me one of her drawings and little stories. I know that you have thought to return here. But Ada, you would be out of the frying pan and into the fire.'

There followed a litany of troubles about inflation, the communists, government mishandling of strikes, and the difficulties of finding servants who these days were indifferent and, even worse, insolent. The cook served up burnt offerings no matter how much Patrick complained, and now that Ahmad had gone with his nephew to relatives in Johore, the new gardener let the lallang grow like a jungle while he gorged on durian and left the husks piled up to attract the flies. And every day there was more bad news to cope with.

'Remember Jimmy, Michael's Chinese friend? I heard a few weeks ago that he died under torture as well. You are far away from all these dark tales. You and Beth have the chance of a much better life. Remember how you coped in Changi. You learned to adapt. Adaptation is the key to survival. Those of us who survived know that.

However, I understand from a previous letter that you find the quarrelsome nature of your sister's marriage distressing, and dislike Beth having to experience this unpleasantness. So, with this factor in mind, combined with what you say about the insularity of the people in a small place, and your own lack of friends, I wonder if it might be a good idea to move to the larger town you tell me you go to sometimes in the bus. You would still be near enough to Vera. Try and see what you can rent there, and let me know. It might be you will need more than I am providing now, but I've recently managed to retrieve most of my money from overseas. I'll be able to give you the money I invested for you from your mother's estate, but there should be no need for you to use that, because in addition I will have money from my house which I'm getting ready to sell. It is far too large for me. And Charmaine and John prefer to have a place of their own, which they intend to buy near me when I move. You must think of yourself in all this, Ada. You need to feel that you can manage. It is not easy being both father and mother.

I gave Amah your love, as you told me to do. She often asks about you both, and I read your letters to her. This time I made some of it up, I'm afraid, because it would upset her to know that you and Beth were unhappy. She lights her joss sticks for you both every day she tells me, to bring you good fortune. Sadly, she will be leaving soon to become an Auntie.'

Ada's cheeks coloured reading about Amah. It was the colour of shame she'd felt before, reminded of Amah's strong independent spirit. Ada imagined the tenement room, the old amahs (known as Aunties now in their well-deserved retirement) cleaning the cramped space, gossiping, playing cards, drinking tea, enjoying their last years, no matter their poverty. She could not help comparing her own friendless state with the companionship the old women would have. Holding the letter, she wandered through the kitchen and out onto the porch steps.

The garden was rough with limp plants injured by frost, and broken twigs and leaves after days of unforgiving winds. The door of the shed, unfastened, swung back and forth. She thought to shut it, but remained where she was. She felt trapped and impotent. Although she was trying not to let Beth sense her anxiety - remembering well how burdensome it was when Elizabeth had allowed hers to be seen - it gnawed away in her guts. Thankfully, Beth was not complaining about being bullied, and had not tried again to coat her face with talc - perhaps because Miss Mathews had promised Ada to keep an eye on the culprits, and Linda had lost interest in Beth. But who knew when Beth would be hurt again?

★ ★ ★

Ada decided to tell Jim and Vera what Patrick had advised the next day, Saturday. Jim had come in from the garden for a cup of tea after tidying up the vegetable patch. Possibly because he was pleased with his efforts, he managed to ignore Vera's indolence when he entered the dining room to put another shovel of coal on the fire. Vera was seated before the fire, drinking coffee and reading a romance novel. Through the window, Ada could see Beth in her coat and striped woollen hat. She was munching a biscuit, and watching the hens pecking for worms in the upturned soil.

"I heard from Patrick yesterday," Ada began.

The two listened attentively.

"I think it would help Beth to be in a larger school, and have a fresh start."

They looked baffled.

"How can a bigger school help?" Vera asked. "There'll be more kids to cope with."

"She'll have more choice of friends," Ada said, thinking of herself as well, how she might have the chance to meet other mothers not in the thrall of Mrs. Watts.

"You won't like it," Jim said. "You'll want to be back here instead of stuck in some pokey flat with a dirt yard out the back." Jim's tone was gruff, and he looked as if he'd been insulted.

"I'm sure I'll miss your lovely home and the garden," Ada said.

"Too right you will."

"Oh, don't go, Ada." Vera looked dismayed. "I'll miss you and Beth like anything."

The words echoed. Hadn't Vera said the same thing when she'd left Singapore for Australia? Ada recalled how Vera had urged her to leave as well. She'd refused because she was afraid of being in a strange place, starting again - and she'd lived to regret it.

"I'm not going back to Singapore. I'm only going to be in town, and I can come into the store. You can call in for tea on your way home if I find somewhere to live on this side of town. And so can you, Jim. Beth and I won't lose contact with you. You're both very important to her. She loves you both."

Jim's face softened. "It'll cost you a bob or two."

"I know. But I don't want much. And...and Patrick will help me a bit more, until I find a job."

"What job?" Jim narrowed his eyes, smiling in disbelief.

Was Jim implying that she was getting above herself? Ada blushed with annoyance.

"There's a part-time job coming up in the lingerie department. They're interviewing next week in fact, though it won't come up until Marg leaves to have her baby," said Vera.

"Lingerie department," Jim scoffed. "Well, that's one way of getting your knickers cheap."

"Yes, if you worked part-time, you'd be home in time to get Beth from school." Vera spoke in a loud confident voice, ignoring Jim's snigger. "Actually, the more I think of it, I'd say you're doing the right thing. I'd give my right arm not to be living out here."

"Right arm, eh." Jim snorted. He said over his shoulder as he began to leave the room, "Yeah, who needs a right arm if you never use it except to powder your nose or wipe your privates?"

"Oh, shut up."

"You're going to have to use it now, though, with your sister gone."

"You're the fuss-pot, you clean the house."

Jim took a couple of steps back.

"What did you say?" he asked belligerently.

Ada heard Beth running into the porch.

"Jim. What are you doing?" Beth called. She burst into the room. "Are you coming, Jim?"

Ada could see him wanting to continue with the quarrel but, perhaps realising that it would be wrong to do so in front of Beth, he followed the child outside, much to Ada's relief.

"I'll miss you, Ada, but go. Go," Vera said. "Only a fool would stay out here. And who knows, I might just join you." Vera picked up her book, and began to read, clearly not wishing to be quizzed or challenged on her remark.

Ada was in no mood to press her, either - she was struggling to work out what she should do next. Would it be wise to find a job first? She did not want to be more dependent on Patrick. But she did not want to remain with Vera and Jim.

"When's the interview in the lingerie department, Vera?"

Ada sat on a customer's chair by the main entrance of the store, waiting for Vera. She fiddled with the strap of her handbag and wished that she could catch the bus home instead of going to the pub with Vera and Jim. They'd suggested a drink after work as a celebration for Ada getting the job. Vera had organised for the teenage daughter of the woman in the village store to fetch Beth from school and babysit, assuring Ada that she knew the family, and that the girl could be trusted for a few hours.

Ada watched Vera take cash out of the till and stuff a metal cylinder, then reach up and fasten it to a wire which carried it speedily to the accounts' office set on a level above. The clock tower across the road struck 5:30, and immediately the other assistants began clearing the counter and putting things away in the glass-fronted drawers behind them. As soon as the last dawdling customer sidled out, they took their handbags from under the counter and eyed themselves in their compact mirrors, dusting their noses and reddening their lips.

Soon, there was a rapid exodus of the entire staff, men coming swiftly down the wide staircase from soft furnishings and fixing on their hats. Amidst a flurry of farewells, Vera came across to Ada.

"So?" she asked. Ada shook her head. "Oh, dear." Vera sounded genuinely surprised.

It had been a humiliation. The woman who had interviewed Ada was quite civil, but it was the slight recoil when she'd held Ada's hand which had been mortifying. The hand must have felt rough, and the critical light in the woman's eyes when she looked up from a covert glance at it told Ada what she already knew. "I used to do a lot of washing and cleaning. I was in Singapore during the war," Ada had said. She did not want pity, and she did not get it.

The woman's neck coloured slightly. "Our hands are always on show, and in the lingerie department when we're dealing with delicate material, well, you know."

Ada explained to Vera about the coarse hands, the thin nails.

"I should've given you a manicure," Vera said. She began talking about the woman who had interviewed Ada. "A bit stuck up. Hubby's only a fireman, too." She adjusted her Ming blue hat with its sprightly feather.

Jim appeared from behind an island of dress materials. He paused and glanced critically at the display of fabrics draped like Grecian togas over gold painted cardboard columns, then strode towards the women at the entrance. He did not greet them. "Are you ready then?" he asked, slamming down the bolts of the doors. "Wait for me outside. I'll get my coat."

Vera took Ada's arm and ushered her through a side-door. While they waited for Jim, Ada glimpsed her reflection in the store window. Among the fanned arrangement of towels and bed linen, a petite woman with sloping shoulders stared critically back at her. You're not going to get any job looking like that, she told herself, and straightened her spine.

"Not sure what people will think of it," Vera said, indicating the window display when Jim joined them.

Jim sniffed loudly.

"The dresser's a queer. Hasn't got any idea. Keeps walking around and flapping his hands all day."

Vera patted her hair, surveying her image in the glass with a pleased smile.

"I like Peter, actually. He's just not suited to the place. Like me. It's a blessing in disguise, Ada, you didn't get the job."

Jim glanced questioningly at Ada, but then started walking briskly ahead. Vera's face was composed into a mask of serenity, although her high heels were snapping along. There was not much time. Ada noticed her reflection again, and felt shaded out, nearly to the point of extinction, in her grey coat and low heels, beside Vera's stylish swagger.

They sped past the open door of the pub, and men's voices blasted out as if someone had turned a radio on full. Ada got a whiff of tobacco and hops. Another door, and Jim pounced on it, tugged it open and led them into a room with a brass plate above the door inscribed 'Lounge Bar.' Jim did not sit, and hurriedly demanded they make their requests. Soon, he came back with two slender glasses of shandy on a tray for the women, a frothing jug of beer for himself, and an empty glass. He was barely seated before he filled it with beer, drank thirstily, refilled, and drank again. It was aptly called the six o'clock swill, Ada thought.

The room had the stale smell of disuse. A raucous hubbub could be heard through the adjoining door. Vera went off to the Ladies; nearby, a couple talked in hushed tones. Apart from them, no one else came in. Ada noticed the fly-dotted parchment shade of the single over-head light, the barred electric heater on the wall, and the faded curtain that hung half-way up the window with the capital letters shaded in black advertising Dominion Bitter. She wondered how Vera could consider being here a treat.

Jim leaned towards Ada, as if about to divulge a secret.

"The job wouldn't have suited you, anyway. They don't get many customers. Women can't afford fancy wear nowadays. Fair dinkum, if it's a choice of a good meal for your family or a lacy pair of pants, what would you choose?"

Ada nodded. She was thinking of alternatives. "I used to do Municipal work. I could operate the Power Samas machine. It did the electricity and water bills."

"Power Samas machine." Jim raised his eyebrows. "You won't find one of those here. People can work things out in their heads over here."

Ada suddenly felt the urge to tip her shandy over his head. She picked up her glass and took a big gulp, then said, "When I get a flat in town it'll be easier to look for work."

Chapter 8

January, 1948

"I've a man who cuts the lawn. But I'm afraid to say that I've let the garden go a bit," Jess said, shading her eyes. Her hair was white, her lined cheeks soft and pink. Ada guessed her new landlady was in her early seventies – as old as Judith had been in the camp, as old as Patrick was now.

"I think it's beautiful," Ada replied.

The garden was long and wide, once part of a sheep farm that had been sold and divided into large sections during the 1920's. Jess told Ada that her house, on one of the sections, was the original nineteenth century homestead. Jess and her husband had been the second owners, and after she'd been widowed Jess had divided a part of it off for a two-bedroom flat. Ada was delighted with it. Jess had furnished it simply – brass beds, a comfortable settee and two small armchairs in the sitting room, a wooden table and four chairs in the kitchen. Ada liked the cheerful red of the cupboard doors, the glint of the brass when the sun shone into the bedrooms. She planned to sew cushions from some batik cloth she'd brought from Singapore, and with a few knickknacks, when she could afford them, it would begin to feel like a home, the very first home of her own. The flat was cheap, cheaper than the ones Ada had seen. Admittedly, Jess's place was near the freezing works, in the poorer part of the town, but Ada suspected that Jess was less interested in the money than in having companionable tenants.

Patrick agreed to continue supporting her. All he desired, he had said, was for Ada and Beth to be happy and well settled in a country of peace. He had written of the strife in Singapore, the aggression of the communists.

It troubled her to think of him having to endure more upheaval in his old age when he deserved a peaceful life. She worried about his safety and wished that she could persuade him to leave Singapore and join her, but she knew that he never would, and that Charmaine and John, whom she thought might like to escape Singapore, also would not come because of him. When she'd written and thanked Patrick for his continuing generosity, she'd pledged to herself that she would not be indebted to him for much longer. She would find a job as soon as she could.

"You've got lots of lovely flowers, Jess." Ada watched the butterflies dancing over the well-stocked beds. Fat hydrangea bushes crowded against the tin fence. A vine was growing up the side of the house, and there were nectarine and peach trees at the far end of the garden. In the fortnight she'd been in the flat, she had been made aware of one neighbour by his smoker's cough, which announced his investigation of the letterbox each morning. On the other side lived a worn-looking woman who'd barely acknowledged Ada's greeting when Ada had passed her standing by her gate a couple of days ago. The snub made Ada wonder how she would ever make a friend. It seemed impossible that she would meet anyone like Melanie again.

Several large bushes in the front garden hid the houses opposite, and provided some privacy from the road, though few cars passed and few people, apart from an infrequent dog walker, a child on skates, or the men – mainly Maoris – cycling home after their shift at the nearby freezing works. They looked round-shouldered with exhaustion, pushing down on the pedals with their heels. Who said Maoris did not know how to work, she thought, watching them the previous day. Jim had, of course.

"I like gardening. Just tell me what you want doing, Jess."

Jess put out her hand and touched Ada's wrist.

"I hope you and your little girl will be happy here."

"I'm sure we will," Ada said. She watched Beth kneel to stroke Jess's black cat, Humphry, lying stretched out like a sleek panther on a bald patch of the lawn.

The child did not complain about leaving Jim's. In fact, she seemed very happy with her own room, the big garden and Humphry, and she liked Jess. Jim and Vera also said that she could visit them anytime. Jim had already called in twice, offering to do any odd job Ada wanted, and on both occasions had brought a book for Beth. He really did spoil the child. On her birthday, he and Vera had prepared a picnic feast: a table laid in the orchard, candles in brass holders, chicken drumsticks with homemade tomato sauce, and an iced fruit cake bought from the newly opened continental shop on the main street.

If Beth did not love seeing him, rushing outside as soon as she heard the bicycle wheels swish past the kitchen door, Ada thought she would do more to discourage him from coming because it had been tiresome hearing him complain about Vera. After talking with Beth for a while, and after she'd gone outside to play, he'd drunk a cup of tea and talked about his work, the fussy customers, the useless colleagues - then about Vera, her continuing laziness, and extravagance.

"It's none of my business, Jim," Ada had said. But she'd hinted that Vera might be keener on working and saving if she had a little more fun with him. There had to be a compromise.

"Yeah. But her ladyship doesn't know the meaning of give and take. All she wants to do is to tog up and gad. The latest plan is to pretend she's someone else." Ada understood this to be the amateur dramatic society Vera had recently joined.

As Ada watched Beth tickle Humphry, obligingly lying on his back, she thought a little anxiously of her claim to Beth that they were moving so she could be happier at school. The teacher, whom they'd met on their initial visit to enrol Beth, did seem pleasant though; she sympathised when Ada had told her about the bullying and Beth's feelings of loneliness. Miss Price, a young and pretty woman, seemed to understand that it was important to keep a look out for bullying, and had assured Ada that Beth would fit in well when the new school year started in February, after the summer holidays. Of course, Ada had not mentioned her own need to move into town.

Humphry righted himself and strolled up to Ada. She bent to stroke him as he began curving his warm, silky body around her legs.

"Come inside and have a cuppa," Jess said, gesturing towards the house. "Beth can give Humphry a bowl of milk." She picked up the cat and led them towards the wooden steps of the back verandah on her side of the house. In the kitchen, Ada sat on the window seat and watched Beth as she carefully poured the milk, then squatted down to observe the contented lapping. "Go through," Jess said to Ada, indicating the living room.

A clock chimed on a side-board made of a rich, blond wood. It was nearly the size of the side-board in Serangoon, and suited the large room. The house was about the same age as Jim's – 'colonial', people called it – with high ceilings and long sash windows, but had not suffered the same neglect over the years. French doors opened onto the side verandah, and light filled the room. It seemed to reach in on all sides, up from the polished floor boards, and down from the snow-white ceiling where bunches of plaster fruit were clustered in the corners above the wallpaper frieze of delicate violets. The airiness provided Ada with a wonderful sense of peace. Books lined the shelves and were stacked in neat piles on the floor. Ada was examining them when Jess returned with a tray.

"You read a lot, Jess?"

"Too much, probably. Should spend more time doing the chores. As you can see, I need more shelves. I'll get my favourite furniture-maker around to take some measurements. He did my side-board. Don't you think it's handsome?"

Ada agreed it was, then said, "You mentioned that you used to be a teacher?" Jess reminded her of Judith. It was a comforting comparison.

"Just the little ones. Loved the little ones." She looked kindly at Beth who was cuddling the docile cat, his soft body spilling over her arms. "Take him outside, Beth, if you want to."

Beth nuzzled her face in the fur. "We're going to find a hiding place."

Beth was darkening with the summer sun, and Ada thought of Evaline with a twinge of guilt, but said encouragingly, "Yes, take Humphry outside, darling." How could you with one breath tell Beth to be proud of her colour, and then with the next tell her to keep out of the sun?

"That shouldn't be difficult," Jess said, her gaze following Beth. The child was chasing the cat, which had slipped from her arms and was racing ahead. "She's a lovely child. It makes me very cross to hear that she wasn't happy. A child deserves the best start in school that anyone can give her."

"I do hope she's not going out of the frying pan into the fire," Ada said, frowning.

"They'll all feel new in the class. The summer break for the little ones is like eternity. She'll have the chance to make friends more easily than starting in the middle of the school year. Don't worry, dear. I always say don't put on the future all the unwanted baggage of the past. It makes travelling forward much more difficult than it needs to be."

"The teacher at her last school said the bullying was because Beth stood out." Ada did not mention Miss Mathews' comment about Beth being well-dressed in case it sounded like boasting, and anyway it was a stupid comment.

"Her work was better than theirs. She'd started to read."

"She'd started to read? My word."

"She couldn't even speak English very well to begin with," Ada began. She'd told Jess that she was a widow, and now passed quickly over the fact of her internment and separation from Beth, then continued to describe the days in the Serangoon house, trailing around the rooms with the doll and coaxing Beth to learn.

After a pause, perhaps noting Ada's brief referral to her internment, and wondering if it would be unwise to question her about this, Jess said, "I hope she hasn't lost her Malay."

"She still has some words, which she uses sometimes. But we discouraged her from speaking it because we were worried that it would stop her from improving her English."

"I hope she doesn't lose it all. Do you speak more than one language, Ada?"

"Malay, and a little Tamil."

"My, how wonderful. You do make me feel small. What little French I learned at school I've forgotten. I only speak English, and I don't do that as well as I'd like." She chuckled, then grew serious. "Few people here can even speak Maori. Isn't that a shame?"

"It's not taught in school?"

"I tried once to get one of the Maori parents to come in each week. Teach the children to name a few things to begin with, and tell some Maori legends, but several of the Pakeha parents – the white parents – complained when they came to hear of it, and the headmaster put a stop to it."

"So what did the Maori parents say about that?"

"Nothing. They accepted that English and not Maori was what their children needed to get on." Jess sighed. "Like you with Beth."

"I suppose it's what many races have accepted. My in-laws told me that mastering the English language helped the

Anglo-Indians to get on. Beth's father was an Anglo-Indian."
She paused. "He died in the war."

"I'm very sorry to hear that, dear."

Sensing the deep compassion in Jess's still quietness, Ada felt a sudden and unexpected urge to cry. She said, her voice breaking a little, "I don't think it was just that Beth could read and write better than the other children that caused her to be bullied. She looks different. She's like her father."

"A very handsome man, then, I take it." Jess said.

"Yes. And clever. Beth's like him in that way, too."

"And you're not clever?"

Ada blushed. "I know I'm not stupid. But I didn't get the chance to finish my education properly. I love to read, though."

"You can always borrow books from me."

"That's very kind. I hope that I can still find the time to read in the evenings when I start working." Jess looked interested. "I'm looking for a part-time job. Once Beth starts school."

"Do you have any idea what you want to do?" Jess asked.

"Not really. I tried for a job as a sales woman but didn't get it. I used to work for the Municipal in Singapore. Making out the bills, that sort of thing," she said off-handedly, remembering Jim's scepticism. "I don't quite know where to start looking."

"The library has a notice board where jobs are advertised. I've never looked at it very closely."

"The job will have to fit with school times."

"I'd be happy to pick Beth up in the afternoons if you couldn't," Jess offered, smiling. "I like to have a walk in the afternoons, and a little chat with a bright young lady would be very nice. I could give her tea."

"Oh, I wouldn't expect that from you, Jess."

"I know you don't expect it, but I love children. My grandchild lives in Christchurch. My son-in-law got a job there a couple of years ago."

Ada wondered if Jess regretted this and was lonely, but there was nothing in the old woman's expression or tone to suggest that she was.

"Anyway, Kiwis like to help one another out when they can," Jess said. "It comes from being pioneers. Having to rely on your neighbour. It's about putting the good words of the Lord into practice. Besides, who knows, you might be able to help me out one day."

*　*　*

Beth sat mutely at the table.

"You haven't done any lessons for a long time, Beth. And it won't be long before you start school. It's a lovely day, and after you've practised your writing, and done your reading, you can go outside."

Beth did not look at her, her features set. Ada felt on edge. She was not in the mood for this, all the persuasion, all the patience. Ada wondered if Beth had too much fun with Jess playing 'Snap' that morning.

Ada had taken up Jess's offer to look after Beth sometimes, and had gone to church for the ten o'clock service. She'd promised herself, and God, that she would go to church when she came to live in town. She no longer had the excuse that the bus did not run on Sundays. The previous week she'd taken Beth to St Matthews, an Anglican church, presumably modelled on an English one because it was not wooden, but grey stone. She'd bought them both straw hats, and Beth had complained that hers was scratchy. The discomfort might have been the cause of Beth's restlessness during the service. The sermon was delivered by a tall thin man with white hair. He'd spoken in a monotonous voice, and what he said drifted over Ada's head. Beth was fidgety; Ada had to give her little warning looks, and a woman glanced disapprovingly down the pew. Afterwards, when the congregation queued to shake the minister's hand, the woman had said to Ada, "children don't generally come to the morning service. They go to Sunday school." The woman did not smile, and her voice was artificial. She sounded like she had swallowed a plum - Elizabeth would say this of anyone who put on airs.

As Beth refused to go to Sunday school, Ada had left her with Jess, and had gone on her own to pray in her stiff hat and uncomfortable shoes. After the service, two women had approached her, welcoming her to the town. But Ada felt they were more interested in impressing her with their own importance – she'd learned that one was the wife of a lawyer, the other of a dentist – than in speaking to a newcomer who did not wear gloves (Ada had noticed them glancing at her hands), and who had a strange accent. She'd been annoyed by this, and felt distracted later by the inner debate she was having about whether she could stop going to church and continue to pray at home in the customary way with Beth before the child went to sleep. Would it really matter to God if she and Beth gave thanks for what they had, and a swift round of blessings for everyone they knew, in a bedroom rather than a church?

Ada pulled out a chair and sat down at the table opposite Beth and looked seriously at her. Beth immediately turned her head to avoid Ada's gaze.

"I've got a lot to do today, Beth. I've got a lot on my mind. We've found you a lovely school, and a lovely teacher who's looking forward to having a clever little girl in her class. You're a lucky girl, Beth."

"Why am I lucky?"

"You don't know what I would've given to have had a good education and become a teacher. If you do well at school you could become a teacher, Beth."

"I don't want to be a teacher."

"Well, there are a lot of other things you can be. There are other interesting jobs clever girls can do to earn money and be very independent, and do some good in this world. Like being a nurse. Even a doctor." She was thinking of Doctor Williams in the camp. Or a journalist, she thought, remembering Freddy Bloom. "But whatever you do you still need to do well at school. You have to read and write very well and know your tables."

"I already know how to read and write very well. And I know my tables."

"I don't know what the matter is with you, Beth. You've always loved your lessons." Worriedly, Ada studied the unhappy little face. "Come on now, let's settle down and…"

Beth got to her feet, knocking over the chair in her haste.

Ada raised her voice, even though she knew that it would only make matters worse. "Sit down, Beth. Now. I haven't the time and energy for this." She put out her arm to catch Beth making for the door. Beth squirmed, and Ada held on tightly. Beth dropped down onto the floor. "Get up, Beth. I've had enough. You're being very naughty." Beth did not move. Feeling impotence, the rage of it, Ada smacked the child's leg, and Beth cried out. Ada stood up, shocked by her own behaviour. She'd never lost her temper before with Beth, had never imagined she would ever hit her child. Michael never used a cane on his pupils; he'd said to do that would be losing the argument. She wanted to apologise, explain that it was tiredness and worry – yes, worry about finding a job without having qualifications - which had made her strike out. Yet at the same time she wanted to scold Beth, force her to do what she was told.

Beth was on her feet, and then she was out the door.

✸ ✸ ✸

"I'm sorry, Jess." Beth was sitting on Jess's settee and drinking a glass of lemonade. "She knows that she's got to be invited." Ada thought Beth might have gone to hide in the garden, but going out to search for the child, framing in her mind an apology that might carry the dual message that hitting someone was not right but then neither was disobedience, she'd heard Beth's voice through Jess's open window.

"She's not pestering, Ada."

Ada wondered if Beth had said that she'd been smacked, and whether there was a soft rebuke in Jess's tone.

"Finish that up and thank Jess, Beth."

Beth looked reproachfully at Ada.

"There's no need to hurry, Ada," Jess said. "Why don't you sit down for a while? Would you like a drink? Something cold. It's such a hot day." For a fortnight now, the days had been growing increasingly warmer, breaking without a flaw in the dazzling blue, holding themselves still and dry so that the earth was becoming nobbled and grey, aging with the flowers and the grass.

"That's why I thought it was a good afternoon to do a little quiet writing and reading," Ada explained. She looked imploringly at Beth, then helplessly at Jess, who raised her brows quizzically.

The sun was streaming through the open French doors. Normally, Beth would be in the garden with Jim on a fine day like this, Ada realised, and they'd not gone for two weekends because of church, plus the fact that school was starting soon.

"What would you like to do then, Beth? Have a picnic in the garden? Or go the park?" Beth did not answer.

Ada moved to the front window to hide her face. She was close to tears, upset because she felt that she had been unfair to Beth. Beyond the shrubs she could see into the street. The red roof of the house opposite glittered in the bright sun. Then a boy in white shorts, wearing a towel draped around his neck and bathing trunks on his head like a party hat, cycled slowly past along the road, the tar seal a shimmering black like a melting strap of liquorice. Through the open window she could hear cicadas drilling away in the long grass. In Singapore, on a day like this – well, later perhaps, when it was cooler – she would go with Michael to swim in the sea. A couple of times she'd taken Beth to Katong, and would have gone again if not for that experience - a man following them from when they'd got off the bus; she'd thought he was going to rob her. Anyway, it had put her off from travelling on her own, and Amah was too busy, Patrick too frail to go to the beach. Thinking back, she felt regret for depriving Beth of an opportunity to learn to swim. Why, Noel had taught Vera and herself by the time they were Beth's age.

"A boy just passed. He looked like he was going swimming," Ada said, turning to Jess.

"There's a swimming pool near Mahora School. I should've told you. How stupid of me. Why don't you take Beth? You can have the togs Susan, my granddaughter, used to wear when she stayed with me. I never throw anything away. Charlie, the man who did my book shelves and side-board, is the life-guard. He could be there today. A big man with a head of curls. Tell him I sent you. He'll show you the ropes. Ask for Charlie Pankhurst."

Ada said to Beth, "Would you like that, darling? Would you like to go to the swimming pool?" Beth looked puzzled. Ada realised that she did not know what a pool was. "A pool is a very big bath that you can stand up in and move around. It'll be lovely on a hot day like this."

"Why are there ropes in the pool?" Beth asked.

Ada smiled. "There aren't any ropes, but it's where you can learn to swim. Like you were beginning to do in Singapore, in the sea."

Mid-afternoon, Beth and Ada made their way across the school playing field, kicking up puffs of dust from the bristly grass. Even from the road they could hear the screams of children and, once they were at the door in the tin fence that surrounded the pool, the air rang with insanity. It was bedlam: boys jumping in off the sides, hugging their legs beneath them for maximum impact and breaking the water into bright jagged pieces; children in groups, or with their parents, springing joyfully up and down. Water heaved and spilled over the sides of the pool, and splashed onto the hot concrete, which gave off a smoky, medicinal smell. Ada looked down at Beth. The child was open-mouthed.

"Do you want to go in, Beth?" Perhaps they could find a quiet corner in the shallow end.

Ada led a dumb-struck Beth into a windowless shed marked for girls. Clothes were strewn along the benches. The sun's heat grilled the tin roof. Sweating, Ada pulled on Beth's costume, then her own, and hand in hand the two emerged into the bright sunlight and stood bewildered at the door of the shed.

"You look lost," a voice said.

Ada saw a tall man with a whistle, hung around his neck on a red cord, walking towards them along the side of the pool. His brown skin and vivid smile instantly reminded her of Ali, who used to bring the fish and vegetables to the boarding house.

"It's our first time here."

"First time, eh. So, do you know how to swim?"

"I do, but my daughter doesn't." The man nodded and put out his hand. His palm was rough and broad. Ada felt hers swallowed up in his firm grasp.

"I'm Charlie." He grinned. "A bunch of us are watching out today. You get everybody on Sunday afternoons."

"I'm Ada, and this is Beth," she said, noting his thick, curly hair. "Are you Charlie Pankhurst?" He nodded. "Jess told me to look out for you. I'm renting her flat. She said that you were the life-guard."

"Jess told you to come, eh." Charlie bent down to Beth. "You look like you'd be a good little swimmer, Beth." He straightened, and said to Ada, "I run swimming classes on Sunday mornings. There's a learner pool down there." He pointed to the far end. Ada could see a rectangle of concrete above ground level. "Next week come along. Nine sharp. Get started." He turned and faced the water, brought the whistle to his lips and blew sharply, just once, but the over-boisterous calmed down immediately. He had their respect. Ada felt Beth would be safe with him. "Bring your togs," he said to Ada. "I don't let parents into the learner pool with the kids while I'm teaching them, but you'll be able to swim in the big pool while Beth's having her lesson."

Ada looked doubtful. Charlie, perhaps noticing her expression, said, "It's much quieter first thing on Sunday mornings. You'll get a good swim."

Ada smiled. "I love swimming. I used to swim a lot before I came here. In the sea, though."

"Ah, nothing beats that."

"I'd love Beth to be able to swim in the sea."

"Well, she best learn how to be a good swimmer. You have to watch out for the currents around here. They can be very dangerous. One of the boys in my class drowned a couple of years ago. Which is the reason I decided to give up some time to help out here during the school holidays."

"You're a teacher?"

"Woodwork at the Boys' High."

"And you built Jess's shelves?"

"I did. As a favour. She's a good woman. A fan of mine." He grinned, then noticed Beth tugging at Ada's hand. "Time to get wet, eh."

Chapter 9

FEBRUARY, 1948

IT WAS A STILL WARM night; the cicadas were making a racket. Ada was reminded of evenings with Elizabeth on the verandah in Geylang, the exquisite pleasure of rest in the cooler air. She gave a small sigh of relief as she sat down beside Jess on the porch steps.

"You sound tired, Ada," Jess remarked, handing her a cup of coffee from the tray beside her.

"I'm grateful to be sitting down. I've got to fit into the afternoons and evenings what it used to take me all day to do."

"You don't have to do the watering you know, dear."

"Oh, no, I enjoy that." After clearing up the supper dishes and hearing Beth read, she did feel tired, but it was a pleasure to see the child running with delight under the spray. Beth loved to grab the hose and hold it up so the water would drum against the tin fence.

"Yes, you've got your time cut out for you now. You must tell me if there's anything I can do to help," Jess said.

"Actually, I feel I can manage if I keep to a routine." A routine which began with the freezing works' whistle announcing the end of one shift and the beginning of another. She used to resent the piercing shriek that would come out of nowhere, but now it sounded like a rallying cry, a prompt to action. "And it's so much easier in the mornings with Beth really wanting to go to school. She gets dressed and has her breakfast without complaining at all.

I think getting her to have swimming lessons was the best thing possible. It's a pity that there were no little girls from her school in the swimming group though. She hasn't mentioned playing with any girl in her class. It's Timmy did this, Timmy said that."

Beth had made friends with Timmy in the swimming group. It turned out that he was in the same class as her at school. A popular child, he was a staunch and useful ally. From what Beth said, he'd allowed her into the boys' games - marbles being the most popular. Jim had bought her a bag of clear glass ones which Beth loved taking out and holding up to the light to see the swirls of different colours inside. It occurred to Ada that Beth might be turning into a little tomboy - apparently she played bull-rush as well, and cowboys and Indians - but she presumed the child was applying herself well in class since Miss Price had not said anything to the contrary.

"Beth can swim…dog paddle, a whole length of the learner pool now. Charlie's been a wonderful teacher. Strict but encouraging."

"He's very good with children. His pupils love him. I got to know him through helping out in the Boys' High library for a little while a few years ago. His father was a school teacher too, from England - hence his surname, Pankhurst. His mother was a Maori."

That explained his looks: the dark hair and brown eyes, with a band of freckles noticeable across his high-bridged nose.

"Has he children of his own? she asked.

"No. Well, I don't think so. He's never mentioned them. Or a wife. Any relative. I get the feeling he's a bit of a loner. Engaging and friendly with people, but there's something reserved about him as well. Not an open book, you might say."

Perhaps he's defending himself, Ada thought. He was of mixed race. He might have experienced a lot of prejudice when he was young. Would Beth grow up to be defensive, too?

Jess continued, "I suppose he hasn't told you about his carvings. He's an excellent craftsman. I didn't expect him to do my bookshelf when I asked him if he knew of anyone who could – one of his ex-pupils, for instance. But he offered himself. He's coming back to measure up for another one too, shortly. Bless him."

"That's good of him. And it's good of him to give up his time to be at the pool. Beth likes him very much, loves to chat to him. I heard her telling Charlie last time about Skippy, one of Jim's lambs that went missing. She still hopes he'll turn up. No one's had the heart to tell her she was eating him at Christmas lunch."

It had been such a hot afternoon, too hot for roast lamb. Ada pictured Jim, sweat on his brow, carving the meat. Thankfully, for all his talk about the need to know where your food came from, he'd not revealed it was Skippy on the platter. But it had been a rather tense occasion altogether, what with Vera speaking longingly of Christmases in Singapore; how they'd return home after carol service at St Andrew's and Noel would hand out the presents dressed up as Santa Claus.

Jim had looked annoyed. He'd got up early to pick the vegetables and made himself responsible for cooking the meal – basted the lamb with loving care, made sure the potatoes were golden crisp – but Vera, after congratulating him briefly on his efforts, was more interested in talking about Singapore. Ada had thought to tell Beth of the Christmas party in Serangoon soon after her birth, soon after the first bombs fell on Singapore, Evaline insisting on the decorations, food, dancing and singing, as in past years. But, aware of Jim, she kept quiet, and then, reminded of what Michael had said that day about his move to the north of the island to supervise the defences, it had been a struggle to appear cheerful for Beth's sake.

It wearied her to think back. She finished her coffee and put the cup on the tray.

"It's such a lovely evening. I could stay out here for ages, Jess. But I need an early night." She reached for the tray to take it inside. "Thank you for the coffee."

"Leave that, Ada. You've had a busy day."

"It's no trouble." The good thing about being very busy was that there was little time to dwell on the past.

✴ ✴ ✴

They set off for school the next morning with Ada pushing the bike and Beth on the carrier. The bike was secondhand, bought from a friend of Vera's. In time, Ada told herself, she would cycle, but she was a novice and did not want to fall with the child.

It was Vera who'd insisted on teaching Ada to ride in order for her to be more independent. Ada, recalling how nervous she'd been, chanted, "One, two, three, four, five."

"Why are you counting, Mummy?"

"I'm remembering my bike lesson. How Vera made me count to five before I put my foot down."

"You were funny," said Beth. "You kept on falling off."

"But I got back on, Beth. I got back on. I proved I could do anything if I was really determined. It made me find the job at the hospital."

The job for a ward and scullery maid in the nurses' home of the General Hospital had been advertised in the library. Ada had hoped for an office job, despite what Jim had said, but the maid's job was the only one for part-time work. She was not afraid of menial work; she'd been accustomed to doing it in the boarding house. And she'd done it in Changi and Sime while she was ill and weak. When Miss Hullet, the supervisor, had heard this at the interview, she told Ada that there was no question of her not being able to manage.

"Have a good day, darling," Ada said when they reached the school gate. Beth kissed her in reply, and, without a glance back, walked into the playground.

Ada clambered on to her bike and rode with care into Cornwall Park, a shortcut to the hospital. The path meandered between banks of rhododendrons, past a pond with two swans, and finally reached an oblong cage housing a peacock and his mate. When Ada slowed to admire the male parading with his tail spread, the female let out a sharp eerie cry as if wanting to gain the attention so readily given to her gorgeous partner. Or perhaps, Ada thought, as she pedalled on, it was a shout of protest. Because what could be worse than being confined forever? She knew about confinement, not only as an internee in Changi, but also as the woman who not so long ago had felt trapped having to live in someone else's home and tiptoe around their lives. Yes, she might only be a hospital maid, but she was going out to work, she was earning her own money, and soon would not have to rely so much on Patrick.

When she reached the hospital, it was early enough to stop at the workers' canteen for a slice of hot buttered toast. A plump, woolly-haired woman with a cigarette stuck on her bottom lip slid the plate across the counter without a word or glance. Ada did not care that she was ignored, although she wondered at the smoking. Miss Hullet would have your head for doing that.

In the ward storeroom, Ada pulled out the mop and bucket and the broom and dusters from the musty cupboard, then unhooked her pink smock from the peg. She was the first to arrive every morning. Miss Hullet, a tall broad-shouldered woman, had already noted in her gruff sergeant major voice that Ada did not keep Maori-time. The comment made Ada feel uneasy. It suggested that the supervisor believed, as Jim did, that the Maoris were lazy. Also, Miss Hullet would nod in a blunt, approving way when she saw her, while she had nothing but a frown for Rangi or Kaia, who always made up for lateness by their hard, efficient work.

Miss Hullet appeared in the doorway. "I want you on the counter today, Ada. One of the servers is off sick for a few days. Finish here a bit earlier and come across to the canteen. You'll be helping Irma."

Fifteen minutes before midday, Ada presented herself in the nurses' canteen and obediently stood beside Miss Hullet as she issued instructions. Irma was nowhere to be seen.

"Today it's roast mutton. We usually have a roast, and most of them will go for that, but there's also a stew, or a slice of fish done in batter. Both very popular. You've got that? The next bit's easy. Peas, potatoes, carrots. Don't daub the plate. We pride ourselves in how we present the food here," Miss Hullet said, adjusting her belt and grimacing, as if reminded of a world of sub-standards which she struggled to combat.

"The nurses help themselves to the pudding. The cooks bring them out on trays. It's steamed sponge today, and custard. No one should go wanting, and there shouldn't be much waste. I keep a strict eye on the quantities." She inclined her head towards Ada, as though imparting a secret. "I used to be a cook here. Got promoted because I never shirked on the job. Hard work gets rewarded." She nodded significantly, before turning to scowl at Irma, who'd sauntered in from the kitchen with a backward quip to the cooks - with an impressive nonchalance, it seemed to Ada.

The nurses came in dribs and drabs. Some of them joked with Irma, a former beauty with a ravaged face at odds with her mane of jet black hair. "Keep an eye on the trolley, dear, and take the dirty plates in to the girls before they mount up," she said. Ada knew the need for this. It was hot and sticky work, washing up, and the bench space was limited. Keeping pace was essential.

When she came to deposit the first load, she was met with a wave of damp air and felt grateful to be working in the airy space of the sunlit dining room. Rangi grinned at her.

"What you done to get a cushy job?"

Ada shrugged and smiled. "I was in first, I suppose."

"Yeah? I think Miss Hullet likes a pretty face on the counter, eh." She turned to Kaia, who was laughing, but in a slightly embarrassed way, as if concerned that Ada might think they resented her being chosen.

Did pretty face mean white face? Irma was white. And so was the absent server. There was a Maori cook, but she was hidden in the kitchen.

"It's just for today," Ada said.

Uneasy about being selected, she returned to the counter. She was careful to serve the food without smudging the plate. Miss Hullet sailed in, her broad back erect, her head at an enquiring angle, her eyes darting. With pursed lips, she watched Ada for a moment, then, apparently satisfied, marched across the shiny lino to a table around which three older women sat. One, with grey hair, wore a short red cape which seemed to indicate her status - she was possibly the matron. Miss Hullet bent to speak to her, inclining her head in an obsequious way.

The next day, while Ada was serving lunch, she heard a loud crash. At first she could not see what had happened. When she handed over the plate and the nurse passed on, she noticed Rangi picking up dishes that had fallen from the trolley. Ada realised that the accident was her fault – she'd forgotten to keep an eye on the pile of plates and the stack had become perilously high. But it was Rangi whom Miss Hullet was pushing before her into the scullery as if she were a thief. The swing doors shut, yet the angry voice carried into the dining hall. Ada was conscious that the dining room had grown quiet, and winced when the words 'fool' and 'savages' rode out on the stream of invective.

Ada glanced at Irma, who seemed to be deliberately ignoring what was going on. Ada left her post at the counter and pushed open the swing doors. Miss Hullet had her back to her and was standing with feet apart, hands on hips.

"It was my fault the plates slipped, Miss Hullet. I let them stack up," Ada said.

Miss Hullet swung round to face Ada. "Get back to the counter, you," she said angrily.

Ada remained where she was. "It's me you should be angry with…"

"You're a foreigner. You know nothing about this country. About Maoris. What the white man has had to cope with. Get out."

"Whatever the white man has had to cope with still makes it wrong to call them savages." The words were out for all to hear; perhaps even the matron had heard. Ada felt her face burn, and the heat creep down her neck.

Miss Hullet raised her arm and pointed her finger at Ada.

"Get out. At once. Now. I don't want to see your face around here. Irma will have to manage on her own. I'll speak to you tomorrow."

Ada, blinded by emotion, pushed through the swing doors of the scullery and dining hall, and strode through the kitchen past the benches, the cauldrons, and the surprised faces of the cooks. She flung off her maid's smock in the storeroom, then headed to the bike shed. She was shaking, and nearly lost her balance as she cycled out of the hospital grounds.

It was only when she reached Cornwall Park that she tried to breathe slowly and compose herself. She imagined Miss Hullet, the following day, imperiously beckoning her into the supervisor's glass box at the back of the kitchen. "Your behaviour was outrageous yesterday, Mrs Wood," she'd bark.

"And yours too, Miss Hullet," Ada muttered to herself as she cycled past the peacock strutting about like a pompous lord. It was disgusting, Miss Hullet speaking to Rangi and Kaia like that. There's no way I'm going to apologise, Ada thought.

She was back too early to fetch Beth from school immediately, as she normally did after the final cleaning up of the canteen following lunch. She had time to rest, calm down. But she could not be calm. Her brave thoughts of standing up to Miss Hullet were rapidly becoming lost with the realisation that tomorrow she could lose her job.

The next morning, Rangi and Kaia arrived after Ada as usual, and in their normal good humour. The events of the previous day did not appear to have marked them at all, whereas Ada was exhausted after a sleepless night. When Rangi said, with a broad grin, "You speak up, real good, Ada. You told her straight," it sounded as if her hot-headed behaviour was being praised because she had stood up for herself, rather than in defence of them. She felt foolish, but troubled as well. Were the Maoris so accustomed to being insulted that they did not question it?

She was not summoned to the supervisor's office as expected. Surprisingly, there was no bulky figure waiting for her as she made her dogged way with mop and bucket down the long corridor, but as the morning passed the knot in her stomach grew tighter. It was while she was polishing the corridor floor that a young nurse hurried up to her and delivered a message. It caused her pulse to quicken. She was to go now and see the matron in her office.

The matron was seated at her desk. Ada recognised her as the woman who'd been wearing the red cape in the canteen, and to whom Miss Hullet had showed such respect. Ada expected that the two women had a high regard for each other. In her agitation, as she waited to be reprimanded for her rudeness to Miss Hullet, it took a while for her to focus on the matron's face, and to discern that the matron's expression was far from hostile.

The matron, seated at her desk, indicated a chair for Ada to sit opposite, and clasped her hands on the clean blotting pad.

"You must be wondering why I sent for you?"

With the merest raise of an eyebrow, the matron said in a gentle voice, "I was in the dining hall yesterday. I heard everything. And I saw you leave looking very upset. I just want to tell you that you have nothing to be frightened of. If you were worried that you were going to be punished for speaking your mind, don't be. It took some courage on your part. And we all know how fierce Miss Hullet can be. She is very..." The matron paused, searching for the next word. "Conscientious. She has very exacting standards." She sighed. "But we all have standards of one sort or another, don't we? I know what mine are, and I appreciate what yours seem to be as well. I've had a little talk with Miss Hullet. I hope such an incident does not repeat itself. I expect it won't."

Ada felt profound relief, and with the concern she detected in the warm brown eyes of the matron, she was led by the matron's questions to talk about herself; about being widowed and leaving Singapore; about coming to New Zealand for Beth's sake, for her education. The matron listened patiently and with evident interest.

"I can see that you've had a lot to cope with, Mrs Wood. I admire your courage. You will need a lot of that as a woman on your own. I know from my own experience." Ada noted the woman's ringless hand. "And I hope that you have ambitions for yourself."

"I'm grateful to be working here," Ada replied, then hesitated, judging whether to say more. The matron nodded encouragingly. Ada continued. "But I don't want to do this forever." The matron smiled. "I'd always thought of trying to become a teacher, but I left school earlier than I wanted to. I was planning to continue my studies with a private tutor before I got pregnant, and the war started. I couldn't have been a teacher, of course, because I was married, but I wanted to complete my education."

The matron bent her head, as if summoning her thoughts. When she looked up, her expression was serious.

"Do you have your School Certificate?"

Ada shook her head.

"You could start there."

"Go back to school?" Ada said. The idea astonished her.

"You could go to night school. At the Boys' High. It's modelled on technical colleges in Wellington and Auckland. Evening classes for those who missed out on their education for one reason or another. Like the war. Think about it. If there's a will, there's a way. It seems to me you have the will. Lots of it. And who knows, you could be a teacher. I know of a married woman…a widow actually, who is teaching. I know that the government gave school boards the discretionary power to dismiss married women teachers during the Depression, and though some boards took advantage of that, others did not. So don't abandon your dreams."

Ada felt a rush of excitement. Was it possible that she could do something with her life of which she was truly proud?

While Ada waited for Beth after school, her thoughts taken up with what the matron had suggested, she was only aware that Beth had not come skipping out when the playground was nearly empty. Perhaps she was helping Miss Price?

The classroom door was open. As Ada drew near, she saw Beth seated beside a little girl, both facing Miss Price at her table. Seeing Ada, Miss Price beckoned her inside. Beth turned around. Her hair was dishevelled, and one hair ribbon was torn. Ada glanced at the other girl, and saw that she was Chinese.

"This is Helen Wong, Mrs Wood." Miss Price smiled and rose from her chair. "Now off you go, girls, and get your things." When the two had gone into the cloakroom, Miss Price said quietly to a worried Ada, "A couple of boys were calling Helen names and pushed her over. Beth came to her defence...verbally, the duty teacher said, and got pushed, too."

"They weren't bullying Beth?"

"No," Miss Price said emphatically. "I told her she must come to me if anyone bullies Helen instead of taking the law into her own hands. Helen's quite capable of standing up for herself, anyway. She's an independent little girl. Her parents brought her the first few days, but she comes back and forth to school on her own now. Not far. Her father owns the greengrocers up the road."

Ada knew it - the only place you could buy root ginger, soy sauce and garlic.

"She's a clever child. Speaks very good English. She went to a missionary school in China. Does well in all her lessons."

The girls appeared, carrying their lunch boxes and squares of paper.

"Show Mrs Wood your drawings, girls." She smiled at Ada as the girls held them up. "Aren't they good?"

"They're excellent," Ada said, noting that the stick arms of Beth's figure were, in Helen's drawing, slender ovals, and the face was framed with recognisable ringlets rather than an untidy scribble.

"Can Helen come and play, Mummy? We want to do some drawing."

"Would you like that, Helen?" Ada asked. It would be good for Beth to have a little girlfriend. Timmy, as he grew a bit older, might only want to play with boys. "Why don't we take Helen home now, and ask her parents if that would be all right?"

★ ★ ★

The girls disappeared behind a curtain at the back of the shop as soon as they arrived, leaving Ada to wait for Mr Wong while he served a customer. When she left, Ada stepped forward.

"Hello. I'm Mrs Wood. Our daughters are in the same class."

Mr Wong regarded her intently through his round spectacles. He seemed puzzled.

"I brought Helen home because she and Beth got into a little scuffle at school today. Y'know, name calling."

"They were calling names? What names?"

"They were being called names. The boys were teasing them, and Beth decided to answer back. She got more than she asked for, I think." Mr Wong nodded, his expression grave. "Miss Price scolded the boys, and she's sure it won't happen again. But if you're worried, just go and see her."

Mr Wong looked serious for a moment, as if reflecting on what Ada had said, then put out his hand to shake hers. "Thank you for bringing Helen home. Usually she walks on her own. Not far."

"Yes, Miss Price said she did. I came though because I wanted to ask if Helen could come and play with Beth one day after school. The girls want to do some drawing together." Mr Wong looked bemused. "Helen is very good at drawing, isn't she?" Ada said. "Where did she learn to draw so well?"

"Her mother helps her. Her mother is an artist."

Ada could hear Helen talking in Chinese behind a curtain at the back of the shop. "She's a clever girl. She can speak two languages fluently."

"Children can pick up quickly because their thoughts are simple," Mr Wong replied modestly, but Ada detected from the spark of light in his eye that he was very proud of his daughter.

"Beth had to learn to speak English, too. But she had to be coaxed. She preferred to speak in Malay."

"You come from Malaya?"

"Well, Singapore. I was there during the war. Interned. So Beth was with my in-laws, but mainly with her amah who spoke in Malay to her. Also, the house was occupied by Japanese officers and they didn't want people to speak English."

Mr Wong looked sombre. "It must have been a very hard time for you. The Japanese make hard masters." He hesitated, then said, "Come. My wife would like to meet you. Come." He drew the curtain aside and ushered Ada before him.

A shaft of light fell from a high window on to a bare wooden floor. There was a table, a stool, and a couple of wooden chairs. A woman sat on one of these. The girls had vanished. Ada could hear them chattering along the corridor.

"This is Beth's mother." Mr Wong gestured towards the woman. "My wife, Kwan." Kwan rose and smiled. She was slim, her hair drawn back tightly from a narrow, finely-boned face. "Kwan speaks a little English and is learning quickly at evening classes at the Boys' High School."

"Special class. Few people. Teacher Chinese too." Kwan smiled again, and added apologetically, "I am, what you call… rusty? After summer holiday."

Ada smiled, and thought to confide her own difficulty in going back to studying with Mr Moses, but decided it was too complicated and said instead, "I heard that you're an artist, Kwan. I think your daughter has inherited your talents. She can draw very well."

Kwan frowned, and Mr Wong said, "Helen is like you, Kwan. She learns from you how to draw well."

Kwan shrugged. "She sit and watch me. She draw and paint too. She bring her book and write when I do English homework."

Ada pictured herself and Beth seated at the table working together. It was an encouraging image, and she smiled broadly at Kwan, who nodded and returned the smile. "She likes to do what you do," Ada remarked.

"Yes, she likes to do what her mother does. Child learn best when parent shows what can be done," Mr Wong said.

Helen called, and Kwan made a little bow to excuse herself, leaving Ada with Mr. Wong. He looked behind the curtain for customers, then gave his attention to her.

"New Zealand is a long way from Singapore. You have relatives there."

Ada nodded. "I have a sister here, though. Which is why I came when I knew I had to leave Singapore. It's not a place to bring up a child nowadays. New Zealand is a safe and peaceful country. Beth will have the chance of a better life here."

"That is what I wanted for my family, too. But it took a long time to get permission for them to come. I was a printer in China, but I put my hand to anything. They need greengrocers, I am a greengrocer. I try now to become a natural citizen. I pay tax. I work hard. But still it is not possible. And it is not even possible for those Chinese who lived here during the war and were called to fight."

"That's not at all fair. I can't understand why the government is being so hard."

"It thinks all Chinese are communists. That we are not loyal to this country."

"I was told when I came that there would be no trouble my staying here for as long as I wanted."

"You are all right. You are a British subject, yes? That is why you were interned, yes?" He raised his arms and shrugged.

"I've got a job working at the hospital, which might help as I can prove that I'm making an effort to contribute something to the country. Even if it's not a very important job."

"All jobs are important."

"I know," she said, nodding in agreement.

Perhaps she looked doubtful, because Mr. Wong asked, "You like your job?"

"Not very much, to be honest. I definitely don't want to do it forever."

"What do you want to do?"

"I'd really like to be a teacher one day," she said. This was the second time she'd admitted this today, she realised, thinking of her talk with the matron. It felt more like a commitment this time, a pledge, than a statement of a wish.

That evening, after Beth was in bed, Ada, her mind full with what had happened that day, sat to write her fortnightly letter to Patrick. She began with what she thought would interest him the most – her meeting with the Wongs – although she decided not to tell him the reason why she'd got to meet them. He'd been so pleased to hear that Beth was enjoying school, and Ada did not want him to start worrying.

She also did not tell Patrick the reason she'd spoken to the matron, but she did write about the conversation they'd had.

'I'd like to do my School Certificate, and if I go to evening classes I think Jess, our landlady, would babysit for a couple of hours. She loves Beth and has always said she would happily mind her. Of course, I would do something for Jess in return, like shopping or gardening. Kiwis believe in helping one another out like that. I think it's very strange to have spoken to the matron and the Wongs on the same day. It's as if I've been given a message from somewhere.'

Ada pictured Michael wearing his white suit and carrying his satchel. She imagined him encouraging her not to give up her studies.

'Classes start next month, but I won't be ready to do the course this year.'

She did not write that she had to find out about the fees, in case Patrick thought she was asking for more support from him.

'At least it's something to look forward to doing next year, and it will give me time to do some reading in preparation. Anyway, I'll have to wait and see how things are. But I must say that Beth is so much more confident these days. I don't think we'll have to worry about her being bullied again. She's growing up very quickly. She's asked to have her hair cut to get rid of the ribbons and have a fringe instead. I think it will suit her.

I must sign off now. It's getting late. I hope I can sleep because I've been given a lot to think about.'

Chapter 10

MARCH, 1948

"OH MY, CHARLIE, IT'S LOVELY."

The house was set in a clearing far back from the road, and they'd approached it, once they'd left the road, down a shingle track bordered on either side by tall trees.

"And you built it yourself?"

"Not finished yet, but I'm getting there," Charlie said, taking a box of provisions from the back of the truck.

It was a timber house, long and low, with tall windows and shutters, and a verandah, wreathed in vines turning gold, running the length. The green corrugated iron roof lost itself in the emerald light cast by the trees and bushes.

As she followed Charlie along the path that led to the house, Ada noticed four wooden figures, two standing on either side. They were the height of Beth, with outsized heads and glinting green eyes made from shells. Their thick torsos and broad arms folded across distended bellies were deeply grooved with whorls and spirals. These also framed the head and encircled the eyes, cut fiercely into the cheeks and knotted on the nose, swirled around the gaping mouth, and coursed over the muscles of the shoulders and thighs.

Beth let go Ada's hand and stood in front of one of the figures. "Are these little men?" she asked.

"They're tikis. They stand for the first person in the world," Charlie replied.

"Why do they have all these?" she said, stroking the lined face.

"Those lines are called moko. They tell you lots of things about the person. They also show when that person has become a certain age. Become a beautiful woman or a handsome brave warrior." He went on ahead. "Now come inside and make yourselves at home."

When she entered and looked about her, Ada sensed a tranquility in the room. It was as if the owner had long since acquired the ability to be alone. It seemed like a place where you could contemplate and be creative.

Beth followed Charlie into the kitchen to make tea, and Ada looked admiringly at the stained floor boards covered in bright rag-rugs, the polished patterned gourds on the window seats, the book-lined shelves. She was examining the titles when Charlie returned to the room with a tray of tea things, and a fruit cake which must have been in the box of provisions. She felt touched that he'd gone to so much trouble, especially since it was Beth who had asked to visit.

"It's very kind of you to have us over, Charlie. Not that you weren't pressured," she said, smiling.

Beth had begged to see Charlie's place after he told her about the swimming hole on his property. He'd been having a break from putting up Jess's shelves and was giving Beth another lesson in how to use the short pois on the back lawn, flicking them so they hit the back of the wrist with a neat slap. He was encouraging her to keep a rhythm by singing a Maori song in a smooth baritone. Ada had noted his patience with the child. He'd said nothing to indicate that he'd ever been married, and she wondered what might have prevented him from marrying because he seemed like a man who would have chosen to do so. He was excellent with children.

"No pressure at all. It's a great pleasure," Charlie said.

"You've got a lot of books, Charlie. You like reading?"

"I love Dickens." He handed a glass of milk to Beth seated at the table. "My father loved him, and I inherited all his books. Thackeray, too. Wilkie Collins…I wish Dad hadn't died before I got a chance to read them and talk about them with him. He was always quoting bits. He was a teacher."

"So was my husband," Ada said, sitting down on an old leather sofa. "He loved Dickens and used to quote bits to me." She pictured Michael with a towel around his waist coming out of the shower. 'It's a far, far better thing that I do…' She shut her eyes to cancel the image.

"How old were you when your father died?"

"My parents were killed together in a car crash when I was eleven. I was brought up by my grandmother. She was a good woman, and I owe a lot to her. She encouraged me to do my best at school, but she couldn't read or write, so was pretty impressed with whatever I did, which sometimes might not have been my best."

Ada wondered how it must have been for him to lose both parents at a young age. "You're a teacher, though."

"Oh, yes. Manual stuff." He tapped his forehead. "Not enough of this."

Ada thought how she would have been happy to teach anything – sewing, for instance, instead of running the boarding house.

"This is an ideal place to read. It's so quiet."

"It's my haven in a troubled world." He was grinning, but Ada felt that he meant what he said. She smiled a little uncertainly in return, and, recalling Jess's remark that he was not an open book despite his warmth and friendliness, looked questioningly at him. He shrugged.

"I prefer a quiet life, and I decided that the best way to acquire it was to find a place like this." He turned his back to her and began pouring the tea.

Ada, sensing that he did not wish to explain further, and discounting her feeling of disappointment that here was another man with secrets, said, "A quiet life, but a busy one, I think. Your carvings are beautiful."

He smiled as he handed her a cup and a small milk jug. "I'm glad you think they're beautiful. For some I expect they're an acquired taste. Some of my pupils, for instance."

"Do you teach them how to carve?"

"Not that sort of carving. They mainly want to learn practical things, things they can use. I don't mind. I like teaching."

"My husband did, too. He worked very hard. His pupils loved him," Ada said, and thought of the Japanese interrogator whose son had loved Michael. "I had a teacher called Miss de Silva whom I adored. I wanted to be like her." She shrugged. "Who knows, perhaps I might be one day. Though it's more likely that I'll get a secretarial job. I'm taking shorthand typing and book keeping as additional subjects. But whatever I do I'm not going to be a maid for the rest of my life." Even if the work was easier these days - she knew her way around, she was fond of Rangi and Kaia, and Miss Hullet was treating them all with more respect. It certainly paid to speak up. If she hadn't, she would not have heard about night school from the matron.

"I couldn't manage it all without Jess. When I knew that I was eligible for free tuition, she was adamant that I go ahead instead of waiting for another year. Strike when the enthusiasm's there, she said. She's really for women getting the best education they can. She told me that New Zealand was the first country to allow women to vote in national elections. She said we should take advantage of every chance we get."

Charlie nodded. "She's absolutely right about that. Some of the strongest and most able people I know are women."

"When I told my brother-in-law I was going back to study, and was especially looking forward to doing English again, he said, 'strewth, why do you want to go back to school to learn

English? You can speak all right. You've just got a bit of an accent.'" She laughed, and Charlie rolled his eyes.

"How are you enjoying night school?" he asked.

"Well, it's early days yet. I was nervous to begin with, but I'm not as daunted now as I was. I did have a tutor for a short time in Singapore, after I got married. My husband knew I regretted not going further at school, and encouraged me to study."

Charlie looked curious, perhaps wanting some more information about Michael. Ada had overheard Beth telling Charlie that her father was dead, and that he'd got a medal for being brave driving hurt people to hospital in an ambulance. The ambulance story was a lie that had to continue, but it occurred to Ada that one day she could tell the truth to Charlie. She believed that he would be strong enough to hear her. But it was only a feeling she had. She hardly knew him at all, and from what Jess had said, she might never know him well.

"What are your main subjects?"

"History, English…The English syllabus is nearly the same as Singapore's. Based on the British one too, I suppose. With a few differences, like Katharine Mansfield." She recalled the librarian at the desk, when she'd stamped the book of short stories, telling her that Mansfield was the country's most famous writer, and that she'd gone to live in England, but wrote marvellously about New Zealand. The librarian had said that it must have helped Mansfield to look back and see the place from a distance because people were often blind to things when they were close to them. Ada had wondered at the truth of this claim in reference to herself. Physical distance might help you to see things more clearly, but only if you could bear to look back and cope with being reminded of what you'd lost.

"I enjoy English the most. I find it the easiest. I think I'll manage geography, if I work hard. And history. The causes and effects of the Maori Wars, we've started that. Anyway, I can repeat the year if I don't pass this time."

She thought of her tutor, a thin, studious-looking man. He'd been the one to interview her for entry, and had set her an essay to write in order to assess the standard of her written expression. He was full of praise for her work. He said she had a natural fluency, a maturity of style. She'd been very gratified to hear this, but wondered if Mr Willis had detected her lack of confidence and was simply being kind. Well, she had spent more time trying to decide what to write about than writing it, and then completed it in a rush.

"You look worried," Charlie said.

"I was thinking of something I wrote and wondering if it really was as good as my tutor said. We were asked to describe a memorable scene in our childhood or growing up. I chose to write about the time my sister and I ran away from Amah – the person who looked after us – on the way home from school one day. We both got into trouble, but I was the one who got most of the blame even though it was my sister who'd been the first to run away." She shrugged, remembering how being the elder child singled you out for punishment as much as for privilege. Noel had not taken her out the next week on his trip into Chinatown.

"My tutor asked me why I'd chosen that to write about. I didn't have an answer then." She paused, and Charlie looked enquiringly at her. "I've always thought of myself as being sensible and responsible - compared to my sister, anyway. So I've been wondering about how I'm changing. Starting at night school, for instance." She frowned. "Of course, I worry sometimes that I won't cope. I haven't studied for so long." Reflecting for a moment on what she'd said, she smiled at Charlie. "But I guess that's why I have to have a go. Risk it. Try not to be the cautious person I've always been." She looked at Beth eating the slice of cake Charlie had cut for her. "And now Beth and I do our homework together, don't we, Beth? Like Kwan and Helen."

"You came over here. That was taking a risk. A fairly brave thing to do, I think," Charlie said.

"Well, Vera was here. My sister. She left Singapore before the war started. And as you can imagine after the war Singapore was in a mess. My father-in-law encouraged me to leave. To me New Zealand is a haven. So you're living in a haven within a haven, Charlie!" She spoke quickly to forestall questions.

Charlie grinned. "Do you want me to show you around?" He glanced at Beth. "Do you want to see the swimming hole?"

"Can I swim?" Beth asked.

"We haven't brought your swim suit, Beth. Anyway, the water will be cold," Ada said.

"When it gets warm again, Beth, you can," Charlie said, ushering them outside.

As they walked, Charlie pointed out the trees, naming each one with pride. His tongue curled around the liquid syllables of the Maori names, and Ada was reminded of the Malay language.

"The man who owned this land knew a lot about native trees. He was a Pakeha, but he got it right. These monsters were planted over fifty years ago. If I ever have to sell, I'll only sell to someone who worships the forest. I'll come back and haunt anyone who cuts one down after I'm gone." Charlie rubbed his hands vigorously together as if relishing the idea.

"Who would want to do that? They're so beautiful. Like ancient gods."

He looked quickly at her and there was an appraising glint in his eyes. Then he walked on, his hands shoved into the pockets of his khaki trousers. He had a muscular, compact body, the beginnings of a paunch. Ada guessed he was in his mid-thirties.

"When the Pakeha came to this country they destroyed the native forest for farm land. What they didn't know was that the plants they brought with them would grow like weeds with the native vegetation gone. Like those." He pointed through a gap in the trees at a hillside, where sheep grazed between clumps of a yellow-flowered thorny bush.

"I suppose they needed to make room for the animals, and plant something to remind them of home," Ada said.

"So much room? So much land? They took more than they should've, more than they needed."

Ada noted the aggrieved tone of his voice, and felt that she'd said the wrong thing in defending the English farmers. "Where did you learn how to carve, Charlie?" she asked, changing the subject.

"At a school for carving. Schools were started up as Maori carving was a dying craft. It was the idea of Puea Herangi. A Maori princess. She decided that the Maori people could regain their pride through practising their traditional skills. Storytelling, as well. Singing. Oratory. Peter Buck and Apirina Ngata also wanted that. They were Maori politicians. Both are heroes of mine, but Herangi, well, she had real vision. She was against the Maori fighting in World War 1, whereas the other two felt that by volunteering they could make themselves equal to the Pakeha, and get back their land and demand help to develop it."

Charlie was silent. Ada glanced at him. He appeared to be resigning himself to accept an unpleasant truth.

"The Maori fought for the Pakeha, but they had to wait until 1935 with the Labour party to get the help they needed, such as medicine and schools, and the subsidies given to white farmers. And even then, their land was not restored to them. Not even after fighting again in the last war. You know, in the Depression, the government gave help to the Pakeha, but not the Maori."

"Did the white man just take the land for himself when he came to New Zealand?"

A flock of birds flew over low, crashed through the trees. Quietness fell again, and Charlie continued.

"The Maori signed a treaty with the British, the Treaty of Waitangi, way back in 1840, because they believed if they gave *sovereignty* to the British – that is, allowed the British to *buy* the land – it would give them the rights of British subjects. Medicine and schools. Besides getting protection against the French, and uniting all the tribes so they would live peacefully together under a British monarch."

He rubbed his chin, and frowned.

"But the Maori did not understand what sovereignty meant, and Maori land is owned by the whole tribe. Each member has got to agree what happens to it. In the beginning, when the settlers came, some of the tribe might have agreed to sell off their land, but some would've considered that the land was still theirs. You can understand why the wars took off. 'Hey, who said you could have that? I didn't say you could. Especially if all I get are a couple of blankets and a few muskets.'"

Charlie raked his fingers through his hair.

"The Maori fought hard. But finally they were defeated."

Charlie looked upwards as if searching the sky for answers, then continued, his tone sorrowful.

"They lost more than their land. They starved and got diseases. And what's more tragic, they lost their mana."

"Mana?"

"Pride. It means pride." He shook his head. "My tribe. You should see the way some of them live. It breaks my heart to see them drinking themselves to death, drinking away their sorrows. Using their anger against one another, and often against their womenfolk. It's hard to believe that they had a lot of spirit once." His tone was bitter.

Ada recalled the drunks she'd seen the previous week. She and Beth had been shopping on the main street. Strong-looking Maori boys in their pink bush singlets sat with their feet in the gutter and ate chips from steaming parcels, which smelled of fried fish and newsprint. They spoke to one another in low easy voices; one played the guitar and sang quietly. Ada had been reminded of the Malays passing the time of day. The boys had smiled and winked at Beth, perhaps believing she was a Maori. It had been a shock to be pushed aside by two drunken Maoris staggering along the street.

"That's a terrible shame. My husband used to get very angry about the land being taken away from the Malays. He said that the Malays were being robbed of their livelihood with all the land speculation. The Malays are fishermen and farmers and want to continue with their traditional way of life."

"They sound like us."

"There's even a similarity in appearance. We knew a lot of Malays. They lived in a kampong...a village near our house. They were very friendly. Although we didn't have them as close friends. We knew more Indians and Chinese. Especially at school. They're keen to have an English education. They see it as a means to getting on. The Anglo-Indians put education first, too. My husband was an Anglo-Indian."

"I agree, education is very important. The Maori would be very unwise not to take advantage of all the education they can get. Education helps people get more power over their lives. And stand up for themselves. The pity is that education is not always used for the good. Very clever, educated people have used their knowledge to destroy. To wipe out millions with one bomb."

"You're talking about Japan? Yes, that was terrible. The whole war was terrible."

Beth was running ahead along the path, leading them out from the forest through a glade of ferns. The ground dipped, then rose abruptly again. Beth scrambled excitedly up the rise. Charlie stepped in front of Ada, turned and took her hand to help her up. Several feet below, she could see a stretch of water glinting as it slowly and relentlessly moved between wide shoals of grey shingle. It was like a powerful beast in a lazy mood.

Beth pointed to a rope hanging from a branch of a tree on the edge of the river bank. "What's that for?"

"You hold the end and use it to swing into the water. The water's deep. You have to know how to swim well. But it's safe. I got someone to dredge the shingle to make a loop, so the water diverts, and the current slows down."

Beth looked at him, her eyes bright.

"After you've had a few more lessons with me next summer, you can come out here, and try the rope."

"Next summer. We won't come back for a long time," Beth said with dismay.

"You won't be able to swim until it gets warmer again. But that doesn't mean you can't come back here before then. You and your mum are welcome anytime you want. Just let me know and I'll come and get you." He looked at Ada and smiled.

She blushed. "Well, that's very kind of you, Charlie. Very kind indeed. But it's an awful nuisance for you to have to drive us here and then back."

"I'll tell you if it's a nuisance." His voice was gruff, but he winked. "Actually, it gives me the chance to see some friends in town. They're teachers too. They're always wanting me to call in. I'm planning to do that today." He looked thoughtfully at Ada. "Why don't you join us, Ada? You'd be very welcome."

"Can I come? Beth cried.

Ada tried to imagine the teacher friends. They'd be friendly and welcoming like Charlie. It would be a chance to meet other people. But she would have to ask Jess to babysit.

"Thanks for the invitation, Charlie," she said, "but I'd have to leave Beth with Jess, and she does enough already. Anyway, I was planning for Beth and me to have a quiet time reading and writing in preparation for Monday."

"I don't want to do my lessons. I want to go with Charlie," Beth said.

"You're not invited, Beth," Ada said. "And if you don't want to read or write, I do. I have homework."

Beth began to protest, and Charlie patted her head.

"That's right, Beth." He looked at Ada. "Another time, eh."

She noticed his expression, acceptance blended with something else. Disappointment? She smiled.

"I'd like to meet your friends one day, Charlie."

Chapter 11

MAY, 1948

VERA THOUGHT IT BEST THAT there should be a few 'drinkies' before the dance so everyone could get to know one another better before they arrived at the dance hall, where it would be difficult to talk properly. Besides, it would help them to get into the mood.

"We'll call round at about 8. We'll bring the booze. Sherry for the girls, and beer for the boys. If you could get a few nibbles? And you can tell Charlie to meet us then too. But of course, if you want some time on your own with him first, he could come earlier. You might want to ask him for supper." Vera jiggled her foot impatiently, and glanced at Jim, who was reading his newspaper at the dining table. She seemed about to say something to him, which by the knit of her brow was probably critical, but then changed her mind.

Ada could see that Vera was anxious that the evening should be a success, so decided not to check her again for thinking Charlie was more than a friend. Of course, Beth had told Vera and Jim about the visit to Charlie's, and how she was going to swim there next summer, and how a couple of weekends ago Charlie had accompanied her and Ada to a matinee. This had prompted Vera to ask, "wouldn't you like to have a proper date?" ignoring Ada's denial that it had been a date at all.

The matinee had again been an outing engineered by Beth, who'd asked Charlie, when he came to put a final coat of paint on Jess's shelves, if he would like to come with her to see a film which had a little girl in it who could tap dance very well. Beth wanted to learn tap dancing. She and her best friend Helen were on the waiting list for classes, which were very popular at the moment. The film was one with Shirley Temple in, *The Little Princess*. Ada had seen it in Singapore before the war. It had surprised her that Charlie accepted the invitation. When she had told him that he must not feel obliged to come, he replied that when the invitation was from a charming young lady how could he refuse?

At the matinee, Beth had sat in the middle - though Ada was very conscious of Charlie, trying not to glance at him over Beth's head to see if he looked bored. She could not believe that Charlie found Shirley Temple as cute as she and Beth did, but as they emerged from the dim cinema into the bright outdoor world, Charlie said that he was very pleased to have seen the movie and wished he could tap dance. He was looking at Beth when he said that.

He bought them thick creamy milkshakes in the milk bar next door, and they took their time talking about the film and Beth's doings at school until the sun began going down behind the clock tower. In the conversation about school, Beth had said in a very grown-up way, which both Ada and Charlie found amusing, that Timmy was only nice to her nowadays when the other boys were not looking, but she did not mind because if she were a boy she would not like being called a sissy for playing with girls. She also mentioned that no one called her a half-caste now. Charlie said that was what he had been called too, which had upset him as well, until his father had told him that he was very lucky to be *both*. Ada thought it was a remark that Michael might have made, and she felt grateful, supported in some way.

She knew that Jim believed Beth's mixed blood was a handicap for the child.

Vera was looking at Ada. "I'm very pleased that you did get around to asking Charlie. I know you don't want to give him ideas, but there's nothing wrong with having a bit of fun now and again. And you don't want to turn up without anyone. There are so many women who go on their own, and then have to sit out all night or partner each other."

"Charlie said he's not been to a dance in years and expects to make a fool of himself." Ada had not been able to tell if the colouring of his cheeks meant he was embarrassed or pleased. She'd wanted to say to him that he was the only man she knew to ask, but decided that would sound rude, even if she had not wished to seem forward.

Vera spread out her fingers and inspected her fingernails. "Val's going to bring her brother. Tom. He's a real dag." Val was Vera's friend on the haberdashery counter whose idea it was, apparently, to go to the dance.

"Dag?"

"You know, a good sport," Vera said. Jim snorted. "You haven't met him, Jim. Give him a chance. You don't want to spoil it for Val. She's been through a lot. It's been a terrible couple of years for her. And she sees this as the beginning of a new life for herself." Vera was referring to Val's husband, who'd died recently from lung cancer. Ada noticed that Jim looked contrite. She wondered if he was trying to change and become the husband Vera wanted because Vera had threatened to leave him if he kicked up a fuss about going to the dance.

"So you've taken up your dress, have you?" Vera said, as Jim left the room with his newspaper.

The dress was one of Vera's, bought on instalment. Ada was as slim as Vera these days, so the dress, a deep midnight blue, only needed to be shortened. The full skirt fell in elegant folds from the waist to a flattering mid-calf length. The brassiere was built-in, and the halter-neck bodice fitted snugly. The first time that Ada had tried the dress on, Vera had insisted on applying Ada's make-up – rouge, red lipstick, blue eye shadow. When Ada stood in front of the full-length mirror, she'd posed like a Hollywood siren - lifting her chin and thrusting forward one shoulder - playing up to Vera's compliment that she would "knock them out." When Ada walked into the dining room to show Beth and Jim, she noticed his eyes flash approval, and for an instant she felt herself to be beautiful and womanly.

Beth appeared as excited as Ada felt with the prospect of visitors, and hearing the knock on the door she rushed to open it. Ada realised that this was the first time Beth had seen her mother entertain anyone. It was a real occasion.

Jim marched in first, carrying a couple of bottles of beer, and dumped them on the table, then removed his jacket as if there was no time to waste. Beth was hovering in the doorway waiting for the others, and cool air crept into the room and curled around Ada's legs, making her feel suddenly more apprehensive than excited about the evening.

"Ah, good, you've got a bottle opener and corkscrew," Jim said, and had the cap off a beer bottle before Vera came in followed by a heavily built man, whom Ada assumed was Tom, the dag, and then a broadly smiling Val.

Vera also seemed in a hurry, plonking a sherry bottle on the table and tossing her stole onto a chair, while introducing Tom at the same time in a brief, off-hand manner.

"Aren't you going to pour the ladies a sherry, Jim?" Vera asked, as Tom grinned at Ada and put out his hand to shake hers - in a less than hearty way, she noted, which did not seem to fit with his burly figure, the red cheeks and broad smile.

"These are pretty glasses, Ada," Vera said, holding a sherry glass up to the lamp light. Jess had lent Ada some sherry glasses, told her to keep them as she did not have parties anymore; in fact, she did not like parties, which made Ada not press her to join them for drinks, although Jess said she would come at the end and take over - would babysit, that is.

"The glass is so fine. Like the ice on puddles in the winter," Vera said. She drew up her shoulders and shivered a little. "Thank goodness we didn't have to bike this evening. There's a definite nip in the air." She was referring to having been brought in Tom's car. "My hair would've been ruined, too."

"You look lovely, Vera," Val said. Ada agreed. Vera's cheeks were flushed, and her hair, brushed from the day's setting in curlers, fell in thick waves to her shoulders. "Those beads go so well with your dress." Vera fingered the beads of her jet necklace, which matched the black trim of her bodice and cream skirt. The black showed off the whiteness of her skin. Her lips were scarlet.

Ada remembered once remarking that Vera was like Snow White. Beth, overhearing this, and knowing the story, had said that she wanted skin as white as snow. "You've hair as black as a raven's wing," Ada had said. "Be satisfied."

Everyone had their glasses filled now. "Let's go into the next room so we can be a bit more comfortable," Ada said. "Beth, could you carry in the cheese straws, please." She'd baked them herself, along with the sausage rolls, from recipes Jess had given her.

Jim went immediately, but the others lingered. Val was admiring the kitchen cupboards, saying that she liked the colour and should repaint hers. Ada considered that Val was quite a beauty in a baby doll, full-lipped way, with wide blue eyes and curly blond hair held back from her forehead by a diamante clip. Tom was grinning broadly at no one in particular, his eyes crinkling at the corners, when suddenly he darted forward and poked Beth gently in the stomach. She looked astonished, yet seeing him nodding happily at her, smiled up at him expectantly as he straightened and pushed back a strand of hair that curled across his brow despite the slick of oil. The women were laughing when Jim returned to the kitchen.

"So are we going to sit down or not?" Jim demanded, and glanced suspiciously about the room, as if something were being planned behind his back. Ada could see that he felt tense, perhaps on trial to prove that he was a man who could relax and enjoy himself.

"Charlie coming?" Vera asked.

"He should be here soon." Ada glanced at her watch.

Jim looked up at the ceiling and announced in a knowing voice, "Keeping Maori-time."

It was the same disparaging term Miss Hullet used for the lateness of Rangi and Kaia, and Ada glared at him, thinking she'd been stupid to have invited Charlie knowing how prejudiced Jim was, and how insulting he could be. Her feeling of apprehension increased, but she did her best to appear cheerful as she handed round the sausage rolls. Everyone told her how good they tasted, so much better than bought ones, and Tom said, "You can ask me over anytime, Ada. You sure know how to cook." He was reclining low on the settee with his legs stretched out in front of him and appeared totally at ease. With a cramped smile, Jim offered to pour him another beer.

"A small one," Tom replied with a grin. "We've got a long night to get through."

"Too right," Jim said, winking at Tom, and tapped a bulge in the pocket of his trousers.

Tom chortled, and Jim left the room. "How ya settling in?" Tom asked Ada. "Too cold for you, I bet. Vera's always complaining of the cold. Very sensitive lady, is your sister." Val leaned forward to corroborate this, while Vera crossed her legs and fluffed out her skirt. Ada, seated upright on the kitchen chair she'd brought in, and alert for the sound of a car drawing into the driveway, wondered how he knew that Vera was always complaining. It could be what his sister related. Or was it that he saw Vera quite frequently? Ada noted Vera's studied indifference to Tom as he continued to tease her, which did not mask her obvious pleasure at being the centre of attention. When Jim returned, Vera looked up at him with an air of disappointment, and could hardly conceal her annoyance when Jim asked Tom about a rugby game.

Tom sat up and directed his gaze at Jim, and soon the two men appeared oblivious of the women. Ada sensed that they were anxious to make a bond, an alliance of some sort, both affirming each other's comments with emphatic grunts and ponderous nods.

Val rolled her eyes. "Listen to them. Rugby's a religion in Godzown," she said to Ada.

This observation seemed to give Val and Vera permission to begin a lively exchange of gossip, seizing greedily on the snippets that were offered - who was pregnant; who wanted to be; who was going out with whom. It was as if they were intent on equalling the men's indifference to them, even though the men were now looking into their beers, searching, it seemed, for something else to talk about.

Ada was becoming increasingly anxious that Charlie might not be coming at all, when she heard a knock on the door. She hurried to answer it before Beth, and seeing him there, holding a corsage of small white flowers, she felt such a rush of relief he'd arrived that she held out her arms in a gesture of heartfelt welcome. He looked both surprised and pleased, then stepped forward and pressed his forehead and nose lightly against hers. She was flushed and smiling when she brought him in to join the others, and was aware that Vera glanced at both of them in a triumphant way, while Jim looked at Charlie as if he were an intruder.

Shielding Charlie from Jim's cold scrutiny, Ada offered Charlie a drink and took him back into the kitchen.

"I had an unexpected guest. I couldn't get away, I'm afraid," he said.

His tone was sincerely apologetic, but his serious expression conveyed a deeper concern than an embarrassment for being late, and he appeared somewhat preoccupied. She wondered if he were thinking about the unexpected guest, but did not ask considering it was none of her business.

"Don't worry, Charlie" she said. "The only thing is the sausage rolls aren't warm." She was still holding her corsage. "Thank you very much, Charlie. This is so pretty."

"Not as pretty as you look tonight."

"Well, thank you," she replied, feeling shy with his gaze taking in her dress, then settling on her face. "Look, I'll just go and get something to pin it on with. Go and join the others."

When Ada returned to the sitting room, Vera was talking about her drama group, how she was going to be a maid in the next play, and had, thank goodness, only to say 'yes, m'lady'. It was not clear to Ada that Vera was genuinely pleased at having such a small part. Vera picked up her skirt and curtsied to each one of them in turn, her head tilted to one side, her smile overly sweet. Tom clapped loudly and said, "I always fancied being an actor. How about you, Jim?" He did not even glance at Charlie, Ada noted.

"You wouldn't see me dead on a stage," Jim replied. "It's for pansies."

"I doubt anyone would want you dead or alive on a stage," Vera said in a withering tone, then, not waiting for a reply, started talking about the other actors, running them down mostly, it sounded to Ada, who wished she and Charlie could go back into the kitchen. Sensitive to how Charlie might be feeling, she was thinking how to manoeuvre their exit when Vera announced, in a loud, American-sounding voice, "Come on, let's break it up and get going." Ada thought she was trying to impersonate someone - Mae West, possibly.

"I'll just fetch Jess," Ada said. Beth, sitting wide-eyed and cross-legged on the floor, began to protest. "You don't have to go to bed immediately, darling. You've got a treat coming. A game of Snakes and Ladders."

✸   ✸   ✸

Charlie followed Tom's car to the hall, not saying much on the journey. From the grave set of his features, Ada wondered if he were still thinking about the person who'd turned up at the house, or was simply dreading the dance, especially the company of Tom and Jim - whose unfriendliness he must have sensed. Concerned that he might be feeling offended, but unable to think how to ask him if he were, she broke the silence by saying, "Have you ever done any acting, Charlie?"

"Not in plays like your sister, but I've had some experience of getting up and speaking in front of people. When visitors came to our village – pa, Maoris call it – I had to greet them and make them welcome in the marae - the meeting place."

"Do you still do this?"

He shook his head. "I left my tribe and came down here."

"Why did you leave?"

"It's a long story."

She could see that he was in no mood to explain, and she wondered again if he'd been upset by either the unexpected guest or by Jim's conduct.

They drove on in silence until Tom slowed and drew up to the kerb. Charlie slowed, too, and parked behind him, switching off the engine. He reached for her hand and squeezed it gently.

"Later, I'll tell you. Let's not spoil the evening, eh."

She climbed the steps of the hall, wondering what Charlie meant by the word 'spoil'. She'd detected a note of regret in his voice and felt uneasy. What was she to learn about him? Would the knowledge alter their friendship? And yet, wasn't it best to find out?

Men were standing on either side of the steps, all of them smoking in a serious, self-absorbed way, as if their very existence depended on deep inhalations of nicotine. There was something raw and uncouth about them, with their big fists and gleaming, oiled hair. Aware of their glances as she passed, and noticing, when she entered the hall, women seated along the edge without partners, she was grateful to have Charlie at her side. Some of the women were attempting to converse with their neighbours, but most gazed into the distance self-consciously, no doubt pretending to be unaware of the men who were assessing them covertly and hedging their bets.

The hall was lit by bulbs painted red. There was no attempt at decoration except for a string of lights around the hatch that led into a kitchen, from which soft drinks were served. Jim looked around the room, a sneer on his face.

"Bloomin' borer," he said, tapping the wall. It was flaking and buckling like one of the old verandah posts of his house where you could pull bits off like honeycomb. Vera, however, laughing at something Tom had said, did not seem to notice how spartan and drab the place was – Vera, who'd frequented the most stylish hotels in Singapore. She was desperate to enjoy herself, Ada thought.

Couples were dancing a foxtrot played by a four-piece band – saxophone, piano, bass, drums. The musicians, all young and slick-haired, looked confident and cheerful in their red blazers. They played well enough, but the dancers were less trotting than walking, and when Charlie led her with a surprising grace around the floor, it seemed to Ada that the other couples looked at them as if offended, as if she and Charlie were showing off. Or was it because Charlie was recognised as being a Maori? She recalled the rudeness of the guests in the Cameron Highlands, and looked at

Charlie as once she'd studied Michael to see if he'd noticed the staring, but Charlie appeared unaware of the attention.

She forced herself to appear oblivious, and congratulated Charlie on his dancing, which he told her he'd learned at school. They did another circuit. When they returned to where they'd started, Ada saw Jim talking to Val on the side-lines. Val looked impatient, perhaps because Jim had not asked her to dance while Tom was partnering Vera. Sighting the two in the crowd of dancers, Ada was struck by Vera's expression of total attentiveness to what Tom was saying. She looked as if she were playing a part: submissive, passive, not like Mae West at all.

After another turn of the floor, Ada noticed Val was dancing with a tall, lanky man, and Jim was making his way to the door. She remembered him in the kitchen tapping the bulge in his trouser pocket and winking at Tom.

"I think Jim's going out to have a drink," she said to Charlie. "It would be better to allow alcohol to be sold on the premises, don't you think? The women could keep an eye. It's more civilised." But she supposed that if people intended to get drunk they would wherever they were. "I hope he doesn't drink too much. He can be unpleasant when he drinks. Quarrelsome."

"He needs courage, I suppose." Charlie said. "It's something you see all the time."

She thought he might be referring to the Maori who'd lost their pride. When the music stopped, he asked if she wanted something to drink.

"That would be nice. It's quite stuffy in here, isn't it?" she said, looking across at Jim, who'd reappeared and was seated on his own. He was staring ahead, his expression sullen. She walked across to sit beside him and followed his gaze. Tom and Vera were standing together, facing the other way. Tom's head was bent towards Vera's; he appeared to be whispering in her ear.

When she looked up at him, his head did not move, so their faces were close, too close. What was Vera getting up to? Didn't she understand how insecure Jim was, that he was coming out tonight to please her? Ada glanced anxiously at Jim.

"It's stuffy in here," she said. Indeed, the windows were steamed up and the air was thick. But it was also the tension she sensed, the weighty currents of Jim's suspicion and misery.

Jim gestured with his head at four men who'd come in through the doorway. They stood in a group with their heads bent towards one another as if planning something.

"They're half-cut already. Can't work out why they bothered to come. Could've done their boozing at home. Probably just looking out for sheilas."

"Well, they're not going to get very far standing over there." Anxious to distract him from Vera, who was still listening avidly to Tom, Ada said, "You don't like dancing at all?"

"Gave it a burl once with Vera. She said it was like dancing with a lump of wood."

Not very encouraging, then, Ada wanted to say. Stupid. If you wanted someone to do something, you had to give them the idea that they could do it.

Jim shuffled his feet. "I need a bit of fresh air."

He was going for another nip? Seeing Charlie approach with two glasses of orange cordial, and knowing he would understand that she did not want Jim to get drunk, she grasped Jim's wrist as the band master announced the next dance, a waltz.

"Come on, Jim, give it another burl. Come on."

He bit the corner of his mouth, and a shadow crossed his face.

"You'll do your block if I tread on you. And what about your boyfriend?"

"Charlie, you won't mind if I dance with Jim?" She looked meaningfully at Charlie, and then behind Jim's back mimed tipping a flask to her lips.

"Not at all," Charlie said, settling on the bench as Ada stood. Jim rose slowly, like a man who anticipated nothing good was about to happen.

They were making laborious progress around the floor when Tom and Vera came up beside them.

"How did you manage to get Jim up, Ada?" Vera gasped.

"Jim told me he was a dreadful dancer. But in fact he's not a bad dancer at all."

Vera pursed her mouth in disbelief. Ada was annoyed at her insensitivity, and wished suddenly that she was not partnering Jim, who held her hand tightly like an anxious child.

"Hey, why don't you dance with Jim, Vera? I should be getting back to Charlie," Ada said. She refused to catch Tom's eye. Damn Tom. She stopped and moved aside, gesturing with open palms for Vera to take her place. Vera hesitated, then, with an apologetic glance at Tom, stepped into Jim's stiff embrace.

Ada did not bother to see how Tom responded, and she headed towards Charlie.

"Well done," he said, handing her the glass of cordial.

Ada sipped her drink and watched Vera and Jim. They were moving but not speaking, each looking steadfastly over the other's shoulder. When she lost sight of them, she turned to Charlie. He looked serious, distracted.

"We can leave whenever you like, Charlie. We haven't been here for very long. But if *you* don't want to stay…"

She looked at the dancers again, and saw Tom dancing with his sister, and then, not far away, Jim and Vera. Vera, to Ada's surprise, was smiling radiantly. But there was Jim, shoulders hunched forward. It did not take a genius to see that he was speaking angrily, and Vera was attempting to appear unaffected. Jim dropped his arms, releasing Vera, and stepped back. His fists were clenched. The couples nearest the pair looked the other way, as though not wanting to cause embarrassment. So you can row on the dance floor, but not dance with a Maori, Ada thought, as Vera approached.

"The bastard's ruined my evening." Vera spoke through clenched teeth.

"I think you ruined Jim's," Ada said. Vera looked mystified, and shrugged at Tom and Val, who'd followed her off the floor. Ada turned to see Jim pushing aside people and striding towards the door. "You laid down the law to him about coming tonight, Vera, but you were dancing with Tom before you had one dance with him. How do you think he felt?"

"Well we're not in Arab land, are we? There's nothing wrong with it, is there?" Tom protested.

Ada ignored him and said to Vera, "Do you think you should go and see how Jim is?"

Vera clicked her tongue and swore under her breath, then stalked towards the door followed by Tom and Val. Ada imagined the scene outside: Jim's anger, Vera defending herself rather than trying to appease him, Tom making useless comments that would anger Jim the more. She said to Charlie, "If we went out there it might help to calm things down." Charlie offered her his arm. "I'm so sorry, Charlie. This isn't what you bargained for."

She heard the raised voices as soon as they came out onto the top of the steps before she saw the four on the street near Tom's car. Jim was swearing loudly at Tom and shaking his fist, and Tom was shouting back.

"Oh, God, I hope there's not going to be a fight," Ada said, alarmed.

Charlie began down the steps in front of her. "Whoa, take it easy," he called out as he approached the four.

Jim turned around. "Piss off. Who told you to interfere?"

"Fighting won't help, man. You need to sit down with your wife and talk about what's getting to you."

"Who the hell do you think you are? A bloody Maori telling me not to fight. That's all your lot ever did. You were bloody cannibals, too."

Ada, who had been standing back, darted forward.

"How dare you speak like that. What cause have you to be so insulting?" Jim looked startled, even sheepish, and stared bewilderedly at her.

Vera said, "Tom, take us home, please. The evening's spoiled. Completely spoiled."

Tom was already unlocking the car, and the women got in behind him. Jim remained on the path. Tom wound down the window and poked out his head.

"You going to walk home?"

Jim swayed backwards a little as if to take stock, and Vera beckoned impatiently at him. Head down, like a man submitting to punishment, he opened the front passenger door.

"Come on, Charlie, let's go," Ada said, turning away with disgust. She noticed people standing on the steps. They'd been watching. She was so angry, she did not care.

"I'm so very sorry Jim spoke to you like that," Ada said, looking anxiously at Charlie as he started the engine. "He's an ignorant bigot."

"He doesn't think much of himself, I'd say. People who speak like that generally don't."

"He saw Vera flirting with Tom, but still there was no cause to make a scene. I'm sorry."

"You don't need to apologise."

"I get so angry when I hear such ignorance," she said, recalling the time in the Great World, when the soldier insulted Michael. "Thank God I have my own home, and don't have to hear Jim talking nonsense, and the two of them arguing."

"Was that why you got Jess's flat?"

"Vera and Jim were very kind to take us in when we came here. But what with their quarrelling, and then Beth not enjoying school…I thought, what was the point? We'd come to New Zealand for a better life after the war in Singapore. And I knew that unless I made some changes it wouldn't be."

"The war in Singapore must've been very hard for you."

"It was." She took a deep breath.

"Do you want to tell me about it?"

He was watching her, but she did not look at him. She was upset by the quarrelling, and Charlie's compassion made her feel like crying. She took another deep breath, steadying herself.

"The British were interned, as you probably know. I was in Changi first, and then in another camp, Sime. We weren't treated like the poor Jews in Europe, or anything like that. We were left to get on with things, but it became really bad, and people began to die because of the lack of food, and disease. I got beriberi. But I was lucky. I received the right medicine straightaway. I always thought it was because…" She clasped her hands and pressed them against her lips, judging whether she should say more, then turned to Charlie. "It's such a long story. We've both got long stories."

Their eyes met. "I'll hear your story first," Charlie said firmly.

She felt overwhelmed with the avalanche of memories, and desperately wanted to share what she'd kept from everyone for so long. She'd sensed before that Charlie was someone who would hear her, *could* hear her.

Her eyes were shut as she spoke of Changi, and, relating the incarceration in Smith Street, she covered her face with her hands recalling the shame she'd felt using the lavatory in a cell of eight men. She became short of breath when she spoke of her fear when waiting to be summoned for interrogation, and remembered how she'd forced herself to think of the small circle, the greater courage she needed to survive. Charlie said nothing, and she continued.

"I wanted to die when I was told that my husband had been executed for being a spy. There was an Indian man in the cell. He reminded me of Michael for some reason. I don't even know his name. He gave me courage." Ada paused, reminded of the Indian mouthing the words 'Hate, Hate.'

Ada continued, "One officer who questioned me had a son who'd been taught by Michael. And he'd loved Michael. The officer remembered that. I like to think that was the reason I was sent back to Changi, and got treatment for the beriberi."

Charlie did not speak immediately, and in the silence, Ada heard the echo of her own voice – the rushed words, the matter-of-fact tone. No wonder Charlie did not know how to respond. Before she could add that she'd nearly gone mad with grief, Charlie said quietly, "What you have gone through, what you have suffered, you and your husband…I have no words to express how sorry I am…It makes everything I've ever experienced which I thought was bad seem completely trivial. You are a very brave person, Ada. I admire you very much. And your husband must have been an exceptional person. You must be very proud of him."

"Yes. I am. When the war came to Singapore he felt he had to do something. He always had a strong sense of duty. He was very clever, and very conscientious. He always tried to do what was right." She went on, speaking slowly as she explained about Michael knowing several languages and learning Japanese, his knowledge of the jungle from scouting days, and the radio messages - the work which had cost him his life.

"He was awarded a medal. I've shown it to Beth, but she thinks he got it for driving an ambulance. When Beth grows up, I'll tell her the truth about what he did."

Charlie drove on in silence, and Ada wondered if she'd said too much, if she had burdened him, as she'd feared burdening Vera.

They were passing Cornwall Park, and Charlie slowed the car and stopped. The trees were a dark, brooding mass, except for some tall cedars showing their girth in the light of the street lamp, and she could see Charlie's eyes as he looked at her; she could see the sadness in them.

"What you tell me about your husband, and his bravery, the way he sacrificed himself, makes me feel ashamed that I have not done more for my people."

"I'm sorry, I didn't intend to do that. And I should tell you that sometimes, and I feel so guilty saying this, I've felt angry with him. Choosing to do the right thing for his country didn't seem to be the right thing for me and Beth. I know that makes me sound like a very selfish person."

"I don't think that makes you sound selfish. It's completely understandable. Men go off and do battle, but it's the women who stay behind and have to cope with the day-to-day. Also, with the fear of never seeing their menfolk again. And they don't get any medals." He smiled gently at her, then looked ahead.

"Being interned wasn't the best time of my life, to say the least, but I know that what I went through made me a stronger person." She realised that she'd not thought of the small circle for a long time. She had changed. She had made the circle grow.

Ada looked ahead at the long stretch of the road's unchartered darkness, dusty gold in patches from the wash of the street lamps.

"I'd like to hear your story now, Charlie," she said. "About your people."

Charlie was quiet for a while, then said, "The visitor I had this evening…it was my cousin. I haven't seen him for several years, not since the end of the war." He was quiet again.

"Where did you fight in the war?" Ada ventured.

"I didn't fight in the war. I chose to work on the land. It was very important work, and I was the oldest of the young men left behind. That's why I was given the role of speech maker when an elder died. Most of my friends, my brothers and cousins volunteered to fight. And though they knew I was doing a valuable job, they found it hard to meet my eye. I come from North Auckland, and my tribe have always been known as good fighters. I'm afraid there's not much warrior blood in my veins. But I also believed, like Puea Herangi, that the Maori should not fight for people who'd invaded their country and taken their land. Anyway, when the war was over, with so many Maori killed, I felt that everyone thought I'd been dishonourable, and when my grandmother died soon after, I left and came down here. I found my little place, and I turned my back on my people." He drummed his fingers on the steering wheel. "Manu, my cousin, said tonight that I was not scorned. He said it was my own guilt that made me believe that." Charlie rubbed the back of his neck. "And now he wants me to return to the tribe and help get back some of our tribal land. He says it's time. Last year official references to 'native' became 'Maori', and the Native Land Court is now called the Maori Land Court. He believes I've got the ability to take things on, and stand up to the government. He says it's more than a struggle about land. Much more. It's a struggle to get back the pride, our mana, that we've lost. We need to fight for our rights. But instead of using our bodies as we used to do, we must use our minds. And sharp tongues."

"Like Gandhi," Ada said. "Look what he did, without any violence. It's a great tragedy he was murdered." She looked at Charlie. "What do you think you'll do?"

"I can't hide away all my life. I have a duty to help my people."

Ada bit her lip. How often she had heard Michael use the word 'duty'. She knew what it meant. "Will you go back to your tribe?" she asked, very quietly, not wanting to hear that he would.

"I need to see how things are."

"Yes. Yes," she said, and spoke more loudly now, forcing herself to sound confident and encouraging. "You said that you would not tell me your story as you did not want to spoil the evening.

Perhaps because you thought I'd judge you. See you as a coward. But you were wrong. You did what you thought was right. You followed your conscience. I admire you for that, Charlie."

"Thank you. It's good to hear you say that." He smiled, but she did not smile back, thinking of his leaving.

"You're looking tired," he said. "I should take you home. I hope talking to me hasn't stirred up too much for you."

"No. It was a relief. Really. You're the first person I've told about Smith Street, Charlie." She managed a smile. "We didn't do much dancing, I'm afraid."

"We shared, though. We said things that mattered, Ada."

"Yes. Yes. We did."

"And I hope we will again."

Did that mean, she thought, as Charlie started up the car, that he would not disappear from her life?

Chapter 12

"**Well, this takes us back** doesn't it?" Vera tapped her chopsticks on the table, and eyed the bowls of sweet and sour pork, steamed rice, and stir-fried vegetables.

Ada poured out the green tea, sipped, and watched Vera carefully for signs of remorse. Did she recognise that her behaviour at the dance had triggered Jim's fury? To confront her directly would spoil the evening, though. It was meant to be a treat, a meal out in the first Chinese restaurant to be opened in the town. Beth was staying the night at Helen's; it was a time to relax. 'Why should I be her sister's Vera's conscience, anyway?' Ada thought.

Vera scooped some rice into her bowl. "Remember that place in Chinatown we used to go to for steam boat?" She selected a slice of pork, took a bite and chewed thoughtfully. "Not bad. But not up to Singapore standards." She helped herself to more pork. "Val's been here. Came soon after it opened. She's quite a girl about town these days. Don't blame her." Vera stared ahead for a few moments, then continued. "In fact, I envy her. She had a good marriage, and she's got that to remember. Much better to be the widow of a man you'd loved, than to spend your life with a man you don't want to be married to."

"So that was what you were trying to do."

"What do you mean?"

Noticing another couple slide into an adjacent booth, Ada kept her voice low. "You were trying to make Jim feel unwanted."

He'd not blamed Vera for causing him to lose his temper, though, when he called around to apologise to Ada a couple of days later. "I was lashing out," he'd explained. "I wasn't thinking. I'm sorry for saying what I did. It was out of order. Tell your friend Charlie I'm sorry I acted like an idiot." He had looked truly repentant, and ruffled his curly hair so it stood up on his head and made him look both anxious and lost. He seemed to care what she thought of him. She refrained from saying that Charlie had not been bothered; he had more important things to think about.

Vera opened her eyes wide, wrist on table, chopsticks suspended. "I wasn't trying to do that at all. If you're referring to my dancing with Tom, well, what was I going to do when he asked me? I was just being polite. Being sociable."

"I don't think Jim saw it that way."

"I can't help that."

Ada filled her bowl with rice, helped herself to meat and vegetables, tasted, and then reached for the soy sauce.

"It didn't look as if Tom was just being polite. Have you got something going with him?"

"Tom?" Vera appeared astonished. "Good heavens, no. If I was going to have a fling, or whatever, it wouldn't be with Tom. If I was going to have a fling, which I'm not, it would be with someone tall, dark, handsome and wise." She paused and smiled faintly. "Someone like Charlie, for instance."

Ada frowned. What was Vera planning? She remembered Vera's designs on Michael.

"Don't worry, I'm not after him, Ada. Even if I was, I wouldn't have a chance. He's only got eyes for you."

"What do you mean?"

Vera did not answer her question, but carried on complaining about being married to Jim. Ada only half-listened, thinking about what Vera had said. Vera was being fanciful, she thought.

The only time Vera had seen them together was at the dance. Of course, Charlie had paid her attention then: any gentleman would have done so, and Charlie was a gentleman. She was aware that he liked her; they had spoken so openly to each other the other night. Undoubtedly, they both felt very close to each other then. They were good friends.

Then Vera said, "I know Mummy used to say that when you'd made your bed you had to lie on it. But I can't see why. I married Jim because he had a bit of go in him. I didn't think he would turn out to be so dull. And he didn't see that I wasn't the little wife he could get to fit into what he wanted. The simple truth is why carry on making each other unhappy? Better to be apart." She shrugged. "Well. We only have one life. And I realise that I've got ambitions, too."

"What are you saying, Vera?"

"Val and I are thinking that we could start up our own little business eventually. We're thinking of moving to Auckland."

"Auckland?"

"We could get a job in one of the big stores, and learn a bit more, then try and get a loan from the bank. And with our savings – Mummy's money, which I haven't spent – set up our own dress shop." She stopped and looked carefully at Ada. "Don't think I'm deserting you. Because you could come, too. You could join us. You know more than me about dress-making, alterations…"

"But I don't want to be a dressmaker." Ada spoke tersely. She felt something had been planned behind her back. It was all rather a shock.

Vera spoke gently. "Oh, Ada, I know you think I'm running out on you, but I need a fresh start." She looked despondent, then her face brightened. "Anyway, you'll have Charlie."

"Charlie's thinking of moving up north of Auckland to be with his tribe. To help them fight for their land," Ada replied in the most even tone she could muster.

"Goodness. How do you feel about that?"

"Well, I'm going to miss him. He's very kind, considerate, and jolly. And Beth loves him. We've had some good times together, the three of us."

"It sounds to me that you're quite keen on him."

"Oh, Vera, you're really jumping the gun. There's a big difference between feeling someone's a good friend, and wanting anything more." She ate some more pork, but she did not feel in the least bit hungry. To tell the truth, she was quite churned up.

"So you're actually thinking of separating from Jim? Does he know?"

"Not yet."

"Do you think he'll agree to it?"

"He's going to have to, as I've made up my mind. I know people will talk, but I can't carry on like we've been doing."

Ada noted the light in Vera's eyes, and read it as the determination to change her life, to try and get the most out of it no matter the scandal, no matter the difficulties she would undoubtedly face.

"You said 'it takes us back' a few minutes ago, Vera. Which reminds me of the last time we sat together in a booth like this. We were having ice-cream sodas in Middle Road. We'd just been to have your passport photo taken. You wanted me to leave Singapore with you, and I said no. God, how many times in the camp did I regret being separated from Beth because I didn't leave when I could've. Not doing what was best for her. I know that I'll never make that mistake again."

"Does that mean you're going to come to Auckland, then? This is a small town. You'll have a better chance of finding the job you want in Auckland. Make use of those qualifications you're getting."

"What I'm saying is that I haven't just got myself to think about. Beth's happy at school now. It would be wrong to unsettle her. Anyway, I haven't passed my exams yet."

★ ★ ★

"We can go and visit Aunty Vera anytime we like. We can go up to stay with her in the school holidays."

"Can we stay with Charlie too? I want to stay at Charlie's."

"Well, he hasn't asked us yet."

"Why?"

"Because he's not living there properly yet. He has to see how things are first."

"I don't want him to live there. Why is he going to live there? I won't have anyone to teach me to swim. And I won't be able to go to the river."

"You'll have another teacher, darling. I've told you that. I can find you another teacher for next summer." Ada paused in her slicing of a carrot and smiled at Beth, who stared glumly back at her. She'd told Beth of the proposed departures of both Charlie and Vera, reasoning that the child should know sooner rather than later so she would be used to the idea before either Charlie or Vera did go. But Beth had been upset at the thought of losing them. The child was still missing Amah and Patrick, Ada realised, and wondered guiltily if her haste to share the news was more to do with trying to manage her own feelings. Possibly for the same reason, she'd told Jess as well, and had invited her to supper with Charlie, who was leaving in a few days. She was attempting to be as positive as possible.

She was preparing the meal - vegetables for a stir fry, to go with the lamb that was braising slowly in stock, sugar, soy sauce and rice wine with a pinch of cinnamon. The aroma of the meat filled the flat. Jess, as soon as she came through the door, sniffed the air, saying "My, that smells good." Ada noticed that she was wearing the pretty mauve voile dress she kept for best; she appreciated the significance of the occasion, even though she'd been told that it was going to be an early meal with Beth there.

"Did you help your mummy to cook the meal, Beth?"

Beth looked thoughtful.

"It's a Chinese recipe. Kwan's," Ada said, as she heard Charlie's car turn into the driveway.

Charlie came into the kitchen carrying a bunch of flowers. He handed them to Ada who fetched a jar of water. "They're beautiful. Thank you, Charlie."

He pressed his forehead and nose against hers, then against Jess's, before patting Beth on the head.

"I went with Mummy to buy the ice-cream," she told him. "It's chocolate," she added triumphantly.

"My favourite," Charlie said, slipping off his coat and hanging it on the peg inside the door. He rubbed his hands together. "Getting a bit chilly."

"It'll be warmer in Auckland," Jess said.

"Yes. It probably will."

"My daughter told me there's been snow in the South Island. Such a variation of climate from north to south. You forget how long a country this is," Jess said.

"Aotearoa. The land of the long white cloud," Charlie said. "Did you know that's the name New Zealand first had, Beth?"

She shook her head.

"Well, it's said that a man called Kupe went out on his boat one day and got lost. But after travelling for a long time on the sea he saw in the distance what he thought was land. His wife was with him and she shouted out, 'a cloud, a cloud', because a peculiar long cloud hung over the land. So Kupe called the land he'd come to Aotearoa, which means 'long white cloud'. Interesting?"

Beth nodded, and said immediately, "Can I have another story?"

"Oh, Beth. Charlie's been working hard all day," Ada said. "And supper's nearly ready."

Beth tugged at Charlie's hand. "Come with me. Come with me."

Charlie allowed himself to be led into the sitting room with Beth chattering excitedly. Ada knew she was going to show off her latest skill, a somersault.

"She's going to miss him," Jess said, as Ada began to lay the table. "I must say, I will. And not just because he fixes my shelves. He's a good man."

Ada knew Jess was watching her. She spoke quietly, under the excited squeals of Beth. "He is. Beth will miss him."

Then there was Charlie at the door again. "Is there anything I can do?" he asked.

"You're doing fine entertaining my daughter."

"Getting her over-excited, I expect," Charlie replied. Beth was clinging to his jacket, drawing him back into the room. "Whoa, whoa," he said, laughing.

"I want another story."

"Please. Say please, Beth," Ada said.

"Please, please, please."

Soon, Beth's chirping gave way to the deep rounded tone of Charlie's voice relating a story about someone called Maui. Jess began talking about something she was going to do in the garden next spring, and Ada thought about Charlie, how she'd miss him.

Ada was expecting Beth to bring up the fact of Charlie leaving, to ask who was going to teach her to swim, for instance, but she seemed to have forgotten – no doubt temporarily – that Charlie was going, and the subject of his departure did not arise during the meal. It was only when Jess took Beth off to read to her and settle her for bed that the matter was touched upon.

Charlie said, as he helped to clear the table, "Real good tucker, Ada. I should ask you for a few lessons. I've never really learned how to cook properly. I can fry a steak, sausages, cook a few spuds, and sometimes I've gone to the trouble of having folks over for a hangi, but I couldn't follow a recipe. Couldn't do anything fancy at all."

Ada wondered how or when he thought she was going to teach him. Did it mean he was not leaving for good?

"What's a hangi?" she asked, turning on the tap to rinse the dishes.

"It's a way of cooking," he said, coming to stand beside her. "You dig a pit and lay hot stones at the bottom of it. Then you put food, like fish, chicken, or kumura – that's sweet potato – wrapped in leaves on top of the stones. Then you cover the hole with a wet cloth and a mound of earth and leave the food to cook for, say, five hours. And, hey presto, when you take it out, the meat falls off the bone. It's delicious. Maoris love it, but Pakehas think it tastes too earthy." He put his hand on the small of Ada's back. "You should try it some time. One day we'll have a hangi, eh?"

She was conscious of his hand, and remembered what Vera had said in the Chinese restaurant. She wanted to turn around and smile at him, say how much she would like that. She wanted to see what his face would tell her. Would his expression match the comforting warmth of his touch? But she waited too long, for when she did turn, he had stepped away. With his back to her, Charlie examined one of Beth's drawings, which was pinned on the cork noticeboard.

"She's a great kid," he said.

Jess came back into the kitchen, before Ada could say that Beth was going to miss him.

Chapter 13

A COUPLE OF WEEKS LATER, after Charlie had left to go up north, Ada returned home from work and found a letter from Patrick waiting for her in the box. She made herself a cup of tea before settling to read it.

'Dear Ada,

I do hope that you and Beth are well. I can't say that I am in the best of health myself, which is not surprising given my age, and all the disturbance from selling the house and moving. It was a greater wrench than I'd anticipated. I'd thought it would be best to be free of the ghosts which seem to hover in the corners on some days when I feel very lonely. But the ghosts are now lost themselves and hold on to me with a desperation that I'd not sensed before. It's because they have left behind the home which they loved, and I loved, and in which we all had more good times than bad. Anyway, although I knew that selling the house was the right thing to do, I found it very unsettling, and I became rather ill. The doctor told me it was a virus, and I had to rest. Charmaine and John have been very good nurses, and I'm indebted to them for their care.

While I was ill, I realised that it was time to write to you and explain matters of much importance. I made a new will some time ago, just after the war, but I didn't tell you or Charmaine the contents of it, because I was waiting for the right time, as I've waited for the right time since you came into our lives, Ada. I know what I'm about to tell you will come as a shock. I pray that you don't take what you now are about to read too badly and will try and understand and forgive me for not explaining sooner. I thought you had enough to cope with, but after my illness I'm more aware than ever that my time on this earth is growing shorter, and knowing that you and Beth are settled now and getting on well in New Zealand (Beth's little story you sent me in your last letter was very good indeed), I feel it should be me rather than a lawyer who conveys what follows.

After my death, you and Charmaine will receive equal proportions of all my money, with the exception of a generous bequest to Amritha Pradu. Who is this girl, you may wonder? She is a child, four years older than Beth. Her mother is Tamil, and I have to tell you now that her father is Michael.'

Ada looked up from the page and caught her breath, then, throat tight with shock, read on.

'The mother was a servant here, and very sadly Michael became too friendly with her. I can assure you that the affair was completely over before he met you. He'd been giving the young woman, Kamala, English lessons, and was impressed by her desire to learn and better herself.'

Ada recalled Michael admitting to teaching the servant woman. Mouth dry, her heart beating fast, she read on.

'I don't know if their brief intimacy – she was dismissed immediately when we detected it – was a result of Michael feeling flattered by her obvious adoration of him, but whatever the reason, he was young and foolish. He wanted to marry Kamala when she informed him of the pregnancy, but we helped him to see that neither of them would have been happy, which he accepted in the end, as he knew that what he felt for her was not love. And what woman is happy living with someone whom they know is with them only out of pity, or duty? They would have been unhappy together, which would not have been good for the child, either. Kamala, to her credit, quickly understood this, got married almost immediately – to a cousin, I believe – and was very satisfied with the money Michael paid in maintenance. In fact, apart from once visiting the house (probably out of curiosity about you having heard of his marriage), which was the time you saw her, she did not want contact with Michael at all. Evaline and I made sure we helped Kamala with money, and with food when supplies became scarce after the war started. Evaline gave clothes, as well. We would leave them at an agreed place and not at the home, of course.'

Ada pictured Evaline pushing a box into a cupboard. Clothes for the orphans, she'd said. And yes, there was the pretty Indian woman standing on the garden path beneath the verandah and looking curiously up at the house. Ada recalled how she'd connected the woman with the black woman in the letter when she heard the Tamil dhobis talking on the path beneath the bedroom window. Hadn't she wondered then if Evaline had given the woman money to shut her up? As it happened, if Patrick was to be believed, it was payment not to come to the house again, no matter how curious she was.

'We never shirked our responsibility. And I am now making sure that the child will have the chance of a good education, and can make a life for herself in this difficult world.

'I know that Michael told you about being the woman's teacher for a short time soon after he'd left college. He wanted to tell you the whole story when he became engaged to you, but we counselled him against doing this because you might have felt it necessary to reject him, which would have hurt you both. We saw that the two of you were very much in love. We didn't know you well enough then to realise that you would not have worried about the possibility of social disgrace, and would have forgiven Michael his transgression. When Michael wanted to tell you on the honeymoon, we advised him against this for the joy he would certainly have robbed you of at a time when a bride deserves to be perfectly happy. Then, when you became pregnant, he wanted to tell you, especially after the letter arrived. (The letter, I can assure you, was not from Amritha's mother. She did not bear ill feelings towards Michael. No, the letter was from a member of her family, angry with Michael for not marrying Kamala and wanting to make trouble for him). Evaline cautioned him against doing this, as she was worried that if you learned about Michael's affair while you were pregnant your physical and mental health would be affected. Then the war came, and you both had enough to worry about. There never seemed to be the right time. I confess that this was the reason, when you were going to be interned, that I did not give you the letter Michael left with me for you before he departed for the north of the island. He wanted you to have it in case anything happened to him. I lost the letter in the turmoil of moving from the main house to the servants' quarters when the Japanese arrived, but I expect it was a full explanation of what had happened - that he had a child; that he was very ashamed; that he never saw her because her mother did not want him to; that he contributed money from his wages for her upkeep; and that he did not tell you sooner because he was protecting you. I imagine, knowing Michael, that he would have taken full responsibility for not telling you. In his usual, honourable way, he would not have mentioned that we advised him to say nothing. I know I could have explained everything when you returned to Serangoon after the war, or before you left the country, but I did not want to do this, and I have given much thought to why I didn't. Besides knowing you had been through so much and did not need anything more to upset you, especially as you were faced with rebuilding your life, and had the worry about the future welfare of yourself and Beth, I simply did not want to tarnish in any way the memory of my beloved, brave son. It seemed to me that his was a small transgression in the scale of events, and especially when measured against the enormous self-sacrifice he'd made.

I am so sorry to have to tell you this now, my dear Ada. But at least I know that you are in a better place, both physically, and emotionally, now that Beth is happy and settled, and with your own plans for furthering your education.

Please find it in your heart to forgive me, and to forgive Michael. He was young and what he did was very foolish, but you were his one true love, Ada.'

Her eyes skimmed the rest of the page. Charmaine and John were decorating a bungalow in Pasir Panjang. The house had been owned by a Chinese family whose taste was not theirs. I overlooked the sea, and had a small garden, three good sized bedrooms - one suitable for Patrick. They'd had to sell much of the furniture from the Serangoon house, for the bungalow was much smaller. The big sideboard had to go, and the piano, which no one touched anyway. The letter finished with the usual reminder that Beth was growing up in the right place, as Singapore still struggled to right itself. And then the words:

'Please forgive me, and Evaline and Michael, for hiding the truth from you about the child. We did it with the best intentions, but it would be very wrong, I realise now, that you should find out from anyone other than myself. Charmaine has also only just learned, and feels for you, Ada. I am sure she will write to you as soon as she can. She sends you all her love, as I send mine.'

Ada threw the letter down, and, elbows on table, clasped her head. The words coursed through her mind - 'forgive, forgive'; 'we wanted to protect you.' But she had suspected something, she had worried, she had felt unbearably insecure at times. Those nights when he'd come home late. Work, ambulance training, he'd said. Those nights he was learning to be a spy, learning how to be a hero. She recalled the words of the letter: 'Your husband has a black woman'. *Has.* The writer had used the present tense, even though the affair had supposedly been over nearly four years before. Could she believe Patrick when he said that Michael did not have any contact with the woman, and gave financial support only? Or had Michael continued to visit her? She sat back from the table and swallowed hard. 'You were his one true love, Ada,' Patrick had written, but could she believe him?

Ada got up from the chair and went to the bedroom for a handkerchief, blew her nose hard, then returned to the kitchen and shuffled the place mats left on the table after breakfast. She picked up the letter, dropped it, and in a daze went into the sitting room and stood at the window to stare numbly into the street. It was a windy day. A newspaper skidded down the footpath, and a man appeared leading a long-legged, mottled grey dog. The man looked very content, and so did the dog. They were companions. She envied the man. She felt so alone.

Ada moved away from the window and went into her bedroom. She sat before the dressing table mirror and, pressing her hands on her cheeks, viewed a woman who looked more than tired, who looked years older than she was. Ada stared at the woman, and the woman stared back. Her eyes were opaque: the eyes of a woman who kept secrets. The women nodded at each other; there was no doubt in their minds. Beth must not be told about Kamala and Amritha.

Ada tried to continue with the chores, but her heart was heavy, and as she tried to match the Michael she thought she knew with the Michael who had emerged, a stream of images passed through her mind - a pretty young Tamil woman seated at a table in the library; Michael standing before her with his hand resting on the piano top; she looking at him with awe and gratitude; he smiling at her; she standing and walking towards him; he smiling and smiling.

"Are you all right, Ada? You look very pale." Jess was seated on a kitchen chair in the sheltered corner of her verandah. "Can I get you something to drink?"

Ada shook her head, sat down on the top step, and leaned back against the verandah post. She felt drained. "I got a letter from Patrick today."

It was exhaustion which made her feel that what she began to relate did not belong to her at all, but to a younger woman with thick blond hair and unlined skin. She imagined herself standing in front of Michael holding a sheet of paper. Pasted on it were the words, cut from a newspaper, that she would never forget. She also remembered lying on a bed with Michael leaning over her, frowning. Had he been comparing her with Kamala?

"Oh, Ada. That's shocking news. I can see how upset you are."

"Yes. I'm very hurt that Michael felt he couldn't confide in me, whatever his parents said, and lived with a secret."

"He lived with a secret. I agree with that."

"He lived with more than one secret," Ada said. "I never knew…he never told me about working for the British as a spy. Dying for the British as it happened. I only found out when I was taken in for questioning by the Japanese after his death. I always thought it was because he didn't trust me not to kick up a fuss that he didn't tell me. I might've tried to stop him."

Jess shook her head. Ada went on, her voice tinged with anger.

"Patrick said that Michael was trying to protect me. And he was trying to protect me by not telling me about the child. Patrick said Michael had been young. Just out of college. Young and foolish to have done what he did. And it was all over before he met me. But if it was all over, didn't he realise I'd have forgiven him, however shocked I might've been?" She remembered Michael saying that in his mind she was not like other English women with their snobbery and social conventions.

Jess was quiet for a moment, perhaps thinking of the best way to answer and to comfort. "If you had been told, do you think that you would've understood without feeling upset? They saw that you were happy, and they didn't want to spoil that. Perhaps they *were* trying to protect you."

Ada shut her eyes against the sun, and visualised Michael pulling off his shoes and complaining of exhaustion. Now he stood at the door of a tenement, like those on Market Street. He was holding the hand of a child. Tears filled Ada's eyes. She brushed them away. It was a form of torture imagining Michael with the other child. Coming home late because he could not bear to leave her – and perhaps the mother, too, because she'd not married as Patrick had claimed, and still wanted Michael. Ada pictured her, Kamala, standing on the path and looking up at the house, her expression full of curiosity. It might have been curiosity that had brought her to Serangoon, but would she not have felt regret as well? Bitter regret that she'd not been considered good enough for Michael, and that her daughter would never know the clever man her mother had so admired? Had she felt angry, too, angry enough to write that letter? Would it have been enough consolation for Kamala to know that the Wood money would enable Amritha to have a good education? Amritha…was she pretty like her mother? Did she also resemble Michael, as Beth did?

Jess rose from her chair and crouched beside Ada. She put an arm around her shoulders. "It's been a dreadful shock, I know. I'm very sorry to see you so upset."

"Beth must never find out."

"Certainly not at the moment." Jess sat beside Ada on the step, and was quiet for a time, then said, "But later perhaps you might want to tell her. Because someone else might. She could return to Singapore one day and discover that she has a half-sister. And then she'll feel what you're feeling now about not being told." A sob caught in Ada's chest. "You want her to think well of her father. Quite right. I heard her telling Charlie about him being very brave. She is proud of him. But perhaps it's hard for children who think their fathers are heroes. Perhaps it would be helpful for her, when she's older, to know that her father was not perfect, so she won't be seeking a husband who is."

"When she's older," Ada murmured, as she tried to take in what Jess had said.

"Ada, dear. It will take time to accustom yourself to this news. We can talk about it again, whenever you want to."

Ada glanced at her watch. She was going to be late for Beth. She rose wearily to her feet.

"Yes, thank you, Jess. I'll need time to think about everything."

✷   ✷   ✷

Ada continued to think as she biked to fetch Beth from school; as she forced herself to chat amiably to Kwan; as she cooked supper and ran Beth's bath; as she had her own bath later; as she prepared for bed; as she lay in the darkness and imagined the time of telling the truth to Beth. First it would be about Michael in the war, how he had been murdered by the Kempeitai. Beth would certainly have to be in her teens for handling that. But when should she be told about her half-sister? Beth would be left with two images of her father - the brave hero, and the man with a transgression. Thinking this, Ada remembered Michael coming out of the shower in Serangoon and quoting from *A Tale of Two Cities*. Certainly, Michael had not been like Sydney Carton, a libertine who'd chosen to go to the scaffold because he wanted to make up for his dissolute life. But still, could it be that it was not simply Michael's sense of honour which had driven him to risk sacrificing himself? Could it also have been guilt?

It was impossible to sleep, and Ada got up for a glass of water. She wished that she could talk to Charlie. It made her feel miserable to think of Charlie, of his absence. She sat down at the table. She felt so tired. At least it was Saturday tomorrow, and she did not have to work at the hospital. But then again, she did not want to be on her own with Beth and trying to hide her feelings from the child. So should she take Beth up to Jim and Vera's? Beth would like that, and if there was a chance, without Beth or Jim overhearing, she could tell Vera Patrick's news. She did not expect Vera to have advice like Jess had, but Vera would be sympathetic, and Ada desperately needed the balm of sympathy. She imagined Vera's reaction. She'd be shocked. And then she'd say 'he was a dark horse, I always thought that. Put it behind you, Ada. Just forget about it. Such a long time ago.'

She realised that she would have to arrive unannounced as there was no phone at Jim and Vera's, but they always said that she could come without warning. Of course, that had been in the days when their marriage was not in its death throes, as Vera had suggested the last time they'd met at the Chinese restaurant.

✯ ✯ ✯

Ada prayed that she and Beth would not arrive on a battle scene, and was much relieved to be greeted by a smiling and calm Vera. Jim was in the vegetable garden, and Beth ran out to see him while Vera remained in the kitchen preparing lunch – a nourishing vegetable soup and sardines on toast, plenty enough for them all, she said. She wore an apron and had a brightness about her, as though happy in the role of housewife for a change. It was too early to eat, so after tasting the soup, she switched off the hot plate, and suggested that she and Ada go outside.

"I've got something to tell you," she said in a confiding tone, "and I don't want Jim, or Beth to come in."

She strode ahead of Ada as if on a mission, towards a bench under pine trees, which overlooked the paddocks with the sheep. Once they were seated, she said, "Jim and I have decided, definitely, to separate. At first Jim was pretty fed up and took some persuading. It was admitting failure, I suppose. As far as it goes, I feel that too. But I think now he's actually quite relieved. He agrees we're not suited. I'm very pleased he's accepting that. It's going to make the whole thing so much easier." She gave a deep sigh, either of relief, or at the thought of what lay ahead, then continued.

"We think the best thing to do will be to tell people that I'm going to Auckland to start up a business, which is true. And that he'll follow at some stage. Perhaps find a property up there. In time, when he doesn't go, people will think that it's a mutual decision to live separately doing what we each want to do. Of course, people will gossip, especially in a small place like this, but they won't be able to label me as some fallen woman abandoning my husband, or Jim as some pathetic chap who can't keep control of his wife."

"Do you really think he's relieved?" Ada had always believed that Jim loved Vera. But then you can love someone and still find them difficult to live with, she decided, as Vera assured her again that Jim was very agreeable to a separation and went on outlining her plans.

"Val's aunt is looking out for a little flat for us in Auckland. Temporary, so it doesn't have to be perfect. But if it suits us, all the better, as we'll have our work cut out for us, finding jobs and everything. I don't want to use up my savings and Mum's money, because I'll need it for the business. But it's there, and Val will have money from her house, which she's selling now. Val thinks we should tell them in the store that we're leaving and make it final, make it real, so we'll have to get on with it. Susan, Val's aunt, is also going to keep an ear out for jobs. She knows someone who works in one of the department stores. Not like the piddly one here. A proper department store. Like Robinson's." Ada remembered when it had been bombed. There'd been glass everywhere. None of that seemed important now.

Vera looked around her as if searching for something.

"God, I can't wait to live in a city. Can't wait."

Vera looked at Ada, and Ada realised that she wanted support, some agreement that the decision she'd made was the best one. But Ada felt unable to give this immediately, being too caught up with her own concerns, besides feeling a little cheated that the space for confiding had been already occupied.

Vera patted Ada's hand. "Don't worry, we'll still see each other, and you'll be coming to join us. I know you will. You won't want to stay here forever. I know you don't want to unsettle Beth, but she'll love it in Auckland. And you'll find it much easier to get the sort of job you want. Make use of all the education you're getting."

The pines creaked in the wind, and the long grass in the paddock flowed like mermaid's hair. Ada was aware that Vera was waiting for an answer, and said, "I'm pleased for you. I'm pleased that you have managed to work something out with Jim. Of course, I'll miss you. Beth will, too."

"It won't need to be for long. As soon as your exams are over, you'll be coming up, I'm sure. And you'll be able to see Charlie too, sometimes."

"I got a letter from Patrick yesterday," Ada cut in.

"Oh yes."

"He told me about his will. About leaving his money to me and Charmaine." Ada's tone conveyed no joy.

Vera leaned forward to look directly into Ada's face.

"That's good news, isn't it?"

"He's also leaving money to a little girl. A Tamil child."

Vera frowned, then drew back as if she already knew what was going to be said next.

"She's Michael's child." Ada hesitated, sighed, then continued. "Patrick told me Michael had completely finished with her mother before he met me, but kept giving support. All the family did. Although he wasn't in contact with the woman. Patrick swore to that. He claimed that Michael never really loved her." Ada shrugged. "But who knows?"

Vera put her arm around Ada's shoulders, but said nothing, which was unusual for Vera.

"Patrick said they didn't tell me because they didn't want to upset me at all. They were trying to protect me." She sighed. "But did I appear to be such a weakling that they thought I needed to be protected?" She wondered if she should tell Vera about the other secret that had been kept to protect her, which she had learned about in Smith Street - Michael's work for the British.

"Oh, Ada, I'm very sorry. You must feel so betrayed."

"At the wedding Patrick said he hoped that I would forgive Michael for his transgressions. I didn't know what he was talking about. But then later, not long after our honeymoon, I got an anonymous letter saying that Michael had a black woman. I asked him if that was right, and he denied it. But even though his relationship was over, he should've told me then that he had a child."

"He must have felt very guilty. But that's no excuse. He should've confessed." Vera removed her arm. "You never told me about that letter."

"Oh, Vera, I haven't told you about quite a lot of things." She stood to see if Beth was still with Jim. He was walking towards the house; Beth was skipping along at his side. "We should go in. They'll wonder what we're up to."

"What things? Come on, Ada. Tell me now."

She spoke quickly. She felt hurried both by the need to get indoors, and by the wish to pass rapidly over a story which had now been replaced, in the forefront of her mind, by the story of Michael's child. Vera was watching her carefully, eyes wide.

"The last time I saw him, just before the British surrendered, he told me that he had work to do. He had duties. I was very upset about being left to cope on my own with a baby. I felt abandoned. But I'd had no idea what he was really up to." She took a deep breath. "I found out that he'd been a spy for the British when I was taken in for questioning by the Japanese military police. It was the worst time of my life. I was terrified. I was in a cell with men. One died while I was in there. He was tortured. I don't know if the others survived."

"Oh, no. Oh, Ada. Oh, God. I can't imagine what you must have gone through. And then to learn about Michael like that. I'm so sorry." Vera's eyes filled with tears. "And you've kept all this to yourself. It makes me feel dreadful to think that I had no idea all this time."

Ada looked towards the house. Jim appeared at the doorway. He shouted, "I'm starving. When are we eating?"

Ada began to walk towards the house, then stopped. Turning to Vera, who had not moved and was looking bewildered, she said, "I just keep wondering if Michael continued to see Amritha's mother."

Vera took Ada's hand and held it tightly. "I realise that you'll never know if he did keep on seeing this woman, but believe me, I saw the way he looked at you, and I was dead jealous. I wanted to be loved like that."

"I remember you saying, when I told you about Michael proposing to me, that he wanted me for my white blood," Ada said, remembering how Evaline would admire her fair skin and blond hair, and how she'd hastened to set the wedding date.

"I didn't believe it. It was a horrible thing to say. I was just so jealous."

The last bus left from outside the village store at five o'clock on its circuit back after delivering the passengers - mainly those who'd been to the two o'clock matinee in town. As she walked down the hill with Vera and Beth, Ada was conscious of how tired she felt. It had been difficult trying to push away her thoughts over lunch and concentrate on what Jim was saying. He'd done most of the talking. Vera had been quiet, as though still absorbing what she'd been told.

Before they got onto the bus, Vera hugged Beth, and then Ada.

"Thank you for telling me, Ada," she said quietly. "I feel closer to you than I ever have, I think." She waved them goodbye. Ada waved back, feeling comforted from having had Vera listen to her and remind her of Michael's love.

Chapter 14

THAT NIGHT, EXHAUSTED, ADA WENT to bed as soon as Beth was tucked in, and this time she did sleep, a ragged sleep from which she woke suddenly, probably from nightmare. It was pitch dark. She switched on the bedside lamp. The clock showed five o'clock. The room was chilly. She pulled on her dressing gown, and felt for her slippers, thinking that this was only a taste of the greater cold to come, all the dismal mornings. Her body ached.

Ada shuffled into the kitchen, flicked the light switch, shut the door into the hallway, and filled the kettle. It was hard to believe that she used to complain of the heat in Singapore. Nowadays, she wanted the comfort of hot tea, and a hot water bottle. Once, all she had craved was the coolness of a dark room, a glass of cold lemon barley water, the swish of a beating fan - especially, she remembered, in the later months of pregnancy. She pictured herself on her way through the dining room to the kitchen for a drink and a biscuit, feeling observed by Michael's forbears - unsmiling, tightly collared men enshrined in dark wooden frames. Anglo-Indians proud of what they had achieved. It occurred to her that perhaps if Michael had not felt there was so much to live up to, he could have told the British officer who had recruited him that he was not prepared to risk his life. He would have insisted on marrying Amritha's mother instead of doing what his parents had no doubt demanded. And I would never have married him, Ada thought. There would have been no need for deception, and none of this hurt from having loved him so much.

She shivered. The cold was deep inside her, and the hot tea made no difference. The extra blanket she threw exhaustedly over her quilt could not stop her body from trembling. Her forehead felt hot and, when she took her temperature, the thermometer read 101. She swallowed a couple of aspirins then dozed. In the distance she heard a flush of water, the tread of bare feet. Put on your slippers, Beth, she thought, you'll catch a cold. But when Beth appeared in the doorway, Ada had no strength to scold her. Instead, she used what little energy she had to sit up.

"I'm not very well, Beth. You'll have to be a good girl to day and play on your own. I'll need to stay in bed if I want to be well for work tomorrow."

"Can I go to Helen's?"

"You were there last weekend. You can't live there."

"I'm not going to live there, Mummy. I'll come back and look after you."

"That's very kind of you, but I'll be all right if I'm just allowed to rest and get some more sleep." She reached for her dressing gown. "You can get yourself dressed, and I'll put out your breakfast."

She left Beth to eat her breakfast and took a glass of water back to the bedroom. Propped up on pillows, she heard Beth switch on the radio. It was the morning service. She closed her eyes to the sound of an organ, a choir drowning the voices of the congregation doing their best to keep in harmony.

A row of soldiers was standing to attention in front of a tall slender man. She could tell, even from a considerable distance that he was wearing a scout uniform. She frowned, straining to see him more clearly in the bright sunlight. You should be wearing a hat, she thought to call to the man, if you don't want to be burned black in the sun. There was a bank of trees behind him, and she saw, to her horror, a tiger lurking in the shadows. She could have sworn that Michael had told her tigers were extinct in Singapore nowadays. The tiger crouched in the undergrowth as if about to rush out and leap at the man. Then, without her seeing the tiger attack, the man was lying on the ground with the tiger prowling around him. But suddenly, to her great relief, the tiger disappeared into the jungle. She ran clumsily to kneel beside the man and saw that he was Michael. He was no longer wearing a uniform, but a white suit. It was torn and dirty, and she took out a handkerchief and began to dab at the stains on his jacket. She was dabbing away, and Patrick appeared. "Forgive me my transgressions", he said. "What do you mean?" she demanded, standing up, and caught sight of a slender woman a few feet away. She was Indian, Ada was sure of that. The woman, aware that she'd been seen, bent over and spat onto the ground as if in contempt of her, so violently that Ada felt the spittle on her cheek. Disgusted, she turned away, her movements slow and laboured. It was like pushing through thick, swampy water.

Sweating, she woke to feel a roughness on her face. At first, she could not recognise the woman above her, but knew that she was European. How disappointing. She wished for a Chinese face, for Amah. She could ask Amah to bring her an iced drink; she could depend on Amah, but she could not ask a stranger, even one that looked kind. The woman smiled, and the sunlight that came in through the window touched her white hair.

Jess put the flannel on the side table and picked up a couple of aspirins and a glass of water.

"Take these, Ada. I've called the doctor. You've got more than a bad cold. The flu, probably. Nasty. But if you stay in bed, drink lots, you'll be up and about soon."

"I can't stay in bed tomorrow."

"You can't think about going to work. What you need is bed rest. Where do you keep your clean nighties? Take that one off. It's soaked." Jess helped her to change then held up her dressing gown. "Here, put this around you while I change your sheets."

"Where's Beth?"

"She's playing with Humphry. Don't worry about her. I'll take her to school tomorrow. And I'll sleep on your settee tonight to keep an eye on you."

"Oh, Jess, you don't have to do that."

"Of course I don't have to, but I'm going to."

Time passed, and Ada drifted in and out of sleep, only vaguely aware in her waking moments that Beth hovered in the doorway, forbidden to approach; that a strange man visited twice and checked her pulse and took her temperature; that Jess or Vera sponged her down, gave her aspirins, tried to spoon soup into her mouth, and made sure she drank frequent glasses of water. And once a man visited whom she could not identify, as it was on the evening the virus was making its final bid to level her completely. He wore a suit and stood in the doorway for a short while. He looked very serious. In her delirium, she thought the man in his formal clothes resembled a funeral attendant. That helped her, she decided later, to fight harder to stay alive.

She told the man this when she was recuperating, and he came again to visit with a bag of oranges and a book for Beth.

"Thank you for coming, Jim."

"You don't need to thank me. Strewth, what are relatives for?" he replied. "Though you might not think I'm a relative now Vera's going."

"Whatever happens between you and Vera, I'll always be grateful for all you've done for Beth and me," Ada said.

"After Vera's gone, I don't want you to think that you and Beth can't visit whenever you like. I can pick you up. I'm getting a truck. I'll need it for the calves I'm hoping to get in."

"Calves. More work for you, Jim?"

"I'm prepared for that. Actually, I'm thinking of putting more of the land to use. Farming full-time." Ada remembered Vera saying that this had always been Jim's ambition. She was aware of Jim watching her carefully.

"You'll always have me around. If you and Beth want for anything, all you have to do is ask. When you're better I'll come down and take both of you up to see the calves." Seeing Jess appear in the doorway holding Beth's hand, he stood quickly, as if embarrassed that his suggestion might have been overheard.

"Must be off to get my dinner." He adjusted the waistband of his trousers. "Vera sends you her love, and says she'll pop in tomorrow."

He did not seem to hear Beth's question about the calves, and left without a backward glance or comment to Jess. Ada felt the need to explain his abrupt leave-taking.

"He's well meaning, but an awkward man. He was kind asking us up." She wanted to add that apart from his mate Bill, he did not seem to have any friends. She felt sorry for him, but he was a difficult man to like whole-heartedly. She detested the way he spoke about the Maoris. It occurred to her that he might know about Charlie leaving, and assumed that she would have more time for him, which was definitely not the case. She certainly did not want him to rely more on her for company when Vera left, though she would not stop him from seeing Beth. He clearly was desperate not to lose her.

"A change of scene will do you good, Ada," Jess said.

"What's a change of scene?" Beth asked, climbing on the bed and positioning herself to comb Ada's hair, as she'd been accustomed to doing since Ada was fit enough to bear the grooming.

"A different place. Jim asked us to visit him. You'd like that, wouldn't you?" Ada answered.

"Yes. Then I can see the calves. When can we see them? And why doesn't Charlie come anymore?"

"Charlie's got work to do up north. You know that, Beth."

"Actually, he's coming down here soon," Jess said. "He rang me last night. Not sure which day next week he'll arrive." She pretended not to notice Ada's blush. "He said he wished he'd known you were so ill. He'd have come down straightaway," Jess said.

"Is Charlie coming back?" Beth asked, excited.

"For a visit. For a few days," Jess answered.

"Will he come and teach me to swim when summer comes?"

Ada felt excited at the thought of seeing Charlie, but she said matter-of-factly, "He's not coming back here to live. He's only coming to visit. But you'll learn to swim, Beth. Someone will teach you."

"Who'll teach me, Mummy?"

"I don't know yet. But we'll find someone." But no one as good as Charlie, she thought sadly.

Despite Jess urging her to take her time and rest for at least a week more, Ada forced herself, a couple of days later, to get up after Jess had gone with Beth to school. It had been two weeks since Ada had first taken to her bed, and she was worried about getting behind with her essays. From the kitchen window, she could see the garden. The sun was shining. She longed to be outdoors in the fresh air, having some exercise, using her limbs. She remembered how, after her ordeal in Smith Street, it had taken some time before she was strong enough to accompany Lucy and watch her gardening in Sime. It took longer before she could do any work at all, and before she could clear the fog in her brain and think for herself, instead of following the patient instructions of others.

Anxious now of being helpless again she began sweeping the kitchen floor, but tiring quickly decided that what energy she did have should not be wasted. So, after making herself a cup of coffee, she dutifully laid her copy of *Julius Caesar* on the table then began to read her essay questions.

1. Referring to the passage below, discuss how Shakespeare explores the interplay between the forces of free will and destiny:

'Men at some time are masters of their fates:
The fault, dear Brutus, is not in our stars
But in ourselves, that we are underlings'
   (Act 1 Scene 2)

2. Using the following passage as a starting point, and from what you have learnt in class discussions about classical Greek tragedy, do you think Shakespeare believed Brutus was a tragic hero?

'There is a tide in the affairs of men
Which, taken at the flood, leads on to fortune;
Omitted, all the voyage of their life
Is bound in shallows and in miseries'
   (Act 4 Scene 3)

She sat, pen in hand, and reread the passages, then looked up at the sun-filled window. Forcing away the inner voice which urged her to go outside, she pulled the chair closer to the table and read the essay questions again. The sunlight slanted across the page and warmed her hands. She noticed her nails needed filing. She put down her pen to examine them more carefully, then glanced back at the window. It was such a beautiful day. Perfect weather for doing a much-needed clothes' wash, she decided. With Jess's new machine it would not be exhausting at all to do, and she could think about which essay topic to choose.

✱   ✱   ✱

As she carried the clothes basket from Jess's washhouse to the washing line, she felt, despite her weakness, that she had rejoined the human race. The air smelled sweet, and her spirits lifted. But as she began to peg the clothes, instead of deciding which essay question to choose, her thoughts returned to how she had been deceived. When she tried to force away the image of Michael returning home late with some excuse about work, she felt an anger grow in her — an anger less to do with feeling betrayed, and more to do with not being able to control her thoughts.

"Ada," a voice called behind her. She turned, and saw Charlie stepping across the lawn. He must have parked his car in the street instead of driving in as he normally did.

"How wonderful to see you, Charlie," she cried. "Come inside. I'll make tea."

"You're taking it easy, Ada?" Charlie asked, when they were seated facing each other across the kitchen table.

"Yes, yes, I am," she assured him. "And you?" She watched him frown and fiddle with his spoon, preparing herself to hear that Charlie had decided, definitely, to move closer to his tribe.

"It's going to be a very long process. There's a lot of mistrust and prejudice. On both sides. I've told you the Maori point of view, what they believed they were going to get by signing the treaty, but the white settlers who came were mainly poor people wanting to make a living. They worked for the wealthy British land owners so that one day they could buy land for themselves and have the chance of a better life. You can understand if the Kiwi of today finds it hard to say, all right, we don't deserve this."

Charlie paused, and Ada wondered if Charlie thought he would not need to live up north permanently, the process being long and difficult, but only visit when necessary. Charlie continued.

"I can't be trying to speak to people all day every day, and I have to feed myself." She watched him expectantly as he looked towards the window. "I decided to visit the teacher who taught me to carve. He runs a small workshop in Ponsonby, which went to in my spare time while I was training to become a wood-work teacher. I learned by helping him with restoration work. Meeting houses, that sort of thing. He said he was looking for someone to take over from him as he's getting on, and asked if I'd be interested."

So, Charlie was leaving for good. She could not help feeling upset. She forced a smile.

"Congratulations, Charlie. You must be very pleased."

"I was in the right place at the right time." Charlie began to talk about his ex-teacher, the high standards he set, the inspiration he provided for his pupils to keep up the traditional crafts. Ada nodded, but she was not taking in what Charlie was saying, and when he appeared to have finished speaking, she asked, "Have you found a place to live in Auckland?"

Charlie shook his head. "Not yet."

"Vera's looking for a place there." She went on to tell of Vera's plans.

Charlie looked surprised at first to hear of Vera's intended separation from Jim, but then nodded, appearing to accept the idea, perhaps because he did not think much of Jim, and said, "Your sister is moving to Auckland, then. So you'll think it worthwhile to come up there? Even call in on me."

"Of course I'll call in on you. You don't need to say *even*," Ada replied.

"I don't expect you'll come up until after your exams."

She put her elbows on the table and cupped her chin. "It scares me to death when I think how much studying I have to do still. It takes me a while to settle down and concentrate."

"You'll be all right. You're a clever sheila," Charlie said with a grin. He put down his mug, and appeared to be thinking carefully about something, then looked steadily at her.

"I've got a friend with a bach by the sea. A few hours' drive out of Auckland. He said I could have it any time. Beth and you and your sister could stay there if you wanted. I'd bunk up in a tent. Keep guard. Catch a bit of tucker for us all. After your exams you might like a break."

Hardly able to believe what she had heard she was quiet for a moment, and then exclaimed, "Why Charlie, what a wonderful idea! The summer holidays seem like a long time away, but it's something to look forward to. The chance to be by the sea sounds perfect. Beth will love it." Ada laughed, "She'll demand swimming lessons."

Charlie smiled. "I'll be more than happy to oblige. She's a great kid. She's getting on all right?"

"She really seems settled and happy. She's made friends with other little girls in her class now. And still plays with Timmy, even though, as she's told you, they don't play together at school. He's come around here a couple of times."

"I remember how well they both got on in the swimming group. Stupid that boys are frightened to be called sissies if they play with girls."

"I agree. I can't understand why females are thought of as the weaker sex. We might be physically weaker, although there are women in Singapore who do men's labouring work." She was thinking of the Sam Sui women with their red scarves. "The trouble is, we're not only supposed to be physically weaker, we're thought of as being less intelligent." She remembered how Jim had derided her for wanting to go back to studying, and how he'd put her off trying for office work. One of the reasons she appreciated Charlie was that he did not seem to think women were incapable. There was that Maori princess he admired, for instance.

"You think it's going to be hard getting back your people's land?"

"Yep." Charlie shrugged. "But then Rome wasn't built in a day."

"That's true."

"If there's a will there's a way, eh."

"If once you fail, try, try, and try again."

"Where there's life, there's hope."

They both laughed. "My mother had a cliché for everything," Ada said. "'Gather ye rosebuds while ye may' was a favourite."

"Too true, though. Make the most of the present." Charlie grimaced. "Which means that you have to try not to dwell on what happened in the past."

Ada was serious now.

"It's easier said than done, I'm afraid."

Charlie was watching her as she judged whether to say more, and she saw the compassion in his eyes. She looked towards the window then back at Charlie, and told him about Patrick's letter.

"I suppose I can't blame them for keeping it quiet. I must've seemed a bit pathetic," she said finally. "I got pregnant very soon after we married. And I was sort of at a loss, coming to live with my in-laws in a very well-organised household, and having nothing much to do. I'd had a lot of responsibility before then, running my mother's boarding house. Then, when the war started, I worried about Michael and what was going to happen."

"That doesn't mean you were pathetic, Ada. You can't blame yourself." Charlie frowned. He looked deeply concerned. "You must be feeling very hurt."

Not only hurt. She was angry, too. Her life had been disrupted by Patrick's news; she could think of little else. She said fiercely, "I'm determined I'll pass my exams. I'll never be dependent on anyone again."

Charlie sat back in the chair. He appeared at a loss as to what to say next. His hands were clasped on the table top. She noticed the scars on his fingers, the tip of one thumb missing. Damage from his work, probably. He was a man with much to do, and he had enough to think about.

"I'm sorry, Charlie."

"What for?" he asked quietly, looking sadly at her.

"I seem to complain to you a lot."

"I complain to you. That's what friends do."

Friends. Yes. Goodness, how she would miss him. He leaned back, and waited for her to say something, but she was shy now, wondering if he could detect what she'd been thinking: the loss she felt at the prospect of his leaving for good.

"It's been a great shock for you, Ada. I can see how upset you are. I'm very sorry. If there's anything I can do you must let me know." She was close to tears. He waited for a while for her to speak, then stood up.

"I can see that you're very tired. It's time I left." Before she could tell him that it was not tiredness she felt, he said, "I'll get home now and start clearing up. I need to put the place on the market as soon as possible."

How final it sounded: he was selling his haven. She rose too, pressing her hands onto the table top, and tried to compose her face so as not to betray her sadness.

"Are you unhappy about having to sell?" she asked. "I know you love your place."

"I guess I can find something like it somewhere else. A place with trees, eh. Real big blighters." He smiled and moved towards the door.

Ada followed him outside. "Thank you for coming to see me. And all the very best of luck, Charlie." She was conscious how calmly she'd said this.

"And the same to you, Ada." He walked down the porch steps, then looked up at her. "I'll be coming back here to keep an eye on things until the house is sold. I'll invite myself over." He raised his brows quizzically.

"Please do, Charlie. Please do."

"Anyway, I'll keep in touch. Ring Jess. We can talk then. Find out how things are going. Complain to each other." He grinned. "Don't forget about staying at the bach. It's a beaut place."

She waved goodbye, tears in her eyes, and walked slowly back into the house, regretting that she had not said how much she'd miss him. He might not ring, believing that it did not matter to her if he did or not. Well, he had plenty to do, enough to fill his day. She blew her nose, sighed, and rearranged her papers. Trying to ignore the ache of loss in her chest, she pulled the chair closer to the table, and read the first essay question again.

'Men at some time are masters of their fate:
The Fault, dear Brutus, is not in our stars,
But in ourselves, that we are underlings.'

She opened the play, and smoothed down the page, looking towards the window, where the blue remained but the sun had passed. Knowing that she was in no mood to concentrate, she pushed back her chair and went into the sitting room for an airmail pad to write to Patrick.

It was a short letter, with the usual news of Beth, and then finally, as if it were an afterthought, she wrote:

'I was taken aback hearing of Michael's child, and am still getting used to the idea. I wish I'd been told before, but I realise that you were all trying to protect me. You have always treated me with great kindness and consideration, Patrick, and I want you to know that I feel very grateful to you for that.

I hope that Amritha will have every chance, like Beth, to get a good education. A good education is absolutely essential. It will ensure a better life. If I know anything, I know that, which is why I must do well in my exams. I'm a bit behind in my studies, though, as I've been rather ill. But I'm all right now, and in fact very keen to get going again, especially with my essays!

I need to sign off now, but will write again when I feel more on top of things.'

On top of things. She put down her pen and folded the letter. On top of memories, and questions, and doubts, she thought. So on top, that I can forgive Michael for hiding the truth from me. So on top, that I will stop wondering if he continued to see Kamala and Amritha. So on top, that I no longer miss Charlie as much as I do at the moment.

Ada made herself a cup of tea, and walked about the flat, then finally sat to work again. She chose the second question to answer, and after Beth had gone to bed wrestled further with the idea of the tragic hero.

It was not surprising that her sleep was dense with dreams. When she woke in the grey morning light, she remembered only one. Michael was standing before her with his arms folded. His white suit was immaculate, his oiled hair gleaming in the sunlight. "I thought you were dead," she said. He looked surprised at her remark, then somewhat amused that she should believe he would do anything as irresponsible as dying. She felt disturbed by the dream. Wondering what to make of it, she recalled that before she was married, as the wedding day approached, it had occurred to her even then that life with Michael would not be straightforward.

Chapter 15

JANUARY 1949

CHARLIE HELD THE STEERING WHEEL firmly, handling the car as if it were a bucking horse. The wheels forged through a thick bed of shingle, the stones viciously battering the undercarriage. They'd left the tar seal of the winding coastal road and taken this rough track that led down to the beach. The window of the car was down, and Ada was half-leaning out to breathe in the air - hot, dry, and faintly scented, possibly from the red flowers of the pohutakawas that decked the trees on the slopes of the hills. She'd been ignoring all Beth's questions coming from the back about how much further they had to go. Vera, beside the child, seemed to be asleep after throwing up again. Ada had thought to offer her front seat to poor Vera (they'd been taking it in turns), but there were some sacrifices you did not or at least could not make if you, too, felt close to vomiting.

Charlie, by contrast, appeared unfazed – his usual, steady self. Once they'd left Auckland, he'd driven for much of the way with only one hand on the wheel, the other hanging out of the window. Mostly they travelled without conversation, which did not bother Ada, and in the companionable silence, she had time to reflect on the past few weeks – the late nights studying, the nerves before the exams, and then her relief and pride when she got her results. Her highest mark had been in English, and she'd done unexpectedly well in history and geography. It had been wise to ask for leave from the hospital so she could focus on her studies in the fortnight before the exams. Miss Hullet had been surprisingly cooperative. Ada suspected the matron had spoken to Miss Hullet about treating her staff with more consideration.

Miss Hullet had said that Ada could return to the hospital after the exams, and she had done so, but with the unvoiced intention that if her results were good she would look seriously for another job as soon as Beth was back at school. She did make enquiries about a clerical job in the hospital, which would have been a first step up from maid's work, but they wanted someone to start straight away, and she'd promised Beth that they would have a summer holiday.

She was imagining herself in an office typing away rather slowly (she'd received the lowest mark for typing and shorthand) when Charlie said, pointing ahead, "Now what do you see?"

"Where, where?" Beth cried.

Ada squinted into the glare. Between the dun-coloured curves of the scorched hillsides was a patch of blue.

"Look. There's the sea, Beth."

"Can I go for a swim? When can I go for a swim?" Beth squealed.

"You can all have a swim while I sort things out," Charlie said. He drove the car to the side of the track. "We walk from here. You can't see the bach. It's around the bend. You can get down to the beach straight from it." He let excited Beth out of the car. "I'll go on ahead, and get rid of the corpses," he said through the window. Ada raised her brows quizzically. "The little furry visitors," he added. Charlie had warned them that they would be roughing it: drop toilet, rain tank water, a stream for washing, and an open fire for cooking. It was like being back in Sime.

The small wooden cabin – the bach – was superior to a leaking hut, but still basic. There were two single beds covered in grey blankets that the women would have, a camp bed for Beth a table and four chairs painted a bright red, and a worn settee. Charlie was sleeping in a tent at the front of the bach, which he always did, he'd said, even when on his own. He loved the smell of the sea, and the immediate sound of the breakers was the best lullaby you could have.

Vera and Beth went in search of the outside toilet – the 'dunny', as Charlie called it – and the stream in the forest behind the bach. While she waited for Vera to help her make up the beds with the clean linen they'd brought with them, Ada stood outside watching the long waves curving in lazily and then spending themselves on the shore.

"I'll teach you all to body surf," Charlie said, coming to stand beside her. "And there's a lagoon beyond those rocks." He pointed to the far end of the beach. "It's very safe for swimming there."

"I love it. It's wonderful."

"I'm pleased you decided to come."

Charlie's property had been sold within six weeks of it being put on the market. Although Ada knew that this meant Charlie would be spared the trouble of checking on the house, she was disappointed. Of course, she could talk to him when he rang Jess and asked to speak to her about out how she was getting on with her studies, and if Beth was all right. But she would not see him. She would not have the warmth from his smile, the support she felt from his presence.

Vera was living not far from Charlie's workshop. Ada was not jealous of Charlie's friendship with Vera, but she did feel envious that Vera was able to see Charlie regularly and enjoy his company.

It was only a small compensation to hear from Vera, when she rang after one of his visits, that he spent most of the time talking about her, Ada.

"What about me?" Ada had asked quickly.

"How well you're doing at night school, and the mark you got for your essay on the Maori wars. He said you put him to shame, the way you apply yourself," said Vera.

Ada did not know what to read into that.

✷ ✷ ✷

After a boisterous throw-over in the stream with Beth following their swim, Vera had changed into a dress. Ada noticed that she was wearing makeup, and that she'd wound her hair up on the top of her head. She looked as stylish as if she were in town and not beside a campfire on a deserted beach. Ada had decided to wear slacks, thinking they would be appropriate, but she felt a little self-conscious, not having worn slacks before, and was unsure that they suited her. She wished that she'd worn a dress, especially when Charlie complimented Vera on her frock, a waisted floral print with cap sleeves and a slim skirt.

Vera smoothed up the hair at the back of her neck. "I get all my clothes at cost price in the store. I'm not spending much at all on clothes. I want to save up for our deposit."

"On your own shop, yeah," Charlie said, breaking up driftwood across his knee and feeding it into the fire. Beside him, on a large flat rock used for a table, lay the fish he'd caught and gutted for the evening meal. He'd thought of everything - kumara to bake in the embers, fresh tomatoes and lettuce from his small city garden. All he'd asked the women to do was to bring something for the pudding. Ada had baked a gooey chocolate cake the day before at Vera's, using a recipe of Jess's. They would go into the nearby village for what fresh food they needed each day, there being no fridge and a high daytime temperature.

Vera began to talk about her plans for her own business, plans that Ada had heard before. She stopped listening and looked across the beach at Beth, washed clean after her swim but now digging a sandcastle near the shoreline. Well, what did it matter if she got salty again? That was the joy of roughing it.

The sun was going down, the water violet rather than green now, and there was a soft pink line on the horizon. Seagulls took flight from the rocks. Pohutakawas cast pale shadows over the sand in the far corner of the bay, and a fish made a quick arc above the water.

Charlie prodded the kumara further into the embers. He was wearing khaki shorts and a vest; his feet were bare. He looked at ease; roughing it suited him.

"Tell me when you want me to get the plates and cutlery, Charlie," Ada said.

"No rush. But someone can get the glasses. I've put a couple of lemonade bottles and beer to cool in the stream."

Ada went inside for the glasses, glancing at herself in the mirror fixed behind the door. She looked pale – she'd spent so much time studying indoors – and wished that she'd thought to put on lipstick.

Charlie poured a beer for himself, shandies for the women, and called to Beth to come and have a lemonade. Vera raised her glass.

"To Ada. To my clever sister, Beth's mummy, Charlie's good friend. Congratulations for passing your exams." After a little cheering, prolonged by Beth, Vera continued.

"Hopefully now, Ada, you'll think of leaving a little one horse-town and coming up with Beth to the big smoke."

"What's the big smoke?" Beth asked.

"Auckland. Where I live," Vera said. "Wouldn't you like to come up to be closer to me, and to Charlie?"

"Can Helen come, too?" Beth asked.

"She'd be very welcome, but I expect she'll want to stay with her parents. But you'd make lots of new friends. And Helen can visit," Vera replied.

"Will Jess be sad if we leave? Can Jess visit too?"

"Jess is thinking of moving one day soon to live with her daughter in Christchurch. Isn't that so, Ada?" Vera said.

Ada nodded. Jess had told Ada that her daughter was urging her to move to Christchurch. She did not feel old, but her daughter thought she was, and worried about her. Ada had said that she would be around, so her daughter had no need to worry. This was after the exam results, and Jess had told Ada that she had to think of her own future, suggesting that she go to teacher training college. Ada was aware that it was possible. Jess said there were government bursaries for trainee primary school teachers. Perhaps not enough to live on, but she still had the money from Elizabeth, which she could use now that she knew Patrick's legacy would be there for Beth's education – piano lessons, ballet, and, eventually, university.

Ada watched Beth run back to her sandcastle.

"I have to think about Beth," she said. "It would be dreadful to have her miserable if she was unsettled again."

"Children are very adaptable. It was a crying shame that she had a hard time when she first started, but *everything* was new then, and she's older now, and a lot more confident," Vera said.

It was surprising, Ada reflected, that the child had not appeared all that bothered about the idea of a move, given how attached she'd become to Helen and Jess. But perhaps she'd not thought what it would mean living over two hundred miles away from them, even if she'd done the journey to Auckland when they'd travelled up last week? It was possible the thought of being closer to her aunt and her beloved Charlie compensated for what she would leave behind. And it was true that she was definitely not the child who'd come home from school unhappy and friendless. Invitations to birthday parties came nearly every week. It had been wise to move into town.

"You'd like to train to be a teacher, wouldn't you, Ada?" Vera said.

"Can't I rest on my laurels for a while?"

"You don't want to get into a rut, settle for a quiet life. W all need to challenge ourselves."

"It's interesting. In the war we didn't pray for anything other than to live. But now just to live isn't enough. We keep on wanting something better," Ada said.

"But that's normal. If people didn't want to improve we'd all still be living in caves. What do you think, Charlie?" Vera asked.

Charlie did not reply immediately, and topped up his glass before speaking.

"It's true we need to progress, like finding better medicines, better ways of living generally. We're a species that's always going to be hankering for a better cave." He took a gulp of beer, and wiped the foam from his lips with the back of his hand. "But it would be good if we reminded ourselves that whatever we do to improve our lives, we should try our best not to hurt anyone else. And, may I say, the land on which we live."

"No more rampant cutting down of trees," Ada said, remembering the first time she'd been to Charlie's property.

Beth came racing back, trailing a branch of kelp. "Look what I've found," she cried.

"You're having a wonderful time, aren't you, darling," Vera said. "Just think, if you got your mum to live in Auckland, you could come out here to the bach as much as you wanted." Vera looked at Charlie for confirmation. He grinned, and winked at Beth.

"I've got the message, Vera," Ada said. "You want us to move to Auckland."

"Val would love it if you shared a flat with us."

As Vera went on to list the advantages of city living, Charlie put out his hand to Beth.

"Come and help me get some more wood for the fire, Beth." Ada noted that he had not endorsed Vera's remarks. She suspected that he felt he'd no right to express an opinion. He was a tactful man.

✳   ✳   ✳

Vera excused herself for bed soon after Beth was settled. Vera claimed to be exhausted, but Ada suspected that she was withdrawing in order to leave Charlie and herself alone together. It made her feel shy thinking this, and when Charlie immediately rose and said he was going to collect more firewood, Ada thought he was feeling awkward as well. Of course, they'd been alone together in the past, and had confided in each other as good friends. But it was different tonight, what with the talk of moving to Auckland. She looked up at the vast sky and felt overwhelmed by the steely brightness of the myriad stars outshining the light of the sickle moon. She wrapped her arms around herself, shivering slightly, feeling a nervous excitement.

Charlie returned, and threw wood on the fire.

"You look cold. Just say if you've had enough and want to go in."

"I'm not cold. I like being outside at night. In Singapore we used to swim a lot at night," she said. "The sea was so silky then."

"I expect you don't want to swim now."

"Yes, I think I've had enough of the water today. I'm happy here."

Charlie sat down on the sand at a little distance from her and crossed his legs. Resting his forearms on his knees, and staring intently into the blaze, he looked grave. Ada suspected he was exhausted after driving, fishing, cooking their supper, and taking Beth for a walk into the forest to look for lizards. Ada was reminded again of how good Charlie was with children.

"I've been thinking seriously about going to night school," he said, not looking at her. "I can see that getting my university entrance for a start, and then going on to do some law, will help in the arguing business."

"To get the tribal land back? That sounds like a very good idea, Charlie. A very good idea."

He turned his head towards her, but did not catch her eye. "I'm not a natural scholar. Like your husband was, for instance. But I guess if I put my mind to it I could manage all right."

~ 390 ~

Ada thought that he sounded defensive.

"I'm sure you could," she said enthusiastically, and recalled that when they'd confided in each other on the night of the dance, she'd said how clever Michael had been. She watched Charlie poking at the fire with a stick of driftwood, and said quietly, "I hope that I didn't give you the impression Michael was a born genius, or anything. He was clever, yes, but he was given every encouragement to do well. Anglo-Indians put a lot of emphasis on education. They attribute their status in a society dominated by whites to their education. Michael's parents expected him to do exceptionally well in his studies." She remembered what Charmaine had written in her recent letter.

Ada had expected to read that Charmaine was relieved to learn that Michael had not been the golden boy everyone had believed him to be, and that she no longer felt condemned to live in his shadow. She'd said, with commendable insight, "I know you're angry with him, Ada, as I would be in the same circumstance, but I suspect that he didn't want to go against what my parents advised as he didn't want to upset them. They always had such high expectations of him."

Ada decided to tell Charlie what Charmaine had said in the letter.

"I realise that I've made Michael out to be a hero to Beth, and I'll have to change the story a bit when she's old enough to understand." She sighed. "Jess said it would be a good idea for Beth to know her father wasn't perfect, so she won't be searching for a hero to marry. What's more, she won't feel that she has to become a heroine. And I must be the one to tell her about Michael's child, and not someone else, if perhaps she visited Singapore one day."

"You don't blame yourself any more for the fact you were kept in ignorance?"

"No, I don't blame myself. Which is not to say that I don't feel resentful and hurt at times. Usually when I'm over-tired and worried. But I don't generally feel as hard done by as I used to." She scooped up a handful of sand and let it drift through her fingers. "I can appreciate more now how difficult it is to get the timing right when it comes to telling the truth. I'm going to have to judge carefully when to tell Beth everything, for instance." She drew up her legs and hugged her knees. "Someone, a parent of one of the children in Beth's class, found out that we were from Singapore, and wondered if I'd been imprisoned in Changi. Beth wanted to know about it, started asking questions. So I thought it wouldn't hurt to tell her about the good times. Like the concerts the men gave. And the classes. There were classes in languages, music, Shakespeare, shorthand typing…dancing classes in the tool shed. They were hilarious. A story Beth loves is the one of the mice a woman called Mary found, and we both ate! She loves being told of the dreadful food. Loves it when I tell her about the weevils in the rice. My time in Changi has become Beth's favourite bedtime story."

"Carefully edited."

"Of course." She noticed that as she edited the Changi stories, her mind seemed to be encouraged to recall what she and Michael had shared in their short time together, from evening swims and going to the pictures – especially during their courting days – to the encouragement Michael gave her to take up studying again. And then there was his love of Beth. It must have been so hard for him to leave her, thinking possibly that he would never return.

"It is difficult sometimes to try and remember the good times amongst all the bad, but it helps if you can, I think."

"I'm sure it helps." Charlie threw some wood onto the fire. It sent up a shoal of sparks and, catching fire, the blaze reflected on Charlie's face. He appeared to be considering what she'd said.

She looked up at the glittering splendour of the sky.

"It's perfect here, Charlie. I could not be more content. The stars, the smell of the sea, the fire…"

"And being with me?" he asked, smiling.

She blushed. "Of course. I was going to say that."

He sat more erect and pushed his hair back from his forehead. She was about to thank him again for bringing her and Beth to the beach, when he said, "What your sister was talking about? You coming to Auckland? I know you don't want to unsettle Beth, but would you consider it?" He did not wait for an answer and spoke slowly as if weighing each word. "It would be great from my point of view if you did." He looked seriously at her. "I'd like us to get to know each other better. I like you very much, Ada."

Ada's heart beat faster. What was he saying, exactly?

"It's a big decision for you to make," he continued. "You've got Beth's welfare to think about. But I just want to say that I won't put any pressure on you, and I would never stop you from feeling independent." He frowned, as if worried that he'd said the wrong thing, but then, seeing her smile, stood up and reached for her hand, pulled her to feet, clasped her shoulders and studied her face for a moment, before kissing her softly on the lips.

"Take your time. Think about it. No rush, eh."

"I will think about it, Charlie," she replied, trying to manage her feelings of happiness and excitement, and match her expression with his. He was not frowning, but he was not smiling either. It was as if he were impressing upon her that he wanted to be taken very seriously.

He nodded slowly, then, without speaking, took her hand and led her the short distance to the bach. He kissed her again at the door, but did not linger, and walked back towards the fire.

She wondered at his abrupt leave-taking and watched him for a few moments as he stood looking out at the sea, hands in pockets, a broad silhouette against the vast blackness of the ocean beyond the breakers. She felt that he was a man with a lot of pride; a lot of mana. It had been an ordeal for him to reveal his feelings, and he needed to compose himself. Or he was simply giving her time to think.

As she prepared for bed, Ada wondered what it would mean if she and Charlie got to know each other better. She imagined Charlie in Auckland. He was in a room much like that in the house he had amongst the towering trees. He was carving the face of a tiki, and she and Beth were seated at a table, Beth colouring a picture in her book, while she was busy writing, presumably an essay. It was a scene of contentment. Resisting the urge to wake Vera and share her news, she lay in bed and imagined a haven, a haven in a city. There were trees in the garden, if not big ones, and lots of flowers, a garden a bit like Jess's. It was perfection.

So, what was it that made the image change? Was it the movement of the moon's shine into the cabin, or was it picturing Charlie still standing on the shore looking out to sea, thinking of his future, thinking of everything he had to do? Because now she thought of him leaving his carving, leaving the house. He had important matters to deal with, duties to fulfil. He had far, far better things to do than to be with her and Beth.

She sat up, feeling a throb of despair. She thought to wake Vera, but that would mean disturbing Beth. Besides, she knew what Vera would say. 'You're thinking like this because of what you went through with Michael. But Charlie's not Michael. And it's different now, Ada. You're not the person you were. Don't let the chance of happiness pass you by for fear of what might happen.'

Of course, you could not account for the future. There was no such thing as a crystal ball. You just had to be as sensible as you could be. Like Patrick, for instance. What would he advise? If nothing disrupted Beth's education, then all would be well. And Elizabeth, what would she say? If anyone would be happy to give advice, it would be her. Ada imagined her mother and Mrs Sinathamby seated on the front verandah of the boarding house overlooking the waste ground. They were talking of the forthcoming wedding, of the Serangoon house, of Ada's good fortune. Ada remembered that neither woman had warned o the difficulties a couple in a mixed-race marriage might face. In their minds, it was unthinkable that a woman should have any doubts if she loved the man.

Love? Respect, certainly, and a deep affection, and a wish for him to be more a part of her life, and she of his. And Beth adored Charlie.

Ada drew up her knees and clasped them tightly. Yes, she was stronger. The small circle, which Michael had told her about so many years ago on Katong beach, that pinprick of glowing light, as she'd imagined it in the camp, nestling near her heart and giving her courage, was bigger now, much bigger. But – and it was this which worried her – was she strong enough to be the supportive wife Charlie deserved as a man with a huge responsibility? Or would she become resentful of him? Would she find herself living in his shadow, and lose her growing sense of being independent, and having her own ambitions? And she'd not met anyone in his family, knew none in his tribe. What would his people think of her? What would they expect from her? Would they distrust her for being a Pakeha?

It was impossible. She would not sleep tonight. She did not need time to think. She needed to talk to Charlie. She got out of bed and, seeing Beth spread-eagled on her camp cot in the trusting vulnerability of deep sleep, thought of what Beth had had to cope with in her short life. Leaving Singapore, leaving Amah and Patrick, being bullied at school. Was it right to unsettle the child again, now that she was happy?

But as she began to dress, she imagined herself - no longer young, typing away slowly, a frustrated woman, full of regrets. A woman who was missing Vera, and, above all, missing Charlie. Missing his solid and supportive presence, his genial nature, his beautiful, wide smile – all because she feared the unknown. Ada remembered how she had been before marrying Michael, and what had happened because she had refused to leave Singapore. How could she ever forget the misery that had followed?

She shoved her feet into her sandals and opened the door quietly. "There is a tide in the affairs of men…" she whispered, stepping outside. The air was cool. She went back inside for her cardigan. Vera turned in her sleep. Ada closed the door behind her. "Which taken at the flood, leads on to fortune…" She slipped her arms into her cardigan and looked towards the ocean. "Omitted, all the voyage of their life…" The stars were blazing. Awed by their magnificence, she hesitated for a moment, saying the words with the breathiness of excitement. "Is bound in shallows and in miseries." There was a light of a torch or a candle in Charlie's tent. She made her way towards it.

Acknowledgements

I COULD NEVER HAVE WRITTEN this book without Martin's belief in me, his encouragement of my writing, and the example he set with his amazing self-discipline in the completion of his own work.

I would also like to thank friends and family who agreed to read my script and risk giving me useful feedback, and John Parker, formerly of MBA literary agency, for his interest in my writing over several years, and agreeing to represent me.

I am indebted to Kate Hopkins for her extremely conscientious and insightful reading and editing of my drafts. I could not have done without her detailed and positive criticism.

Two diaries directly informed my account of life in Changi Gaol: *Dear Phillip. A diary of captivity, Changi 1942-1945* by Freddy Bloom; *Diary of a Girl in Changi* by Sheila Allan. Both women were interned with my mother, whose stories of her own experience in prison enthralled me, whose courage and fortitude I have always admired, and whose ability to forgive I will never forget.

About the Author

ISOBEL SCHAREN WAS BORN IN Singapore, where she was adopted by a mixed-race couple. She was educated in New Zealand before settling in England. She divides her time between London and Bristol.

Printed in Poland
by Amazon Fulfillment
Poland Sp. z o.o., Wrocław

53763108R00240